Praise for *Unnatural Death*

How can scriptural claims that "God did not make death" (Wis 1:13) and that "death came through sin" (Rom 5:13) be squared with what seems evident from evolutionary science: that death not only long predated the appearance of human beings on earth, but also is itself integral to the emergence of the human species, as a part of the process of natural selection? Many theologians, without rejecting evolution, have managed to avoid grasping the nettle of this challenge, or if they have, they have tended to presume that the Christian tradition offers scant resources for addressing it. In *Unnatural Death*, Philip Porter takes up this challenge by turning to figures in the Christian tradition—Augustine, above all—to address how death can haunt all creaturely existence from the outset and yet still not be "natural." This genre-defying book manages to be at once philosophical, historical, and literary, but above all, theological, inquiring into God and God's ways with the world.

—Frederick C. Bauerschmidt, professor of theology,
Loyola University Maryland

There is no stronger biblical pairing than the intertwining of sin and death, and yet it is now routinely dismissed because it is thought to violate scientific theories of human origins. There could be no more timely book than this one. As it "seeks understanding" of this mystery of the faith, it provides intellectual insight allowing those tempted by scientific reductionism to see the compatibility of faith and reason even here, without rationalizing the mystery away. This will appeal not only to theologians and teachers, but to pastors and anyone else charged with offering a compelling defense of Christian faith.

—John C. Cavadini, professor of theology,
University of Notre Dame

Porter's *Unnatural Death* is a learned and creative contribution to a surprisingly understudied topic: the Christian theology of death. At its heart lies an analysis of angelic sin and the disorder that flows from it, evident principally in the universality of creaturely death. Porter's writing shows on every page an unusual and lovely combination of conceptual precision, stylistic elegance, and intellectual energy.

—Paul J. Griffiths, author of *Israel: A Christian Grammar*

UNNATURAL DEATH

UNNATURAL DEATH

CREATION, SIN, and THE ANGELIC FALL

PHILIP G. PORTER

FORTRESS PRESS
Minneapolis

UNNATURAL DEATH
Creation, Sin, and the Angelic Fall

30 29 28 27 26 2 3 4 5 6 7 8 9

Library of Congress Control Number: 2024055035 (print)

Cover image: The First Day, The Second Day, The Third Day, The Fourth Day—Old Testament Miniatures with Latin, Persian, and Judeo-Persian inscriptions. Paris, France ca. 1244–1254; sourced from The Morgan Library and Museum
Cover design: LUCAS Art & Design, Jenison, MI

Print ISBN: 979-8-8898-3529-5
eBook ISBN: 979-8-8898-3530-1

For my wife, Kristi

Si enim rebus deessent animae quae ipsum fastigium ordinis in universa creatura sic obtinerent, ut si peccare voluissent, infirmaretur et labefactaretur universitas, magnum quiddam deesset creaturae: illud enim deesset, quo remoto stabilitas rerum atque connexio turbaretur. Tales sunt optimae, et sanctae, et sublimes creaturae coelestium vel supercoelestium potestatum, quibus solus Deus imperat; universus autem mundus subjectus est. Sine istarum officiis justis atque perfectis esse universitas non potest.

For if the souls which occupy the very highest of ranks in the whole creation really had failed—if they would have willed to sin—the universe would have been weakened and ruined. Creation would certainly lack something great. For it would lack that thing the absence of which would have disordered the stability and connection of things. Such are the best, holy, and sublime creatures of the celestial and supercelestial powers, whom God alone rules, but to whom the whole world is subject. Without their just and perfect service the universe could not be.

St. Augustine, *De libero arbitrio*, 3.11.32 (*PL* 32:1287)

CONTENTS

ABBREVIATIONS

General Abbreviations

CCL	*Corpus christianorum, series latina*
CSEL	*Corpus scriptorum ecclesiasticorum latinorum*
DS	Denzinger *Symbolorum*
NRSV	New Revised Standard Version
PG	*Patrologiae cursus completus, series graeca*
PL	*Patrologiae cursus completus, series latina*
RSV	Revised Standard Version
Vulg.	Vulgate

Alcuin of York

in Apoc.	*Commentariorum in Apocalypsin*

Augustine

civ.	*De civitate Dei*
conf.	*Confessiones*
div. qu.	*De diversis quaestionibus octoginta tribus*
doct. chr.	*De doctrina christiana*
Gn. c. Man.	*De Genesi contra Manichaeos*
Gn. litt.	*De Genesi ad litteram*
Gn. litt. imp.	*De Genesi ad litteram imperfectus*
Io. ev. tr.	*In Evangelium Ioannis tractatus*
lib. arb.	*De libero arbitrio*
ord.	*De ordine*
pecc. mer.	*De peccatorum meritis et remissione et de baptismo parvulorum*

retr.	*Retractationes*
trin.	*De Trinitate*
util. cred.	*De utilitate credendi*

Cyprian

dom. orat.	*De Dominica oratione*
zel.	*De zelo et livore*

Gregory the Great

mor.	*Moralia in Job*
reg. past.	*Regulae pastoralis*

Gregory of Nyssa

De hom. op.	*De hominis opificio*

Jerome

in Esaiam	*Commentariorum in Esaiam*

John Cassian

con.	*Conlationes*

Thomas Aquinas

pot.	*Quaestiones disputate de potentia*
SCG	*Summa contra Gentiles*
ST	*Summa Theologiae*
super Iob	*Expositio super Iob ad litteram*

All translations are my own unless otherwise noted. I have used the Revised Standard Version (RSV) of Scripture for all biblical citations unless otherwise noted. When I have used another version of Scripture those citations are given in line with the chapter and verse.

ACKNOWLEDGMENTS

I am grateful to all who have made this book possible. Fritz Bauerschmidt, Jim Buckley, Angela Christman, Fr. John Conley, Steve Fowl, Claire Matthews McGinnis, and Trent Pomplun each contributed significantly to my grasp of the work of theology. They helped me see what it is you are doing when you are asking and answering questions about God, and why it might be worthwhile to do so. Sarah Beckwith, Maria Doerfler, Susan Eastman, Reinhard Hütter, Thomas Pfau, and Warren Smith offered me new perspectives on the set of problems I would confront while imagining this work. Each introduced me to new skills not only in theology but also in history, literary studies, philosophy, and scriptural exegesis. Bruce Marshall, in whom I have found an exemplar of precise theological thinking and writing, offered astute criticisms that have improved this book at each stage. I owe special thanks to Paul Griffiths and Stanley Hauerwas. Their respective influences were acutely felt throughout the writing of this book. Without them this project could neither have been started nor finished. Finally, and above all, my wife Kristi and our four children, Oliver, Evelyn, Aidan, and Hugh, who sacrificed much to help me make this book a reality.

INTRODUCTION

This book originated in a fascination with the deaths of the martyrs of the early Church. The ways their deaths imitated Christ's own compelled me to look closely at what it means to die as a Christian. It also turned my attention back to the passion and death of Jesus on the cross. Looking closer at the martyrs and Jesus, it became clear that understanding what death was and where it came from deserved specific attention. Further research into this question yielded an interesting gap in contemporary theology. There is little written on the topic of death itself. There are many books dealing with death under different aspects—how to die well, how to deal with the deaths of loved ones, the medicalization of death, and so on, are all topics that have been explored at length. The questions being asked about death were primarily ethical in nature and in scope. There have been fewer studies about what death is, where it comes from, and why we die. Conceptual theological work on the topic of death was lacking.

This book is a theology of death that considers death's place in the doctrine of creation. Writing on this meant confronting a problem with a few different aspects. Here is a sketch of the problem. The cosmos in which we find ourselves is, on the best accounts available, just shy of fourteen billion years old. The last three-and-a-half billion years on earth have been the scene of the evolutionary development of all sorts of living things. This began very early, with protein chains coalescing into single-celled organisms, and these went on to evolve into multicellular organisms, plants, animals, every different kind of living creature.

Death belongs to that process as an integral, structural feature that makes biological evolution possible. Living things must kill other living things or outcompete them (killing them indirectly) in order to survive and pass on their genetic material to succeeding generations. Likewise, preceding generations (though there are some interesting exceptional cases here) die, making room for the following generation. Creaturely adaptations that make them capable of outcompeting others for limited resources or in the predation game results in the process of biological evolution. Charles Darwin called this process "selection," and though his heirs in the field of evolutionary biology have rightly complicated his ambitiously parsimonious picture, one thing remains true: death plays an integral role in the evolution of species and is bound up with the processes by which the whole panoply of living things has come to be. Death belongs to the biological machinery of planet earth.

This observation can be scoped out even further. Not only must successive generations of species be done to death in order for all the kinds of creatures there are to come to be. It is also the case that we live in a dying cosmos. The tick of the clock only counts down. At some point, entropy and decay will take their toll even on the life of the stars. The heat death of the cosmos—if not preceded by the second coming—will mean a barren, cold, lifeless universe. Utterly devoid of light and heat, the universe will also be necessarily devoid of life. This process of decay and death at the cosmic level also belongs to the conditions for the possibility of life as we know it. The repeated death of stars over the course of billions of years creates the heavier elements on the periodic table. Without entropic decay there would be no life because there would be none of its building blocks.

Given the truths of the faith, reflecting on this set of conditions for life as we know it should bring Christians up short. Take the book of Wisdom, where we hear, "God did not make death, and he does not delight in the death of the living. For he created all things so that they might exist; the generative forces of the world are wholesome, and there is no destructive poison in them" (Wis 1:13–14). If death looms large over the "generative forces of the world" by doing all things to death, it is unclear what it means to say, "there is no destructive poison in them." That is the first aspect of the problem.

Its second aspect is found in St. Paul's Letter to the Romans, where he says, "the wages of sin is death" (Rom 6:23). Or again in the First Letter to the Corinthians, where he says, "The last enemy to be destroyed is death" (1 Cor 15:26). Death is not only not made by God, it is also intimate with sin—the turning away from God by rational creatures. Death's intimacy with sin means, on Paul's account, that death is an enemy in need of destruction. If death is something that needs to be destroyed it is hard to explain how it is part of the proper functioning of the created order. The third aspect of the problem is also found in the book of Wisdom, which has more to say on the origins of death. God did not make death. Death comes into the world through the action of God's creatures: "through the devil's envy death entered the world" (Wis 2:24). The problem is further complicated, because Scripture also tells us, "sin came into the world through one man, and death came through sin" (Rom 5:12).

To sum up this multifaceted problem: We have reason to believe that death is integral to the processes that have brought about all the different kinds of life there are. But God did not make death. Death is an enemy of life, something caused by sin. The origin of death by way of sin is attributed to both angelic and human sinfulness. This is a muddle, and Christians should attempt to see how these disparate data points can be held together. That is the problem informing this work from beginning to end, through which I attempt to chart a speculative theological path.

In order to answer this set of questions posed to theology by the natural sciences, I have turned to the Christian theological tradition, the philosophy of language, and some works of literature. Latin Patristic texts, especially those of Augustine, form the backbone of the theological grammar of creation, sin, and fall laid out here. In his latest and most thorough commentary on Genesis, *De Genesi ad litteram*, Augustine argues for the importance of reconciling what can be known by faith and by reason, even when they appear to be at odds. Two facets of Augustine's theology of creation are important for accomplishing this goal with respect to the problem of death. The first is the concept of the *rationes seminales*—the seed-like rules at the heart of creation—which norm and govern the development of all creatures in time and space. The second involves how these *rationes* should be understood in relation to the order of eternity (which I call the *conditio*) and the order of time (which I call the *administratio*).

Angelology is an important, though of late underrepresented, area in theology. My contention is that the angelic fall damages not just angels but the whole created order. The angels play an important, governing role in the cosmos. When some of them rebel, the intrinsic relationships between them and all other things are damaged. The *rationes seminales* function differently in a universe that is out of alignment, and the effects are devastating. Showing how this could be so and what the extent of those effects is offers part of a solution to the question of the origin of death that is compatible with Christian thought and the best scientific accounts of the origins of life and biological evolution. Along the way, the problem of evil and the permission of sin present certain obstacles to the main argument about the origin of death. In response, I describe the relationship between natural and voluntary evils as meaningfully distinct. But this distinction is often forced to do more work than it can. To combat this tendency, I suggest that natural evils have their ultimate origins in the free choices of rational creatures. That is to say, natural evils are the result of voluntary evils. In the first case, the freely chosen rebellion of some of the angels.

This presents another angelological difficulty. What is the nature of the primal, angelic sin? Angelic sin is a topic that has received repeated attention throughout the tradition. It is a question with ecumenical appeal, and my claims about angelic sin look within and beyond the Catholic theological tradition, including the way the cause of evil and the rebellion of angelic beings have been represented in literature. Cyprian, Gregory of Nyssa, Augustine, Gregory the Great, Thomas Aquinas, Francisco Suárez, Jonathan Edwards, and Matthias Scheeben each treat the angelic fall. Putting Shakespeare, Tolkien, and Milton in conversation with these theological writers helps to elaborate the origins of voluntary evil and natural evil. Angelic sin, on the account offered here, has an explicitly christological character. It is shaped by some of the angels' negative response to the incarnation.

By offering a coherent view of the origins of angelic sin, the role angelic beings play in the cosmos, and the effects of angelic sin on the fundamental order of the cosmos as a whole, it is then possible to offer a picture of how these events, which occur outside time as we know it, unfurl in the temporal order. The grammar of creation, which allows us to speak of creatures *sub specie aeternitatis*, leads ineluctably to certain descriptions of creatures in the order of time. Pushing back against the tendency in contemporary theology to naturalize death, I instead use the grammar of creation already established to affirm doctrines essential to Christian orthodoxy. Embracing an Augustinian theology of creation leaves us better able to affirm both the positions taught definitively and repeatedly by the Church throughout its history and what the best scientific investigation teaches about the natural world.

My argument also shows the value of taking seriously the worries scientists, poets, and novelists have articulated, each in their own genres, about the problem of death. I show how death plays an integral role in the shaping of the fallen cosmos guided by God's providential care for all things. God does not straightforwardly undo the evil of death, but puts that evil to good use in a way analogous to the instrumental use of the evil of Christ's passion to bring about salvation. I also put Darwin into conversation with some of his early Catholic respondents. Critical and appreciative, these sources help show where the difficulties with Darwinian evolutionary theory lie and where they do not. In the end, I offer a speculative account about the origin and nature of human beings which shows where we stand in relation to nonhuman creaturely death and how human sin fits into the picture offered.

This investigation is likely to generate as many questions and points of departure as answers. This is a good place to have ended up, as it is how Augustine understands his own *De Genesi ad litteram*. Looking back upon it in his *Retractationes* he says, "Many more questions than answers were found in that work, and of those that were found, fewer were certain, the rest having been put down so as to be looked into as they need to be."[1] With all this in mind, I offer this work to the Church, submitting to her judgment my speculations and suggestions, claiming all the errors as my own. I only hope it serves as a goad to further thinking and writing on the topic, including writing critical of what I say here.

1. Augustine, *retr.*, 2.50, *CSEL* 36:159–60: "in quo opere multa quaesita quam inventa sunt et eorum, quae inventa sunt, pauciora firmata, certera vero ita posita, velut adhuc requirenda sint."

CHAPTER ONE

On the Meaning of "Literal"

READING SCRIPTURE *AD LITTERAM* means attending to "the way the words run."[1] This attention is rooted in a theological assumption. It assumes the words of Scripture are God's words and that they manifest the will of God to their reader. This assumption does not undermine the fact that the words of Scripture are human words, with human authors. Like Jesus Christ, the Word of God, Scripture, the word of God, is at once divine and human. Augustine affirms this noncompetitive account of divine and human authorship in *De doctrina christiana*, a text that would inform the Western Church's mode of scriptural interpretation for over a thousand years. Scripture offers salvific knowledge. That knowledge is "nothing other than the thoughts and will of those who wrote it, and through them the will of God according to which we believe such writers have spoken."[2] Attending to the text of Scripture *ad litteram*, to the way the words run, is to attend to God's salvific will for humans made knowable in human language.

In *De genesi ad litteram*, Augustine attempts to read God's will in the act of creation. Looking at how the words run does not necessarily mean equating every passage of a scriptural narrative with a discrete, historical event. Here, Augustine's *ad litteram* shows its distance from modern "literal" readings

---

1. Stanley Hauerwas, "Why 'The Way the Words Run' Matters," in *Working with Words: On Learning to Speak Christian* (Eugene, OR: Cascade Books, 2011), 108. See also Lewis Ayres, *Nicaea and Its Legacy: An Approach to Fourth-Century Trinitarian Theology* (Oxford: Oxford University Press, 2004), 32; and Eugene Rogers, "How the Virtues of an Interpreter Presuppose and Perfect Hermeneutics: The Case of Thomas Aquinas," *The Journal of Religion* 76 (1996): 64–81, at 74. Rogers translates "litterae circumstantia" as "the way the words run" from Thomas Aquinas's *De potentia* (q.4, a.1, c., *post init.*).

2. Augustine, *doct. chr.*, 2.5.6, *PL* 34:38: "Scriptura divina . . . qua opportune potuit per orbem terrarum disseminari, per varias interpretum linguas longe lateque diffusa innotesceret gentibus ad salutem: quam legentes nihil aliud appetunt quam cogitationes voluntatemque illorum a quibus conscripta est, invenire, et per illas voluntatem Dei, secundum quam tales homines locutos credimus."

of Scripture. Rather than prizing a fundamentalist commitment to *the* literal meaning of Genesis, Augustine gives the Church a way to read Scripture according to the letter which prizes the authority of Scripture rather than a particular interpretation of Scripture. His investigations into the days of creation lead him to conclude that Genesis 1 is not a straightforward account of events in time and space. Instead, he argues, it is a recounting of God's simultaneous and atemporal act of bringing into being all that is from nothing. To learn this is to learn something about the will of God and the way that will is present in the created order.

I find Augustine's claims about creation powerful and convincing. And his way of approaching Scripture and teasing out this interpretation is as interesting and informative as what he finds there. It is important for the argument that follows to learn from Augustine's assumptions about Scripture and to see how some of them have been formally taught as Catholic doctrine. Once I have shown this, I will explain how those assumptions fund Augustine's decisions as he reads Genesis 1 *ad litteram*. Augustine insists that his interpretation is not figural or allegorical, but *literal*. Augustine's view of literal interpretation comports well with what Stanley Cavell, Donald Davidson, and Cora Diamond have to say about metaphor, interpretation, and meaning.

That said, Augustine's interpretation of Genesis is startlingly innovative and does not always meet with approbation in the later tradition, though it is sometimes domesticated by treating it as a spiritual rather than literal reading of the text. With that in mind, I will turn to Thomas Aquinas's reception of *De genesi ad litteram* to highlight what is unique about Augustine's interpretation. The aim of this chapter is exegetical and critical. I exposit Augustine's mature reflections on the book of Genesis to present its enduring value to Christian reflection on creation. I will go on in the following chapters to extend Augustine's thought in directions warranted and in some cases entailed by his positions. In this way, Augustine's thoughts on Genesis and his way of arriving at them will lay the foundations for a superstructure of my own theological speculations on the origins of death in the created order.

The Two Authors of Scripture

The Second Vatican Council formalized Augustine's noncompetitive account of the two authors of Scripture, human and divine. The Dogmatic Constitution on Divine Revelation, *Dei Verbum*, affirms the Augustinian claim that the human will and divine will are present in the text of Scriptures, codifying this position as Catholic doctrine.[3] We must hold, *Dei Verbum* teaches, the books of the Old and New Testaments to be inspired texts. Because the Holy Spirit inspires them "they have God as author."[4] This must be taken together with the affirmation of the following section, "God spoke in Sacred Scripture through humans in a human way."[5] For this reason, the interpreter of Scripture "ought to investigate attentively what the holy writers in fact intended to signify and God was pleased to manifest by their words."[6] Augustine's own search for the literal meaning of the days of creation in Genesis 1 is mindful of Scripture's human and divine authorship. By investigating Scripture in this way he discovers how to read the creation account of the first chapter of Genesis so that it coheres with the second chapter and with other explicit teachings in the biblical canon.[7]

---

3. Cf. Augustine, *doct. chr.*, 2.5.6.

4. *Dei Verbum*, 3.11, *DS* §4215: "Libros enim integros tam Veteris quam Novi Testamenti, cum omnibus eorum partibus, sancta Mater Ecclesia ex apostolica fide pro sacris et canonicis habet, propterea quod, Spiritu Sancto inspirante conscripti . . ., Deum habent auctorem, atque ut tales ipsi Ecclesiae traditi sunt."

5. *Dei Verbum*, 3.12, *DS* §4217: "Deus in Sacra Scriptura per homines more hominum locutus sit."

6. *Dei Verbum*, 3.12, *DS* §4217: "attente investigare debet, quid hagiographi reapse significare intenderint et eorum verbis manifestare Deo placuerit." Nicholas Lash has commented on the importance of not separating the "*quid*" of the holy writers' intention from what "God was pleased to manifest to us by their words." I have therefore left the translation somewhat awkward (excluding the second "what" that often appears before "God"). This preserves what is clearer in the Latin, i.e., that we are not dealing with two things, "what" the writers wrote and "what" God intends to manifest. Rather, these levels of meaning are inextricably linked. For more on this see Nicholas Lash, "On Re-Reading Vatican II," in *Theology for Pilgrims* (Notre Dame: University of Notre Dame Press, 2008), 250–51.

7. Although standard scholarly practice is to divide the two creation narratives of Genesis 1–3 into the "priestly" and "yahwist" accounts, Augustine's impulse is to harmonize them. He is aware that they are distinct, but he takes this to indicate that the accounts have different purposes. He treats it as a theological, not a compositional, difficulty. Augustine harmonizes Genesis 1–3 by holding to the atemporality of God's work in creating everything that is as described in the first chapter along with the temporal unfolding of that work in the second and third. Cf. Augustine, *Gn. litt.*, 5.1.1–3. The clearest scriptural support for Augustine's reading is found in Ecclesiasticus (Sirach) 18:1, which in the Vulgate reads "Qui vivit in aeternum creavit omnia simul."

Reading Genesis 1 *ad litteram*, Augustine concludes that "creation" names God's atemporal act of bringing the cosmos into existence. God's creative work occurs in eternity, outside of all time. He begins the line of reasoning that leads to this conclusion in the opening chapters of the commentary. Connecting Genesis 1 and the Prologue of the Gospel of John, Augustine claims God's first utterance in Genesis, "Let there be light" (Gen 1:3), just is God the Father speaking the Word of God himself. The Word of God is God, and so the Word is spoken in God's own eternity. Because, Augustine claims, "Let there be light" is an eternal utterance, our normal manner of speaking begins to break down. We cannot arrive at the "when" of it, because the word "when" is already indexed to time. Instead, Augustine says, "the 'when' wherein something must be made is eternal in the Word of God, and 'then' it was made 'when' it must have been made in that Word, in whom there is no 'when' or 'sometime,' since that whole Word is eternal."[8] From the start, he is bumping up against the boundaries of human speech about God and God's creative act. He returns repeatedly to this difficulty throughout the commentary. What he thinks this indicates, however, is that the first verses of Genesis ought to incline the reader away from an interpretation that would take what follows to be a straightforward description of a historical sequence of events in time.

As both Augustine and *Dei Verbum* make clear, the words of Scripture are human words given to humans so that they might understand the things of God. The language in the opening chapter of Genesis uses spatiotemporal categories to describe something for which humans do not have categories, God the Father's utterance of the eternal Word.[9] Talk of "days," therefore, should not be taken to refer to twenty-four-hour solar days. But Augustine does not simply dismiss that thought. Instead, he tries it on to see what it would be like if it were the literal meaning of the text. It seems straightforward

---

8. Augustine, *Gn. litt.*, 1.2.6, *PL* 34:248: "Quod si ita est, aeternum est quod dixit Deus, *Fiat lux*; quia Verbum Dei Deus apud Deum, Filius unicus Dei, Patri coaeternus est: quamvis Deo hoc in aeterno Verbo dicente creatura temporalis facta sit. Cum enim verba sint temporis, cum dicimus, Quando, et aliquando; aeternum tamen est in Verbo Dei, quando fieri aliquid debeat: et tunc fit quando fieri debuisse in illo Verbo est, in quo non est quando et aliquando, quoniam totum illud Verbum aeternum est."

9. Edmund Hill, "Introduction" to *The Literal Meaning of Genesis*, in *On Genesis*, ed. John E. Rotelle (Hyde Park, NY: New City Press, 2002), 160.

enough that talk of "day" and "evening" and "morning" would lead an interpreter to think of the length of time we call a day. But reading the text this way causes more problems than it resolves. Augustine carefully points these out, one after another.[10]

Augustine asks questions of the text, and he is not overly concerned with coming to an answer quickly or definitively. One of the most distinctive and attractive features of *De genesi* is Augustine's willingness to let himself be led by the process of questioning without feeling the need to provide an irrefutable answer that would settle the matter of interpretation for all time. He also cautions fellow interpreters of the text of Scripture against rashness or stubbornness in their own readings of the Bible.[11] A through line in this mature exegetical work of Augustine is the courage to dwell faithfully and humbly with Scripture. As he says about this process in his *Retractationes*, "many questions were asked, fewer answers were found."[12]

The questions do lead him to posit some answers about what it means for God to create by speaking the Word. The answers are a long time coming, though he hints at them in the second book.[13] In book IV Augustine returns to his initial line of questioning about the meaning of "day," "evening," and "morning." There he suggests, "maybe God just created one day, so that by its repetition many things called 'days' passed by and ran along, so there was no labor that created the seventh day, as it had been created, surely, by the seventh repetition of this single day?"[14] He then expands on some earlier observations about the nature of the light spoken into being in Genesis 1:3. Given that there were no heavenly bodies on the first day, Augustine thinks that light is best understood as the beginning of the spiritual creation.[15] Now he gives a fuller

---

10. Augustine, *Gn. litt.*, 1.9.17–1.10.21.

11. Augustine, *Gn. litt.*, 1.18.37, 20.40.

12. Augustine, *retr.*, 2.50, *CSEL* 36, pp. 159–60: "in quo opere multa quaesita quam inventa sunt et eorum, quae inventa sunt, pauciora firmata, certera vero ita posita, velut adhuc requirenda sint."

13. Cf. Augustine, *Gn. litt.*, 2.6.13.

14. Augustine, *Gn. litt.*, 4.20.37, *PL* 34:310: "An unum tantummodo diem creavit Deus, ut ejus repetitione multi, qui dicuntur dies, praeterirent atque transcurrerent; nec opus erat ut septimum diem crearet, quia illius quem creaverat, septima repetitio hunc utique faciebat?"

15. Augustine, *Gn. litt.*, 1.10.22, 17.32.

account of the movement from evening to morning and how the succession of days of Genesis 1 is to be read on those terms.

Augustine's reading of these verses is ingenious and strikingly beautiful. The light God creates when he says "Let there be light" is the spiritual light of the angels. The angelic creation is called into being and receives its form as created light by contemplating the uncreated light that God is.[16] Enlightenment by the Word of God suffices to give them form. The angels have the form of created wisdom, a participation in the begotten but uncreated Wisdom who is the Word. This Wisdom is made in them and conforms them to that same Word. In book IV, Augustine then shows how the created wisdom in the angelic intellect relates to talk of "evening" and "morning" in the succession of days. "Evening" and "morning" mark a back-and-forth movement in angelic contemplation. It is an oscillation between contemplating themselves and the rest of the created order and contemplating God. Contemplation of creaturely realities in themselves, angelic or otherwise, corresponds to "evening" knowledge. Contemplation of those created realities in God corresponds to "morning" knowledge. Augustine explains it in this way:

> So if that light which was created first is not bodily but spiritual, it was made after the darkness where it is understood that it turned from its own formlessness toward the creator and was formed. And so after the evening, morning was made when, after understanding of its own proper nature (that by which it is not God), it brings itself back to praise the light which is itself God, of which it is formed by contemplation. And because the other creatures, which are made below itself, are not made without its knowledge, certainly for that reason the same day is repeated in each place. So, by that day's repetition as many days may be made as there are kinds of created things to be distinguished, to be finished by the perfection of the number six. The evening of the first day, then, is also knowledge of itself, that it is not what God is. On the other hand, the morning after this evening, by which the one day is concluded and the second day begun, is its turning, by which it was created, to the praise of the creator, and that it might take into itself from the Word of God knowledge of the creature which it made after itself, that is, the firmament. That

16. Augustine, *Gn. litt.*, 4.22.39.

> firmament is made first in its knowledge when it is said, *And thus it was made*, and following that the firmament in its own nature, which was made when just after it is added by saying, *And thus it was made, And God made the firmament*. Then the evening of that light comes about, when it knows the firmament itself in its own nature, and not in the Word of God as before. Since it is a lesser knowledge, it is rightly signified by the name of "evening."[17]

This turning back and forth between knowing things in themselves and knowing them in the Word issues in the succession of the days of creation. It does this by way of *repetition* of the "one day" of Genesis 1:5, and does not indicate a sequence of events in time and space.[18]

Augustine goes on to insist that this reading of the six days of creation is *not* a figural or allegorical interpretation.[19] It is instead a reading *ad litteram*. Attending to how the words run in this text pulls the reader along toward the edges of words. This does not mean these words are signifying something by association, something other than they are saying. But how exactly do we go about speaking of the bringing into being all that is from nothing? One would expect language to feel stretched here. We should not assume, however, based on what is said of the spiritual light in Genesis 1 that we are "to come to the understanding of 'day' and 'evening' and 'morning' figurally and allegorically,

---

17. Augustine, *Gn. litt.*, 4.22.39, *PL* 34:311–12: "ut si lux illa quae primitus creata est, non corporalis sed spiritualis est, sicut post tenebras facta est ubi intelligitur a sua quadam informitate ad Creatorem conversa atque formata; ita et post vesperam fiat mane, cum post cognitionem suae propriae naturae, qua non est quod Deus, refert se ad laudandam lucem, quod ipse Deus est, cujus contemplatione formatur. Et quia caeterae creaturae, quae infra ipsam fiunt, sine cognitione ejus non fiunt, propterea nimirum idem dies ubique repetitur, ut ejus repetitione fiant tot dies, quoties distinguuntur rerum genera creatarum, perfectione senarii numeri terminanda: ut vespera primi diei sit etiam sui cognitio, non se esse quod Deus est; mane autem post hanc vesperam, quo concluditur dies unus, et inchoatur secundus, conversio sit ejus, qua id quod creata est, ad laudem referat Creatoris, et percipiat de Verbo Dei cognitionem creaturae quae post ipsam fit, hoc est firmamenti: quod in ejus cognitione fit prius cum dicitur, Et sic est factum; deinde in natura ipsius firmamenti, quod conditur, cum additur etiam postea, jam dicto, Et sic est factum, Et fecit Deus firmamentum. Deinde fit vespera illius lucis, cum ipsum firmamentum, non in Verbo Dei sicut ante, sed in ipsa ejus natura cognoscit: quae cognitio quoniam minor est, recte vesperae nomine significatur."

18. Augustine, *Gn. litt.*, 5.3.6.

19. Augustine, *Gn. litt.*, 4.28.45.

only not properly."[20] The very nature of the object of the discussion, God and how God creates, means we ought to *expect* it to require an odd use of language. This use of language "is certainly different than the idiom in which we speak of everyday, corporeal light, but not such that here is the proper and there is the figural."[21] Since this might all seem like a very odd way to speak of literal interpretation of Scripture, I will now turn to what some contemporary philosophers of language have to say about metaphor. This will help support Augustine's contention that his reading is neither allegorical nor figural.

On Metaphor, Interpretation, and Meaning

In a section of *The Claim of Reason* called "The allegory of words; interpretation; seeing something as something," Stanley Cavell works through the concept of metaphor.[22] He discusses how we speak about mind and soul. Something about "mind" and "soul" makes us feel as though much of what we say about them is metaphorical. He provides a few examples: "grasping an idea," "holding a belief," "searching one's memory."[23] But what does it mean to say that these concepts are metaphorical? Cavell digs deeper:

> If someone says "The mind has mountains," I will not understand unless I know that this is a metaphor (i.e., that it is meant metaphorically), and not because its topic is the mind. It would not be quite right to say that I must *take* it metaphorically, because it is not quite clear how else I might take it. Sometimes the matter is not so clear. If I tell you that I tripped him up or waved a red flag at him I may not mean you to take me literally. How then?[24]

20. Augustine, *Gn. litt.*, 4.28.45, *PL* 34:314–15: "Nec quisquam arbitretur, illud quod dixi de luce spirituali . . . non jam proprie, sed quasi figurate atque allegorice convenire ad intelligendum diem et vesperam et mane."

21. Augustine, *Gn. litt.*, 4.28.45, *PL* 34:315: "sed aliter quidem quam in hac consuetudine quotidianae lucis hujus et corporalis; non tamen tanquam hic proprie, ibi figurate."

22. Stanley Cavell, *The Claim of Reason: Wittgenstein, Skepticism, Morality, and Tragedy* (New York: Oxford University Press, 1979), 354–70.

23. Cavell, *The Claim of Reason*, 361.

24. Cavell, *The Claim of Reason*, 361–62.

Cavell uncovers something about metaphor and about *taking* something metaphorically. He has also something important to say about metaphor's relation to literal meaning. Saying I *take* something metaphorically presumes that it would be possible to take it some other way, for the statement to be put otherwise. The example, "The mind has mountains," is apt because it is not clear what one would have to say to convey the literal meaning of this phrase. On the other hand, it is clearer where the difference lies between being "tripped up" literally or metaphorically.

But this picture of metaphor gets still more complicated when Cavell brings in Wittgenstein's comments on "private language" and "aspect-seeing." He says this: "The idea of the allegory of words is that human expressions, the human figure, to be grasped, must be *read*."[25] Is this a metaphor? For what exactly? "Surely," Cavell goes on, "there can be no doubt that *that* is merely a metaphor? But I ask again: What is this idea of metaphor? The suggestion seems to be that my expression must be translated into others, even perhaps *reduced* to others."[26] What are we asking for when we ask for the literal meaning of a metaphor? Perhaps that we speak more plainly. But it is clear from Cavell's emphatic "*reduced*," that there is a danger in the demand for translation or plain speech. The danger is that translation into the literal from the metaphorical will miss something. We will fail to mean what we have properly meant to say.

It may be that translation is not the right way to put it. Cavell tries "paraphrase" instead. "Certainly," he says, "it is essential to an expression's counting as a metaphor that it *can* be paraphrased. It is equally essential that the paraphrase not be treated as a reduction but rather as a certain sort of instruction."[27] In instruction the aim is not to show you what I *really* meant by my words. Extending Cavell, I would say "instruction" is a form of invitation. My paraphrases are not for my benefit but for yours. Or, rather, they are for *our* benefit. They are a kind of training in the use of the metaphor, so that you might understand how it is used and so understand me. As he put it much earlier, "our ability to project appropriately is a criterion for our having learned

25. Cavell, *The Claim of Reason*, 356.

26. Cavell, *The Claim of Reason*, 363. Emphasis original.

27. Cavell, *The Claim of Reason*, 363.

a word."[28] "Projection" here means a certain kind of know-how. It is knowing how to use a word in different contexts, including metaphorical ones.[29] Part of learning a language is learning how to go on in this way. As Cavell says, "After a while we are expected to know when the words are appropriately used in further contexts."[30] The need for instruction in a metaphor marks a boundary of our common use of language. But the possibility of instruction means boundaries like these are not static.

Looking back to Cavell's "allegory of words" we find him saying something more about the idea that human expressions and the human figure must be read. It is not enough to say that by "read" he means that "it can be interpreted, understood."[31] It is not enough because "the idea of reading seems to tell me what *kind* of understanding or interpretation I might aspire to."[32] Here is the danger of reduction to paraphrase. Cavell does not just mean to say that the human figure can be interpreted or understood. He means to say that it will be interpreted or understood *by reading it.* The way someone will come to understanding is related to the interpretation of texts. To figure out what the word "read" calls out, "what I need is not a paraphrase or translation of the word 'read', but an account of why it is that *that* word is the one I want."[33] That kind of an account involves an initiation into a form of life, a

28. Cavell, *The Claim of Reason*, 169.

29. In this earlier discussion Cavell is commenting on a remark from Wittgenstein's *Blue Book*: "we learn words in *certain* contexts." Cavell elaborates, "This means, I take it, both that we do not learn words in *all* the contexts in which they could be used (what, indeed, would that mean?) and that not every context in which a word is used is one in which the word *can* be learned (e.g., contexts in which the word is used metaphorically)" (Cavell, *The Claim of Reason*, 168–69). This would seem, on the face of it, to argue against what I am saying about training in metaphorical usage. Is he saying we cannot learn how to use these words metaphorically in the way I'm describing? But this would, in fact, render the whole concept of "projection" nonsensical. The point is not that we cannot learn how to deploy words in metaphorical contexts, but that we cannot learn all of the contexts in which a word might be used metaphorically *in advance*. Cavell's use of "projection" points to the futurity of words. They might come to mean something that it is not entirely obvious they could mean at present. Hence the impossibility of learning "every context."

30. Cavell, *The Claim of Reason*, 169.

31. Cavell, *The Claim of Reason*, 363.

32. Cavell, *The Claim of Reason*, 363.

33. Cavell, *The Claim of Reason*, 363.

form of life in which it makes sense to say that human expressions and figures can and ought to be read. This kind of initiation is integral to our life with words. As Cavell explains, "You cannot use words to do what we do with them until you are initiate in the forms of life which give those words the point and shape they have in our lives."[34] The world, the life, and the words that go with them are a package deal.

Another, perhaps more controversial, way to understand how metaphor functions comes from Donald Davidson. His position is coordinate with the one proposed by Cavell, but he pushes the position further. The insight is this: the meaning of a metaphor is its literal sense, and only its literal sense.[35] He contrasts this with theories that claim an additional, metaphorical sense attributable to words used in certain circumstances.[36] Davidson canvasses the various manifestations of this initial error of attributing additional senses, dismissing each in turn. We cannot account for metaphorical uses by attributing their sense simply to the extension of a word in a new context.[37] This might seem to run afoul of Cavell's interpretation of Wittgensteinian "projection," but I think not.[38] Metaphorical use also cannot be attributed to ambiguity of

34. Cavell, *The Claim of Reason*, 184.

35. Donald Davidson, "What Metaphors Mean," in *Inquiries into Truth and Interpretation* (Oxford: Oxford University Press, 2001), 245.

36. Davidson, "What Metaphors Mean," 246–47.

37. Davidson, "What Metaphors Mean," 248.

38. What I have already said above on Cavell and "projection" is principally concerned with the possibility of the *use* of a word in new, metaphorical contexts. Davidson's disagreement with theories of metaphor that rely on "extended meaning" deals with something different. Extending the meaning of a word occurs when a word can apply in a *proper* sense to whatever it is someone is talking about. In this case, "there is no difference between metaphor and the introduction of a new term into our vocabulary: to make a metaphor is to murder it." Davidson, "What Metaphors Mean," 248–49. An example of a dead metaphor makes this point clearer. Davidson looks at the cases of rivers and bottles. Davidson, "What Metaphors Mean," 252. Both have mouths, and they have them literally. These are dead metaphors, supposing that is, that rivers and bottles did not always properly have them, but rather had them metaphorically at one time. The same might be supposed of heads of lettuce, eyes of needles, spines of books, etc. The point is, that no one thinks of these uses as metaphorical. They are properly said of all these things. This differs from Cavellian "projection" in that the possibility of the use of a word in a new context does not hinge on that word being properly attributable to the subject under discussion. When Chaucer says, "fields have eyes and woods have ears," it is not necessary—the metaphor would be dead if it were—for fields to have eyes or for woods to have ears. Compare the fields' eyes to the needles' eyes, and mark the difference.

meaning, as it is not always the case that metaphors are ambiguous. And of course, not all ambiguity is metaphorical, it may simply be a double entendre.[39] Related to the ambiguity approach is to suppose a word or words to have both a literal and a figurative meaning at the same time. But in this case we encounter something similar to the extension of meaning, and then there is nothing interesting to say about the difference between live and dead metaphors.[40] Finally, we end up with the position Cavell exposes as a confusion, where the "figurative meaning of a metaphor is the literal meaning of the corresponding simile."[41] The problem with this is that it makes the meaning of the metaphor too easily discernible and accessible.[42] This is Cavell's danger of reduction to paraphrase all over again.

How, then, are we to take Davidson's assertion that the meaning of a metaphor is its literal meaning? And why would this be controversial in a discussion of Scripture? I will take the second question first. What makes his point controversial is his explanation of metaphor in terms of "patent falsity."[43] Davidson explains that this is the usual case with metaphor. Metaphorical sentences are most often just clearly false in their literal sense. In that case, "the ordinary meaning in the context of use is odd enough to prompt us to disregard the question of literal truth."[44] It is important that Davidson is relying on a distinction between the meaning of a word (or words) and the use of those words.[45] Davidson also distinguishes the metaphor from the lie. But in doing

39. Davidson, "What Metaphors Mean," 249–50.

40. Davidson, "What Metaphors Mean," 250–52.

41. Davidson, "What Metaphors Mean," 253.

42. Davidson, "What Metaphors Mean," 254.

43. Davidson, "What Metaphors Mean," 258.

44. Davidson, "What Metaphors Mean," 258.

45. Davidson, "What Metaphors Mean," 247. Does this run afoul of a Wittgensteinian approach to language? The likeliest candidate for the relevant disjunction between Davidson and Wittgenstein would be §43 of Wittgenstein's *Philosophical Investigations*, the locus classicus for the "meaning is use" theory of language. But to talk of a theory of language is already to have made a mistake when reading Wittgenstein. Rather, we must take Wittgenstein's advice that we "look and see" both what he has written here and to what he is pointing us. Ludwig Wittgenstein, *Philosophical Investigations*, trans. G. E. M. Anscombe, P. M. S. Hacker, and Joachim Schulte (Oxford: Wiley Blackwell, 2009), §66. Concerning what he has written, Wittgenstein says, "For a *large* class of cases of the employment of the word

so, he only treats one part of the equation adequately. In the lie, he rightly clarifies, the key is "not that what you say be false but that you think it false."[46] He does not go on to say what I take to be the obverse of this statement, which is that in metaphor it is key that what you say be patently false but that you think it true. Or, in the case of a patently true metaphor—Davidson gives the example "Business is business"—you think it a truth worth saying.[47] I suspect the idiosyncrasies of Davidson's own theory of truth keep him from wanting to say this explicitly. But I think it is a warranted extension of his position and necessary if we are to apply his theory of metaphor to our discussion of Augustine and Scripture.

Are we, then, to take it that Scripture is in the habit of proposing patent falsehoods that we are to take as truths? Maybe we are. "The LORD is my rock, and my fortress, and my deliverer, my rock, in whom I take refuge, my shield, and the horn of my salvation, my stronghold" (Ps 18:2). I do not take it we ought to think "rock," "fortress," "shield," "horn," or "stronghold" are properly predicable of God. These are metaphorical uses that are patently false, and yet we think them true, we affirm them as true. The metaphors in these cases only do their work because they call to mind the literal sense of the words. So, what kind of truth are we dealing with in this case? Clearly it is not the same thing we mean when we call a proposition true. Instead, we can relate the sense in which the metaphors we utter are true to a different, but common, usage of the word "true." In addition to characterizing propositions, we also use the word "true" to describe relationships between persons.

An example of the use of "true" to describe human relationships can be found in the Catholic marriage rite. In it, both groom and bride must give their consent to the marriage, and a key element of this is a promise to be true. So, each in turn, they say, "I promise to be true to you in good times and in

---

'meaning'—though not for *all*—this word can be explained in this way: the meaning of a word is its use in the language." Wittgenstein, *Philosophical Investigations*, §43. Emphasis original. Concerning the phenomenon he is pointing out to us, it is clear that this is not a *theory* at all, but rather an empirical observation. I take Davidson's drawing upon the still relevant, if attenuated, distinction between meaning and use as an example of just this descriptive drive. In metaphor, Davidson has located one of the cases of employment where meaning and use are not the same thing.

46. Davidson, "What Metaphors Mean," 258.

47. Davidson, "What Metaphors Mean," 258.

bad, in sickness and in health."[48] In this context, we should not take "I promise to be true" to mean "I promise to only utter true propositions." Rather, this is something more like a promise of faithfulness of one person to another. And because the sacrament of matrimony is understood by the Church "to signify and share in the mystery of the unity and fruitful love that exists between Christ and his Church,"[49] it also makes sense to look to the person of Christ to understand further what the promise to be true might mean.

The promise to be true in the context of matrimony is closely related to Jesus's self-identification as the truth. When Jesus says, "I am the way, the truth, and the life" (John 14:6) he is revealing to us something about what truth is. As Bruce Marshall explains, "if Jesus Christ is the truth, then truth is borne, not only or chiefly by sentences and beliefs, but by a person. More than that: if the New Testament is right, then in the end the truth *is* a person."[50] This understanding results in a more rather than less expansive concept of truth precisely because it is not only sentences that may be true, but persons as well. Persons will be true when they are conformed to the person who *is* the truth, Jesus Christ. This conformity makes human persons into "Christ's icons," and as such they may "be seen as truth bearers."[51] This relationship with truth is not just a matter of the conformity of the intellect but of the whole self. "As whole selves, they can become 'true' when the action by which the triune God enables them to have the relevant true beliefs brings about their conformity to the risen Christ."[52] It is in this sense of "true" that we should take the promise to be true in the wedding vows. The promise is best understood to be one of mutual conformity to the truth of Christ and so to one another as his icons and truth bearers.

But what does this all have to do with the truth of metaphors? I am suggesting that a metaphor is true when I utter it in good faith, with the intention of sharing something with you. What is being shared is a particular vision of

48. International Commission on English in the Liturgy ICEL, "Rite of Marriage," in *The Rites of the Catholic Church* (Collegeville, MN: The Liturgical Press, 1990), no. 25, p. 727.

49. International Commission on English in the Liturgy ICEL, "Rite of Marriage," no. 1, p. 720.

50. Bruce Marshall, *Trinity and Truth* (Cambridge: Cambridge University Press, 2000), 242.

51. Marshall, *Trinity and Truth*, 268.

52. Marshall, *Trinity and Truth*, 268.

the world. This will be the case even if the sentence I speak is patently false. In this sense, what I am sharing when I share a metaphor is something of myself. Encounters with metaphor, their particular brand of patent falsehood, are encounters with persons. And because persons as well as propositions can be true, though in different ways, what makes the metaphor true is not the sense of the sentence but the intention with which a person speaks it.

For this reason I find a number of commonalities between this way of putting things and the way Cora Diamond has described Wittgenstein's use of the term "nonsense" (*Unsinn*) in his early and late work. A key difference between her position and Davidson's lies in the characterization of metaphorical sentences given so far. Davidson's description of metaphorical sentences as "patently false" could be reasonably said to run afoul of Diamond's reading of Wittgenstein on "nonsense," especially as it is used in the *Tractatus Logico-Philosophicus*. For Wittgenstein, Diamond explains, "if a sentence makes no sense, *no* part of it can be said to mean what it does in some other sentence which does make sense—any more than a word can be said to mean something in isolation."[53] Metaphor would seem to be a case in point for this understanding of nonsense. But I think there are grounds for taking what Diamond and Davidson have said to be compatible on this point.

If we take Davidson's adverbial modifier "patently"—as in "patently false"—to distinguish the sort of falsehood he means from other kinds, we can connect it with Diamond's "nonsense." There remains, however, one further obstacle. For Davidson, metaphors have a literal meaning, albeit a false one. The metaphor's literal meaning is given by the literal meaning of the words that comprise the metaphor. On Diamond's view, if the sentence is nonsense the words in it do not mean what they do elsewhere. Except they sort of do. In another essay, Diamond shows that the sorts of images a word conjures up for us when we hear a nonsense sentence do not do anything to change the logic of the sentence. They do not take it from nonsense to sense. But, "it is exactly those familiar mental accompaniments of the sentence that may give us the illusion that we mean something by a sentence which contains some familiar word, even though the word is not being used in its familiar logical

53. Cora Diamond, "What Nonsense Might Be," in *The Realistic Spirit* (Cambridge, MA: The MIT Press, 1991), 100.

role, and has not been given a new assignment of meaning."[54] Nonsense sentences can trade on these mental accompaniments "in the service of an imaginative understanding of persons."[55] Nonsense sentences, and our imaginative engagement with them, might help us to see others and the world as those others see it. In this way, I find Diamond's "nonsense" and Davidson's "patent falsehood" to be in the same ballpark even if not identical.

To return to Davidson, we find him asserting something close to this. Metaphors are distinguished not by their meaning, but by their use.[56] The various theories of metaphor Davidson dismissed were describing the effects metaphors have on us, even as they aimed to "provide a method for deciphering an encoded content."[57] This returns us to the Cavellian description of metaphor. Like Cavell, Davidson thinks there is a role for paraphrase. It is important to note, however, that "what we attempt in 'paraphrasing' a metaphor cannot be to give its meaning, for that lies on the surface; rather we attempt to evoke what the metaphor brings to our attention."[58] And so Davidson's account of paraphrasing a metaphor also includes the idea of initiation or invitation.

Metaphor brings something to our attention by way of a literal statement.[59] Usually, Davidson has shown, that statement is patently false. We can also follow Diamond and call this statement nonsense. Those patent falsehoods or nonsense sentences are frequently in need of elucidation, and this task is performed by paraphrase. The paraphrase is not meant to replace the metaphor, but to help the reader to see what effects the metaphor produces.[60] As Davidson puts it, "The legitimate function of so-called paraphrase is to make the lazy or ignorant reader have a vision like that of the skilled critic."[61]

---

54. Cora Diamond, "Ethics, Imagination and the Method of Wittgenstein's *Tractatus*," in *The New Wittgenstein*, ed. Alice Crary and Rupert Read (London: Routledge, 2000), 159.

55. Diamond, "Ethics, Imagination and the Method of Wittgenstein's *Tractatus*," 161.

56. Davidson, "What Metaphors Mean," 259.

57. Davidson, "What Metaphors Mean," 261.

58. Davidson, "What Metaphors Mean," 262.

59. Davidson, "What Metaphors Mean," 263.

60. Davidson, "What Metaphors Mean," 264.

61. Davidson, "What Metaphors Mean," 264.

In other words, metaphors will not be pellucidly clear to everyone. Those for whom they are can share that vision with others through the use of paraphrase. The aim of paraphrase in those instances is not to replace the metaphor but to help others see word and world differently.

Augustine, Interpretation, and Initiation

These thoughts on metaphor and meaning help make sense of Augustine's reading of Genesis 1. Augustine repeatedly warns his readers that he is not offering the definitive explanation of the text.[62] At the same time, he clearly thinks what he is offering is an interpretation that says something true about God and creation. But who is it for? In book VIII, as he is discussing the narrative of Genesis 2, he says: "You see, I am speaking to those who obey the authority of these writings [Scripture]. Because some of them want to understand paradise not properly, but figuratively."[63] He also says explicitly who it is not for:

> But for those who are completely opposed to these writings, we have had it out with them elsewhere and otherwise. Yet as much possible in this work of ours, we also aim to defend the literal meaning (*ad litteram*) of these writings. In this way those who, moved not by reason but by a stubborn or dimwitted mind, refuse to believe these things may find no reason at all by which they could show them to be false.[64]

Augustine has two purposes. The first tells his reader what a text like this does for someone who grants the authority of Scripture. The second purpose is apologetic. I will concentrate on the first, since there the

62. Cf. Augustine, *Gn. litt.*, 1.18.37, 1.20.40–41, 4.28.45, 5.1.1, 7.28.43 *inter alia*.

63. Augustine, *Gn. litt.*, 8.1.4, *PL* 34:373: "Ad eos quippe loquor, qui auctoritatem harum Litterarum sequuntur: eorum enim quidam non proprie, sed figurate paradisum intelligi volunt."

64. Augustine, *Gn. litt.*, 8.1.4, *PL* 34:373: "Nam qui omnino adversantur his litteris, alias cum eis atque aliter egimus: quanquam et haec in hoc ipso opere nostro, quantum valemus, ita defendamus ad litteram, ut qui non rationabiliter moti, propter animum pervicacem vel hebetem, credere ista detrectant, nullam tamen inveniant rationem unde falsa esse convincant."

resonances with our contemporary philosophers' understandings of metaphor and the interpreter's task are most pronounced.

I am suggesting that Augustine understands his reading of the text of Genesis 1 as a form of training. The language of the first chapter of the Bible is metaphorical, but it is so in a way that it does not make sense to say that we ought to *take* it metaphorically. What would it mean to say that I ought to *take* the ascription of "evening" and "morning" to the "one day" of creation metaphorically before the sun and the moon exist? Augustine's point on this is the same as Cavell's: "it is not quite clear how else I might take it."[65] As Augustine says, the language in the opening chapter of Genesis employs an unusual idiom, "but not such that here is the proper and there is the figural."[66] The language is clearly metaphorical, but it is not for that reason allegorical or figural.

Part of what the concept of metaphor helps us to understand is the metaphorical quality of so much of language. The language of Scripture is no exception. We can take as an example Jesus saying, "Destroy this temple, and in three days I will raise it up" (John 2:19). One way to hear this would be—as John tells us the crowd did (John 2:20)—as referring to the temple in which they were all standing. But John goes on to provide the reader with a piece of instruction about this saying, "But he spoke of the temple of his body" (John 2:21). Would it then be right to call John 2:19 allegorical or figural? It is surely metaphorical, but that does not mean it was ever referring to anything other than the death and resurrection of the Christ. We might instead call it a statement in need of a context. After the resurrection the disciples have that context. "When therefore he was raised from the dead, his disciples remembered that he had said this; and they believed the Scripture and the word which Jesus had spoken" (John 2:22). If I am right to connect the thoughts of Augustine with those of Cavell, Davidson, and Diamond on metaphorical usages of language, then Augustine is providing the instruction necessary for "those who obey the authority of these writings."[67] That instruction trains readers how the words of Genesis are being projected into a metaphorical context. Training readers in this way is meant to show them how to grasp the impact of these words and attend to their effects.

---

65. Cavell, *The Claim of Reason*, 362.

66. Augustine, *Gn. litt.*, 4.28.45, *PL* 34:315: "non tamen tanquam hic proprie, ibi figurate."

67. Augustine, *Gn. litt.*, 8.1.4, *PL* 34:373: "qui auctoritatem harum Litterarum sequuntur."

I take Augustine to have noticed some features in the text of Scripture that push him toward a Davidsonian position on the words of the first chapter of Genesis. Augustine treats the light in Genesis 1:3 as spiritual rather than physical. To establish this, he interrogates the alternative, running a *reductio ad absurdum* on the idea that we are dealing here with physical light.[68] Augustine's rhetorical strategy in these chapters makes it clear that he understands the words, in Davidsonian terms, as patent falsehoods. To be convinced that Genesis 1 is a straightforward description of solar days is to miss the point of the text, which is to elicit particular effects from the reader. A further connection with Davidson's thoughts on metaphor lies in the role of the interpreter. Metaphors, like Scripture, require interpretation. Those who are competent to do so can help others to see what truth the metaphor conveys. If the truth of metaphor is true not like propositions are true but the way people are true, what the good interpreter of metaphor helps a reader to see is the intention of the author in uttering it. When that author is the author of Scripture, what the interpreter helps a reader to see is the will of God.

Augustine's reading of the first chapter of Genesis is meant to show his readers God's intentions. The truth of Scripture is preserved by distinguishing the metaphor's meaning and its use. In order to know the *persons*—Father, Son, and Holy Spirit—who used the metaphors of Scripture to express themselves, it is necessary to attend to the effects those metaphors are meant to produce. Those effects are produced by, yet separable from, the meaning of the metaphors themselves. Augustine's interpretation of Scripture is an attempt to initiate his readers into a way of seeing and so into a form of life. His aim is to bring about an awareness of the effects Scripture induces in just the way a skilled reader helps the less skilled to grasp a metaphor that has eluded him.

It is still possible that someone will not or cannot accept Augustine's instruction on Genesis, just as it is possible for someone to refuse Cavell's paraphrases in his allegory of words. In this case the boundary of words and worlds remains in place. The invitation refused, the reader remains outside. What has been marked out here is a disagreement in judgment. In remark 242 of his *Philosophical Investigations*, Ludwig Wittgenstein explains the problem this way: "It is not only agreement in definitions, but also (odd as it may sound) agreement in judgements that is required for communication by means of

68. Augustine, *Gn. litt.*, 1.9.17–1.17.35.

language."[69] Toril Moi explains disagreement in judgments by appealing to Wittgenstein's notion of "criteria" in her book, *Revolution of the Ordinary*. Our disagreements in judgment make it evident that we do not "*share criteria* for when and how to apply concepts."[70] That is, we do not accept or cannot see how a particular word can be projected into a new context of use. In this case, the metaphorical context of Genesis 1. Augustine recognizes this possibility, and he is happy to offer instruction to those who want to grasp the truth of Scripture *ad litteram*. He also does not expect that everyone will be able to understand or accept what he has said.

Augustine does not think disagreement in judgments when interpreting Genesis 1 means those who disagree with him are consigned to the outer darkness. In book V of *De Genesi*, where he summarizes the findings of his investigation into the days of creation, he explains that it should now be possible to understand how the text of Genesis speaks of a simultaneous creation. The "one day" of Genesis 1:5 is repeated timelessly six times to create all things. "If you can," he says, "grasp it. If you cannot yet," then,

> leave these things to be discerned by those who can. You, on the other hand, may make progress by walking more slowly, with Scripture not deserting you in your infirmity but keeping a motherly pace alongside you. She speaks in such a way that she jeers at the proud by her height, frightens the attentive by her depth, feeds the grown by her verity, and suckles the little ones by her courtesy.[71]

Scripture is the agent in this passage. It works to chastise us if we have begun to think too highly of ourselves and our own comprehension of all it contains. Scripture also gently leads those who are not *yet* able to sound her depths. She takes us by the hand, as our mother, to show us the

69. Wittgenstein, *Philosophical Investigations*, §242, p. 94.

70. Toril Moi, *Revolution of the Ordinary: Literary Studies after Wittgenstein, Austin, and Cavell* (Chicago: University of Chicago Press, 2017), 224. Emphasis original.

71. Augustine, *Gn. litt.*, 5.3.6, *PL* 34:323: "si possis, apprehendas; si nondum possis, haec relinquas conspicienda valentibus: tu autem cum Scriptura non deserente infirmitatem tuam, et materno incessu tecum tardius ambulante proficias; quae sic loquitur, ut altitudine superbos irrideat, profunditate attentos terreat, veritate magnos pascat , affabilitate parvulos nutriat."

way and nourishes us according to our capacity. But supposing we do take ourselves to have grasped what Augustine is offering, what then? What are the implications of Genesis 1 narrating the all-at-once creation of everything that is not God? What does it mean for angels, the heavens, earth, plants, animals, and even humans to be created by God's eternal utterance? Before answering these questions, I will first investigate how Augustine arrives at his conclusions concerning the simultaneity of creation and show how unique this view is.

Augustine's Interpretation of Genesis

Augustine's interpretation of the six days of creation is radical. But insisting on the simultaneous creation of all things is a decision he makes for a number of theological and scriptural reasons. His distinctive reading of the creation account in Genesis 1 flows out of his conviction that "creation" names God's bringing into being *everything* that exists out of nothing. Genesis, he reasons, is a description of the creation of all things in the movement from the first day to the sixth. He emphasizes the importance of God resting from all his works on the seventh day—nothing new is created on it or after it. Angelic creatures, as he says in *De civitate Dei*, form the "the greater and more blessed part" of the heavenly city, and must be accounted for in this sequence of days.[72] He has to show where in the text describes the angelic creation. Augustine thinks the most probable candidate for this is the light spoken into existence and separated from the darkness on the first day.[73]

A second theological conviction is that God is the Lord of time. To argue that creation took place at *a* particular time is to make God subject to time. It would make the question, "What was God doing before he created the world?" something intelligible to ask. Augustine thinks this question is nonsensical, and explains why in *De Genesi contra manichaeos*. In that text, he say that God makes time along with the heaven and earth.

> We cannot, therefore, say there was any time when God had not yet made anything. For how was there time that God had not made,

72. Augustine, *civ.*, 11.9, *CSEL* 40.1:522: "quae huius civitatis et magna pars est et eo beatior."

73. Augustine, *civ.*, 11.9, *CSEL* 40.1:523.

> when he himself is the maker (*fabricator*) of all times? And if time began to be with heaven and earth, it is not possible to find a time at which God had not yet made heaven and earth.[74]

On the contrary, as he says to God in book XI of *Confessiones*, "eternity is yours."[75] This commitment to time's creatureliness makes saying what needs to be said about creation very difficult. As God's act in eternity, it makes no sense to speak of a before and after with respect to creation. And yet, that very same act gives rise to the whole succession of times, which are not themselves eternal. Augustine sums up the conundrum this way:

> And therefore you say everything you say simultaneously (*simul*) and eternally (*sempiterne*) by the Word coeternal with you. And whatever you say shall be made is made. You do not make in any other way than by speaking. Yet not all things you make by speaking are made simultaneous (*simul*) and eternal (*sempiterna*).[76]

---

74. Augustine, *Gn. c. Man.*, 1.2.3, *PL* 34:175: "Non ergo possumus dicere fuisse aliquod tempus quando Deus nondum aliquid fecerat. Quomodo enim erat tempus quod Deus non fecerat, cum omnium temporum ipse sit fabricator? Et si tempus cum coelo et terra esse coepit, non potest inveniri tempus quo Deus nondum fecerat coelum et terram." Cf. Augustine, *Gn. litt.*, 5.5.12.

75. Augustine, *conf.*, 11.1.1, *CSEL* 33:280: "tua sit aeternitas."

76. Augustine, *conf.*, 11.7.9, *CSEL* 33:287: "et ideo verbo tibi coaeterno simul et sempiterne dicis omnia, quae dicis, et fit, quidquid dicis ut fiat; nec aliter quam dicendo facis: nec tamen simul et sempiterna fiunt omnia, quae dicendo facis." One of the manuscripts cited in the *CSEL* has both instances of *sempitern-* rendered *sempiterne*, in an adverbial use. I prefer to read both *sempiterna* and *simul* as substantive uses. They are a matched pair for Augustine in this discussion. Translators have dealt with this in different ways. Henry Chadwick prefers to render both the first and second instances of *simul et sempiterne/a* as "in simultaneity and eternity." Augustine, *Confessions*, trans. Henry Chadwick (Oxford: Oxford University Press, 1991). Sr. Maria Boulding translates the first and second instance "you speak all that you speak simultaneously and eternally" and "things which you create by speaking do not all come to be simultaneously, nor are they eternal." Augustine, *Confessions*, trans. Maria Boulding (Hyde Park, NY: New City Press, 1997). I think both of these fail to capture something important about what's being said here. God speaks simultaneously and eternally but not everything God speaks into existence is for that reason simultaneous and eternal. This does not necessarily exclude creatures from simultaneity and eternity (see n77 *infra*), it just means God's eternal

The key distinction in this passage is between what is and what is not simultaneous and eternal. The speaking of the Word happens at once (*simul*) and eternally (*sempiterne*). What comes of that speaking does not necessarily have the character of being *simul* and *sempiternus*. God's act of creation in eternity brings everything that exists temporally into existence.[77]

These informing convictions lead to Augustine's *sui generis* interpretation of creation. "Light" is taken to mean angelic creatures, "evening" and "morning" and the succession of "days" describe a timeless event. The event does not occur in time but is the presupposition for all times. One way to show how distinct Augustine's reading is, and to understand it as a significant theological achievement, is to examine Thomas Aquinas's articles in the *Summa Theologiae* on the same subject. To keep the comparison manageable, I will look at question 67 of the Prima Pars, which along with questions 68 and 69 treat the work of the first three days of Genesis 1. Thomas calls this the work of distinction (*opus distinctionis*) in his introduction to question 67.[78]

He begins this series of articles with a discussion of whether "light" is used metaphorically or properly when speaking of spiritual things.[79] In the *respondeo* of this first article, Thomas explains how the name "light" may be used in two ways, "according to its first ascription" and "according to the use

---

speech act does not only make simultaneous and eternal things. It is instead the eternal ground that holds all things—eternal and temporal alike—in existence.

77. NB Augustine does not by this statement rule out the bringing into being things that exist simultaneously (*simul*) and eternally (*sempiterne*). The likely candidate for a class of things that might exist this way is the angels. Augustine says more than once in *De Genesi ad litteram* that the angels enjoy God's own eternity. They do not partake of it by their own nature but rather by their contemplation of God—cf. Augustine, *Gn. litt.*, 2.8.17, *PL* 34:269: "qui ex quo creati sunt, ipsa Verbi aeternitate sancta et pia contemplatione perfruuntur"; *Gn. litt.*, 4.29.46, *PL* 34:315: "Simul hoc totum possint, simul hoc totum faciant; possunt tamen et faciunt. Simul ergo habent et diem, et vesperam, et mane." In the latter citation we find the capacity for simultaneous (*simul*) contemplation attributed to the angels. The key distinction in the case of angels, bearing in mind Augustine's talk of the act of creation, seems to be that they are not *coaeterni* while still being *sempiterni*.

78. Thomas Aquinas, *ST*, I.67.

79. *ST*, I.67.1 1, *sed contra*.

of the name."[80] What he says here is broadly congruent with the description of metaphorical usage as explained by Cavell and Davidson. In particular, what he says about speaking according to the use of a name comports well with what Davidson has to say about usage and "dead metaphors." By this Davidson means the transition in language that takes place when usage changes from metaphorical to literal. "Once upon a time, I suppose," Davidson muses, "rivers and bottles did not, as they do now, literally have mouths."[81] Thomas says something nearly identical about the word light: "For it was first instituted to signify what the sense of sight makes manifest, but afterward it was extended to signify everything that any kind of cognition makes manifest."[82] Whether what you say about light is said "properly" (*proprie*) or "metaphorically" (*metaphorice*) has everything to do with how the word is used.[83] For Thomas, as for Cavell and Davidson, the lines separating these uses will be fuzzy. Sometimes it will be clear that what is said about light falls under the rubric of "first ascription" (*secundum primam impositionem*) or "use of the name" (*secundum usum nominis*).

In the following two articles, Thomas meditates on the nature of light in its first ascription.[84] He seeks to resolve whether light is a body or a quality. This sets the stage for what will come in the fourth article and beyond. Augustine's *ad litteram* reading of Genesis stands apart for Thomas, and in many ways requires its own treatment and commentary. In this article and the articles of the following questions treating the days of creation, the florilegial quality of Thomas's *Summa* is on full display. Augustine's reading of Genesis is presented alongside those of Basil of Caesarea, John Chrysostom, John Damascene, Origen, and Maimonides.[85] These sections of the *Summa* are interesting not only for the many interpretations presented but because Thomas appears less interested to resolve all of the differences between them.

---

80. *ST*, I.67.1 *resp*: "secundum primam eius impositionem" and "secundum usum nominis."

81. Davidson, "What Metaphors Mean," 252.

82. *ST*, I.67.1 *resp*: "Nam primo quidem est institutum ad significandum id quod facit manifestationem in sensu visus, postmodum autem extensum est ad significandum omne illud quod facit manifestationem secundum quamcumque cognitionem."

83. *ST*, I.67.1 *resp*.

84. *ST*, I.67.2–3.

85. Cf. *ST*, I.67–74.

Even so, it is clear that Thomas hews closer to some interpretations of creation than others.

In the fourth article of question 67, Thomas presents the first of the two theological principles discussed above—the necessity of accounting for the creation of the angels—which govern Augustine's interpretation of Genesis. He explains, "For it seems to Augustine that it would not have been fitting for Moses to leave out the production of the spiritual creation."[86] This, Thomas says, leads Augustine to say that the light of the first day is spiritual light, the created light of angelic intelligence.[87] Thomas does not end the discussion there, ruling one way or another on the soundness of this interpretation. Instead he presents additional possible interpretations, introducing them with a telling, "But, it seems to others . . ."[88] He goes on to show how Basil's and Chrysostom's readings support, for various reasons, an omission of the angels in the narrative of creation. With this setup, Thomas presents his own positions on the matter in the replies to objections two and three. These replies indicate his preference for a less exotic interpretation of the days of creation than the one Augustine provides in *De Genesi*.

Perhaps even more telling is Thomas's presentation of one of Augustine's concerns about reading the days of creation nonmetaphorically, as an objection in question 67. Augustine decided that trying to connect the days of creation to solar days causes more problems than it resolves. This is especially true given the nonexistence of the heavenly bodies before the fourth day of creation.[89] Thomas presents this concern as the second objection in article 4 of question 67: "It is through light that night is distinguished from day. But this is brought about through the sun, which is set down as having been made on the fourth day. Therefore the production of light ought not to be put on the first day."[90] Thomas replies to this objection, which can clearly

86. *ST*, I.67.4 *resp*: "Augustino enim videtur quod non fuerit conveniens Moysen praetermisisse spiritualis creaturae productionem."

87. *ST*, I.67.4 *resp*.

88. *ST*, I.67.4 *resp*: "Aliis autem videtur . . ." It would be possible to translate this even more strongly, perhaps, as "On the contrary, it seems to others . . .," but I'm not entirely sure contrariness is what's at stake here.

89. Augustine, *Gn. litt.*, 1.10.21.

90. *ST*, I.67.4 2: "per lucem distinguitur nox a die. Hoc autem fit per solem, qui ponitur factus die quarta. Ergo non debuit poni productio lucis prima die."

be attributed to Augustine, by doubling down on the "light" of Genesis 1:3 being light of the first ascription. He answers, citing Dionysius, "that the light was the light of the sun, still formless as of yet, but that it was already the substance of the sun and had a general illuminative power."[91] In this same reply, he affirms precisely those things Augustine finds problematic with the position that the days of creation are solar days. In particular, he affirms talk of illuminating the different hemispheres and so of the division of time according to solar days.[92]

My exegesis of the *Summa* shows Thomas as a subtle critic who gives careful attention to multiple strains of argument in the tradition of interpretation. Reading him closely, it is clear that he has major disagreements with Augustine's interpretive strategy. He names it here and elsewhere as something that stands apart from other major figures.[93] Basil and Chrysostom are much closer in agreement about the literal meaning of the days of creation. Thomas locates himself among their ranks by opting to read the *ad litteram* signification of "light" in its first ascription. These disagreements are not cosmetic but substantive in nature. Thomas does not say Augustine's reading is wrong, but he certainly thinks there is something more edifying to be gained by taking Genesis 1 to be referring to something occurring in the order of time. This preference is apparent in his discussion of illumination from "solar substance." One of the distinctions already in play with God's creation of light is a distinction "quantum ad tempus"—as to time.[94]

Immediately following his disavowal of the Augustinian atemporal creation narrative comes an important tip of the hat to the validity of Augustine's interpretive strategy. Though there are fundamental disagreements at stake, Thomas has a clear vision of what that disagreement does and does not mean. In the first article of question 68, Thomas cites some important Augustinian principles of scriptural interpretation, taken directly from *De Genesi ad litteram*. "As Augustine teaches," Thomas begins,

91. *ST*, I.67.4 *ad* 2: "quod illa lux fuit lux solis, sed adhuc informis, quantum ad hoc, quod iam erat substantia solis, et habebat virtutem illuminativam in communi."

92. *ST*, I.67.4 *ad* 2. He elaborates this position further citing Basil in I.67.4 *ad* 3.

93. Cf. esp. *ST*, 1.74.3

94. *ST*, I.67.4 *ad* 2.

> two things are to be kept in mind in questions of this sort. The first is certainly that the truth of Scripture be unshakably held. The second is, when Holy Scripture can be laid open in manifold ways, no one should cleave absolutely to an exposition such that if it were shown to be false by certain reason, someone might presume to assert it to be the sense of Scripture. So that Scripture might not be for this reason derided by the unfaithful, and that the way of believing might not be closed off to them.[95]

By disagreeing with Augustine, Thomas shows that they do not share the same judgment about the meaning of the text of Genesis 1 *ad litteram*. What he does not mean is that this disagreement in judgment settles the matter or that it would be prudent to press this disagreement. This is precisely because "Scripture can be laid open in manifold ways."

Truth in Interpretation

I suggest we take Thomas to be rising to a challenge Augustine levied in *De Genesi*. In a number of places throughout the work, Augustine explains the method of his commentary as one that avoids hasty or rash conclusions.[96] What he means by this is precisely what Thomas outlines in I.67.1: the readings we give of Scripture must be provisional without in any way thinking the truth of Scripture itself to be provisional. As Augustine puts it in *De doctrina*, when we do not understand the meaning of Scripture, we still ought "to think and believe what is written there to be better and truer—even if it is hidden—than what we ourselves can discern."[97] In *De Genesi* Augustine challenges others to offer a better, more edifying, interpretation.

> As far as I could, I unfurled and brought forth the many possible senses of the words in the book of Genesis, which were set down obscurely to discipline us, not rashly affirming any particular one so as

95. *ST*, I.68.1 *resp*.

96. Cf. Augustine, *Gn. litt.*, 1.20.40, 5.1.1, 7.28.43, 12.1.1, 7.28.43.

97. Augustine, *doct. chr.*, 2.7.9, *PL* 34:39: "cogitare potius et credere id esse melius et verius quod ibi scriptum est, etiam si lateat, quam id quod nos per nosmetipsos sapere possumus."

> to rule out another, perhaps better, explanation. So that each person may pick out by his own lights what he is able to grasp.[98]

He later affirms that his explanations are put forward "without preventing anyone the freedom of understanding it better."[99] Thomas accepts this challenge to understand the words of Genesis better than Augustine. Augustine himself encouraged this, so long as the interpretation did not become an idol and so a stumbling block.

How might an interpretation of Scripture become a stumbling block? There are, I think, two interrelated ways of answering this. First, in relation to a person's own faith, and second in relation to the faith of others. If an interpretation of Scripture is held in such a way that upon learning that it cannot possibly be true someone feels inclined to abandon her faith altogether, the interpretation is clearly a stumbling block. Take, as a hypothetical, Thomas holding to his explanation of the creation of the *substantia solis* on the first day, along with his contention that its general illuminative power shone upon the earth and divided day and night. If Thomas, upon learning the earth would not be around for, roughly, nine billion years following the birth of the cosmos, took it to mean not that he was wrong but that Scripture was untrue, he would have a problem. This would indicate a malformed relationship to Scripture from the start. It would show that he thought that Scripture was subject to his interpretations rather than his interpretations being subject to it. Second, and in a related way, it would indicate a lack of trust in God and God's words. It would show he considered the truths of Scripture themselves liable to disproof by the discovery of facts about the world.

There is a flipside to this particular deformity. It still involves making the truth of Scripture subject to disproof via the natural sciences. It simply refuses to admit the necessary evidence has been produced to disprove it. Cleaving to interpretations in this way attempts to settle the meaning of a particular scriptural text in such a way that no other interpretation of the text is possible.

---

98. Augustine, *Gn. litt.*, 1.20.40, *PL* 34:261: "librum Geneseos multipliciter, quantum potui, enucleavi, protulique sententias de verbis ad exercitationem nostram obscure positis; non aliquid unum temere affirmans cum praejudicio alterius expositionis fortasse melioris, ut pro suo modulo eligat quisque quod capere possit."

99. Augustine, *Gn. litt.*, 5.1.1, *PL* 34:321: "nulli intercludens melius intelligendi licentiam."

The interpretation of Genesis is a notoriously fraught example. Those who have succumbed to this particular form of idolatry maintain that *this* (*this* can be whatever you like) is the meaning of the text, and as goes the truth of the interpretation, so goes the truth of Scripture as a whole. When confronted with well-founded evidence that contradicts this explanation of the text, this kind of interpreter refuses to admit it as valid. There is something admirable, if extraordinarily misguided, about this kind of relationship to Scripture. To hold its truth so strongly as to reject all evidence that might undermine it indicates a rugged determination to follow Christ whatever the cost. But this way of reading the Bible is not founded on the truth of Scripture. It is founded on the truth of an interpretation of Scripture. Their fate is that of all idol makers and worshippers: "Who fashions a god or casts an image, that is profitable for nothing? Behold, all his fellows shall be put to shame, and the craftsmen are but men; let them all assemble, let them stand forth, they shall be terrified, they shall be put to shame together" (Isa 44:10–11).

The properly Christian way to read and interpret Scripture weaves together the strengths of both these positions—pugnacious tenacity in the face of contradiction combined with a docile receptivity toward revisionist readings. It does so by insisting on the truth of Scripture. This is distinct from an insistence on the truth of a particular interpretation of Scripture. At root, this is a conviction that God is the truth (John 14:6). The words that pour forth as a gift from him cannot be untrue. By this principle—the principle of gift—the same applies to the created order as a whole. In other words, the truth of Scripture and the truth of creation cannot contradict one another, as both have their origin in God's own truth. Bonaventure, in the *Breviloquium*, puts this point beautifully,

> The first principle may make himself recognizable to us through Scripture and through creation. He shows himself through the book of creation as the effective principle, through the book of Scripture as the restorative principle. That restorative principle cannot be known unless the effective principle is known as well. For that reason Holy Scripture, although it may principally deal with the works of restoration, ought to deal nonetheless with the work of creation, insofar as it may lead to knowledge (*cognitionem*) of the first making and remaking (*efficientis et reficientis*) principle. Therefore that knowledge

> is sublime and salvific: sublime, because it is about the effective principle, which is God the creator; salvific, because it is about the restorative principle, which is Christ the savior and mediator.[100]

Knowledge of creation and knowledge of Scripture may both provide knowledge of God as *primum principium*. We relate to God as first principle in different ways, as the creator and as the restorer of all things. It follows that different ways of knowing will be suitable to these different modes of relation. In no way, however, can the truths discerned in creation or Scripture contradict one another. In that case, they would not be truths at all.[101]

I have already given an account of the concept of truth as it relates to persons. Central to that argument is the idea that truth is a person, Jesus Christ. Part of the point of that discussion was to show how truth remains an important concept in the deployment of metaphor. The sort of truth dealt with was not propositional but the sort of truth that obtains between persons. I illustrated this with the example of marital vows. The promise to be true involved conforming oneself to the person of Jesus Christ. I now intend to return to Marshall and Davidson for help in discussing propositional truth. This part of the investigation aims at coming to terms with our failures to know the truth. In other words, I want to show how we can be and often are wrong about what Scripture or creation are telling us. Further, I hope to make clear that these epistemic failures do not undermine the truth of Scripture or creation.

The truths of Scripture and creation are often opaque to us. That this is so does not damage either of their claims to truth. Something similar happens

---

100. Bonaventure, *Breviloquium*, in *Opera Omnia*, vol. V (Quarrachi: Typographia Collegii S. Bonaventurae, 1891), II.5: "primum principium reddat se nobis cognoscibile et per Scripturam et per creaturam, per librum creaturae se manifestat ut principium effectivum, per librum Scripturae ut principium re- parativum; et quia principium reparativum non potest cognosci, nisi cognoscatur et effectivum: ideo sacra Scriptura, licet principaliter agat de operibus reparationis, agere nihilominus debet de opere conditionis, in quantum tamen ducit in cognitionem primi principii efficientis et reficientis; et ideo ipsa est cognitio sublimis et salutaris: sublimis, quia de principio effectivo, quod est Deus creator; salutaris, quia de principio reparativo, quod est Christus salvator et mediator."

101. Cf. Leo XIII, *Providentissimus Deus*, *DS* 3287: "Nulla quidem theologum inter et physicum vera dissensio intercesserit, dum suis uterque finibus se contineant."

when examining the truth content of a sentence in an unfamiliar language. There is no requirement that I understand "Le chat est noir," to be translatable as, "The cat is black," in order for it to be true. The truth conditions for this sentence can be identified using what Donald Davidson calls "T-sentences."[102] The truth of the statement can be framed in this way: "'Le chat est noir' is true if and only if le chat est noir." This tells us something about how the concept of truth is operative for this sentence, that is, what makes the sentence true. T-sentences also gives us some information about the range of the concept of truth in a particular language. Each T-sentence marks out some territory for "truth" as applicable to this or that sentence in the language.[103] What this definition provides us is a "purely extensional" approach to truth, by showing where and how it applies.[104]

What this definition of the concept of truth does not give is a way of knowing whether and when we have got it right apart from knowing something about the language in which a sentence is uttered or written. So "Le chat est noir," may be true and may be so based on conditions entirely independent of my knowing what those conditions are. Consider the following thought experiment. Suppose I am learning French. Once a week, I go to my tutor's house and in this house there is a black cat. The tutor provides me with some of the rudiments of the language by pointing at everyday objects and saying something about them: "Le fourchette est dans l'évier," "L'arbre est en dehors de la fenêtre," "Le chat est noir." But each time she points to the cat, it is sitting on a mat near the back door. Let us assume that I have correctly grasped the meaning of the other two sentences—"Le fourchette est dans l'évier" and "L'arbre est en dehors de la fenêtre"—but that my grasp of them has also led me to make a mistake. The mistake I make is thinking "Le chat est noir" is meant to indicate spatial relations just like the other two sentences. My tutor's black cat is always seated in the same place, on the mat, and so I take "Le chat est noir" to be translatable as "The cat is on the mat." Another way to put this using the T-sentence formula is to say I have made a mistake concerning the sentence's truth conditions. I think "'Le chat est

102. For the background of this whole discussion, see Marshall, *Trinity and Truth*, 233–41.

103. Marshall, *Trinity and Truth*, 234.

104. Marshall, *Trinity and Truth*, 234.

noir' is true if and only if the cat is on the mat." I am wrong about this, but so far I do not suspect it and so do not see a need to go searching for a different definition of "noir."

What would it take for me to see that I had made a mistake about the truth conditions for "Le chat est noir"? Suppose the next time I go to my tutor's house, the cat is now on the window sill. Without missing a beat, my tutor points to various objects, rattling off French sentences. This time when she points to the cat, she says again "Le chat est noir." Puzzlement ensues. Perhaps I ask "Le chat est noir?" pointing at the cat. Maybe I also gesture toward the mat. It is now clear to me and to my tutor that I have misunderstood the sentence. It becomes reasonable to ask in English, "Well, then what does 'noir' mean?" When my tutor says, "It means black," I quickly grasp the nature of my mistake. Because I am learning the language, it will not be hard to revise my sense of "noir." Language learners expect these kinds of mistakes of usage to occur. The revised T-sentence that properly represents the truth conditions would go, "'Le chat est noir' is true if and only if the cat is black." This was always the case for this sentence. My failure to know it was an epistemic failure. The sentence's meaning did not depend upon my knowing what it meant but instead on what "Le chat est noir" means in French.

This vignette is meant to illustrate something analogous that might occur when trying to grasp the truth of the book of creation or the book of Scripture. Neither depends on me knowing or understanding the truth in order for it to be true. To stick with the case of the black cat, it will sometimes happen that we realize our error. I was certain that "Le chat est noir" could be translated as "The cat is on the mat." In a similar way, I might read the book of creation and be led to think a hierarchical cosmos composed of heavenly spheres rotating around the earth makes a lot of sense. Like the other French sentences—"Le fourchette est dans l'évier" and "L'arbre est en dehors de la fenêtre"—uttered around the same time as "Le chat est noir," I might be fooled by the context of my investigation of creation. From my perspective, it seems quite right to say the heavenly bodies rotate around the earth. Realizing this is analogous to realizing I was mistaken about the meaning of "Le chat est noir." It might involve a great deal more puzzlement than for someone learning a foreign language, who expects these kinds of mistakes. What is required, though, is the same thing required of the language-learner. It requires a revision of the criteria used in applying my concept of creation. This is not a revision of the truth of creation but of my grasp of that truth.

The same is also true of the book of Scripture. This is what Augustine and Thomas Aquinas mean for us to understand when they describe the kind of assent we ought to give to particular interpretations of Scripture. Just as I do not doubt the truth of my tutor's statement, "Le chat est noir," even when I realize I have failed to interpret it correctly, neither do I doubt the truth of Scripture, even when facts come to light that make a particular interpretation of it untenable. Augustine makes this point in the first book of *De Genesi*. He explains that in the case where it is unclear what Scripture means, where various interpretations can account for the way the words run, it is possible to hold to either one. An interpretation may be held, "so long as it is not against the faith, until it is refuted by most certain (*certissima*) truth. If that were to occur, then this [interpretation] was not contained by Holy Scripture, but had been supposed by human ignorance."[105] What might count as a definite refutation "by most certain truth" of a particular interpretation of Scripture? Augustine takes up this point and explains that Christians do not necessarily have any special insight on these matters. The knowledge that may be read from the book of creation is just as well had by pagans as by those who worship the Triune Lord.[106]

There is a structural point here as well. However provisional our interpretations of the book of creation and the book of Scripture are, it is important when possible to show that they are compatible. Neither of the interpretations may be *contra fidem*, and when the chips are down, Augustine is clear on where his trust lies. But there is something worthwhile in looking into pagan explanations of created phenomena and showing how they can be understood to comport with the Catholic faith. So, Augustine says,

> we should show that whatever they have been able to demonstrate about the nature of things by way of accurate sources is not contrary to our literature. But whatever they may have produced from any

105. Augustine, *Gn. litt.*, 1.19.38, *PL* 34:260: "tamdiu non est contra fidem, donec veritate certissima refellatur. Quod si factum fuerit, non hoc habebat divina Scriptura, sed hoc senserat humana ignorantia."

106. Augustine, *Gn. litt.*, 1.19.39.

> of their volumes contrary to our literature (that is, the literature of the Catholic faith) we should either deftly show, or believe beyond a shadow of a doubt, to be absolutely false.[107]

Augustine is clearly committed to the priority of the faith. But there is something else at stake here, too. The theological point is that there can be no contradiction between the truth of creation and the truth of Scripture because theirs is a participation in God's truth. As Herbert McCabe has put it, Scripture is itself a theological interpretation of history, and "here we have a uniquely authentic interpretation because the author of the interpretation is also the author of the facts themselves."[108]

This does not shield our interpretations of either creation or Scripture from error in the order of knowing. Augustine's final point about believing *nulla dubitatione* is an assertion about the order of being. His clarity of conviction is rooted in the proper place, God's own truth, rather than human interpretations of that truth. And for this reason Augustine can affirm the following:

> It is commonly the case that even a non-Christian will know something about the earth, the sky, the other elements of this world, the motion and revolution or even the magnitude and distances of the stars, the precise eclipses of the sun and moon, the cycles of years and times, the natures of animals, fruits, stones, and other things like this. And he knows these things by most certain (*certissima*) reason or experiments.[109]

---

107. Augustine, *Gn. litt.*, 1.21.41, *PL* 34:262: "ut quidquid ipsi de natura rerum veracibus documentis demonstrare potuerint, ostendamus nostris Litteris non esse contrarium. Quidquid autem de quibuslibet suis voluminibus his nostris Litteris, id est catholicae fidei contrarium protulerint, aut aliqua etiam facultate ostendamus, aut nulla dubitatione credamus esse falsissimum."

108. Herbert McCabe, *The New Creation* (London: Continuum International, 2010), 6.

109. Augustine, *Gn. litt.*, 1.19.39, *PL* 34:261: "Plerumque enim accidit ut aliquid de terra, de coelo, de caeteris mundi hujus elementis, de motu et conversione vel etiam magnitudine et intervallis siderum, de certis defectibus solis ac lunae, de circuitibus annorum et temporum, de naturis animalium, fruticum, lapidum, atque hujusmodi caeteris, etiam non christianus ita noverit, ut certissima ratione vel experientia teneat."

Augustine uses the same adjective, *certissima*, which he used to describe the possibility of refutation in the preceding paragraph of *De Genesi*.[110] The nonexhaustive list of things pagans know also includes a specification of how they know them. And so, the *certissima* truth that shows an interpretation of Scripture to be false comes through *certissima* reason or experiments.

If it is the case that reason and experimentation have shown ancient cosmology to be defunct, where does that leave us? What follows, in other words, if we accept the conclusions of modern physics that indicate a universe that is around 13.7 billion years old, that the earth itself is some 4 billion years old, that the heavens are not comprised of celestial spheres rotating around the earth but rather planets and stars and galaxies dancing to gravity's tune in vast deserts of interplanetary, interstellar, and intergalactic space? It seems that certain interpretations of the first chapter of Genesis are off the table. This in no way impugns the truth of the narrative, but places it in a new context. This context is informed by our complementary grasp of the truths of the book of creation. It makes no sense to say Genesis 1 narrates the beginning of division of times if by that you mean, as Thomas explains he does, light shining upon the surface of the earth. Neither does this mean Thomas's explanation was a bad one. He offered it provisionally, in light of what he knew about the physical world. We cannot, however, be happy with the same explanation. Something else must be offered if Christians are to keep from scandalizing pagans in ways that prevent them from trusting the truth of what Scripture says elsewhere.[111]

We need an interpretation of Genesis that can bear the weight of a cosmos of unfathomable immensity. The readings proposed by Thomas and the Fathers he follows, who take the *ad litteram* meaning of the text to indicate a temporal unfolding over a week of solar days, buckle under this burden. What I will show going forward is that Augustine's *ad litteram* reading *can* bear this weight. Because it can, it also provides the conceptual resources to answer pressing questions about the origins of death and death's relation to the double fall of angels and humans.

110. Augustine, *Gn. litt.*, 1.19.38.

111. Augustine, *Gn. litt.*, 1.19.39.

CHAPTER TWO

What Are the *Rationes Seminales*?

What Does Augustine Mean by "Ratio"?

"*Ratio*" does a lot of work in theological Latin. One of Augustine's translators has noted how its plural form, *rationes*, dominates the whole of *De Genesi ad litteram*. At the same time he confesses, "no single satisfactory translation can be provided."[1] Given what we have already seen of Augustine's interpretation of Genesis, something about *ratio* in the singular should stand out, the connection of the Latin *ratio* with the Greek *logos*. As I made clear in the last chapter, Augustine ties the "Let there be light" of Genesis 1 to the Prologue of the Gospel of John. In translation, the Greek *logos* of John's gospel becomes the Latin *verbum*. The Son is the Word, and the Father's uttering that Word is the timeless act of creation. But in addition to *verbum* or "word," some of the valences of *logos* are better captured by the Latin *ratio*. As Hill notes, this word cannot be translated into English without loss—much as *logos* loses some of its connotations when rendered into Latin as *verbum*. In order to understand how Augustine uses the concept of the *rationes seminales*, I will first attend to the different ways he uses the term "*ratio*" in the text of *De Genesi ad litteram*.

The first way Augustine uses *ratio* is one I have already pointed out. He uses *ratio* to mean "reason" in the sense of human reckoning or cogitation. In book I of *De genesi*, he explains that *certa ratio* (sound reason) can show an interpretation of Scripture to be true.[2] On the other hand, an interpretation is shown to be false "certissima ratione" (by most certain reason).[3] This usage

1. Augustine, "The Literal Meaning of Genesis," in *The Works of Saint Agustine: A Translation for the 21st Century: On Genesis*, ed. John E. Rotelle, trans. Edmund Hill (Hyde Park, NY: New City Press, 2002), 175n9.

2. Augustine, *Gn. litt.*, 1.19.38, *PL* 34:260.

3. Augustine, *Gn. litt.*, 1.19.39, *PL* 34:261.

shows up in a number of places in the work,[4] and in each case refers to something humans do.

A second, related, sense appears when Augustine is investigating the meaning of the "evening" and "morning" of Genesis 1. He has given some possible interpretations of these words. But now he wonders whether "there may be some other *ratio* of these words to be sought out more diligently."[5] Because he is discussing the words of Scripture, this use is slightly more complicated. As I have shown, Augustine and the Catholic magisterium have affirmed the divine and human authorship of the Bible. At the same time, this authorship cannot be parsed, here the divine, there the human. The words of Scripture are divine and human all the way down. When it comes to speaking of the *ratio* of these words, how are we to take it? That these words are human words argues for a fit with the first sense of *ratio* understood in terms of human reckoning or thought. That these words are divine inclines toward a sense of *ratio* understood in terms of the divine *logos*. This does little to clarify things, as I have yet to show how Augustine uses *ratio* in the divine sense. For now, I will settle on *ratio* used here to vaguely indicate "meaning," with the caveat that the meaning of the words of Scripture is both human and divine.

The third use of *ratio*, pointed out in the last paragraph, is the one applicable to God. In this case, the *ratio* under discussion is *in* the Word of God. The *ratio* that is in the Word of God is the *ratio* of the things made through him, which is to say, the whole of the cosmos, "things visible and invisible" (Col 1:16). I will enumerate a few of Augustine's uses of *ratio* in this sense in order to achieve conceptual clarity. In book II of *De Genesi ad litteram*, Augustine wonders how the text of Genesis 1 might indicate the three persons of the Trinity. He moves the discussion to the Prologue of John, verses 3 and 4, where his text diverges from modern versions. Asking whether the repeated "fiat" of Genesis 1 is the Word of the Father, he explains that in this Word, the Father's only begotten Son, "are all created things, even before they are created."[6] "Whatever is in him," and here he is referencing his version of

4. Cf. Augustine, *Gn. litt.*, 8.8.16, 11.8.10, 11.16.21, 12.11.22.

5. Augustine, *Gn. litt.*, 2.14.28, *PL* 34:275: "aliqua alia ratio sit horum verborum diligentius vestiganda."

6. Augustine, *Gn. litt.* 2.6.12, *PL* 34:268: "unigenitus Filius, in quo sunt omnia quae creantur, etiam antequam creentur."

John, "is life, because whatever was made through him is, in him, life—life the creator, though when below him, life the creature."[7] This phrase, "life the creator" (*vita creatrix*) is an affirmation of divine simplicity. Created things in God must in some sense be identical with God if we are not to introduce composition into the divine nature. In him, in other words, created things just are life, the life that the Word of God is.

Divine simplicity does not exclude the difference between created things and God. Augustine explains that the things made through the Word are in him in one way, while what he is himself is in him in another.[8] But what are we to make of this? The passage that asserts the existence of created things in the Word of God—as distinct from what the Word himself is—also describes how this is the case. The things made through him are in him because the Word "rules and holds them together."[9] The word "rules" (*regit*) in this passage could be translated as "governs," "guides," or "controls"; my choice to translate it as "rules" is deliberate. This word links up with Augustine's third use of *ratio*, which appears in the very same paragraph of *De Genesi ad litteram*. The *ratio* of created things is in the Word of God and alive with the very life of God. Were it not, nothing at all could be created.[10] Here *ratio* also has the sense of "rule." And so "creandi ratio" can be Englished, "the rule of things to be created." These two uses of "rule" fit together well. When this connection between *regit* and *ratio* is drawn out, it shows us how created things are in the Word of God and yet are in him otherwise than he is in himself.

To summarize, the "rule" (*ratio*) of all created things is in the Word of God as their measure. The Word "rules" (*regit*) them by being that by which

---

7. Augustine, *Gn. litt.*, 2.6.12, *PL* 34:268: "et quidquid in illo est, vita est; quia quidquid per eum factum est, in ipso vita est, et vita utique creatrix, sub illo autem creatura." For more evidence of this textual variant, see also Augustine's Tractates on the Gospel of John, e.g., *Io. ev. tr.* 1.16 citing John 1:3, *PL* 35:1387: "Omnia *ergo, fratres*, omnia *omnino* per ipsum facta sunt, et sine ipso factum est nihil. *Sed quomodo per ipsum facta sunt omnia?* Quod factum est, in illo vita est."

8. Augustine, *Gn. litt.*, 2.6.12, *PL* 34:268: "Aliter ergo in illo sunt ea quae per illum facta sunt . . . aliter autem in illo sunt ea quae ipse est."

9. Augustine, *Gn. litt.*, 2.6.12, *PL* 34:268: "quia regit et continet ea."

10. Augustine, *Gn. litt.*, 2.6.12, *PL* 34:268: "Quia ergo nihil creari posset sive ante tempora, quod quidem non est Creatori coaeternum, sive ab exordio temporum, sive in aliquo tempore, cujus creandi ratio, si tamen ratio recte dicitur, non in Dei Verbo Patri coaeterno coaeterna vita viveret."

they are made and reckoned—reckoned being a way of saying at once set right, known, and measured all at once. This use of *ratio* shows up repeatedly throughout *De Genesi ad litteram*.[11] But Augustine's argument began on a note of identification. And it is worth dwelling on the precise wording of a citation I only paraphrased above, where Augustine observes, "nothing could be created . . . the rule (*ratio*) of which—if it is rightly called a rule (*ratio*)—was not enlivened with coeternal life in the Word of God with the coeternal Father."[12] The life of these *creandi*, things to be created, is the life of the Word of God. In a very real sense they are identical with that Word. They have the "*Logos*" as their "*ratio*."

I have identified three distinct usages of *ratio*, which Augustine deploys for different purposes throughout *De Genesi*. One refers principally to cognition, and can be understood as way of saying "reason" as in, "It can be known by human reason." The second use, *ratio horum verborum*, when referring to the words of Scripture, could most nearly be translated as "meaning."[13] And now we are in a slightly better position to understand what the *ratio* of the words of Scripture is in divine terms. The *ratio* of Scripture's words, their rule, is the Word of God, the *Logos*. The third use of *ratio*, comes in the *creandi ratio*, the rule of things to be created, which is coeternal with the Word without simply being identical with him. These three uses of *ratio* are not exhaustive of the term's connotations, even in Augustine's text, but they give a sense of its range. The "family resemblances" between these three uses are all directly connected to this investigation.[14] Moving forward, I will emphasize the third connotation in order to account for the relation between *ratio* in the Word and *rationes seminales* in the created order.

Augustine on the Divine Ideas

Identity and difference are each transcended by linking *ratio* in the third sense with the divine *Logos*. The *creandi ratio* is God. And in that sense, all the things that are not God are also in God. They only are and only can be by

11. Cf. *inter alia* Augustine, *Gn. litt.*, 2.8.17, 3.12.18, 4.32.50, 8.26.48, 9.2.3.

12. Augustine, *Gn. litt.*, 2.6.12, *PL* 34:268: "nihil creari posset . . . cujus creandi ratio, si tamen ratio recte dicitur, non in Dei Verbo Patri coaeterno coaeterna vita viveret."

13. Augustine, *Gn. litt.*, 2.14.28, *PL* 34:275.

14. Wittgenstein, *Philosophical Investigations*, §67.

virtue of this rule, the *Logos*, the Word of God who is with God and is God (John 1:1). The things that are not God exist because they have been created. The *ratio* that is in God and so identical with God also has a differentiated existence in created things. Those created things have been given their existence by this *ratio*, which is "enlivened with coeternal life in the Word of God with the coeternal Father."[15] God wills the existence of created things within and without himself. Within himself, they exist by virtue of their coeternality with the Word of God. Without himself, they exist by virtue of the gift of creation. This is not the conferral of independent existence—whatever that would mean—but of dependent existence.

Created things come to be and are preserved in being by God's gratuitous gift of self. God is, as Thomas Aquinas puts it, "to be itself, subsisting through itself."[16] God gives of his selfsame act of subsistent being to call creatures into existence out of nothing. He is the *ratio* of all things that are not God because he gives them a share of this same *ratio*. Within him this *ratio* is the rule that is the Word of God. Without him, in the multiplicity of created things, this one *ratio* becomes many *rationes*. They are participations in the one *ratio* received as gift. The gift grants them existence not as absolute beings but as beings reliant on the continuous outpouring of God's own act of being. This outpouring is the act that constitutes them as creatures. All creaturely powers and potencies are downstream of God's gift of self.

We can also consider the plurality of the *rationes* within God. The *ratio* does not simply go from unity to multiplicity in the act of creation. The created *rationes* have their source in the uncreated *rationes*, which Thomas Aquinas calls the "rationes ideales."[17] Augustine treats these uncreated *rationes* in question 46 of his *De diversis quaestionibus* by explaining their connection to the Platonic ideas.[18] It is clear, Augustine says, that "*rationes*" is not a literal translation of Plato's term "*ideae*" since *rationes* are called λόγοι in Greek.[19]

15. Augustine, *Gn. litt.*, 2.6.12, *PL* 34:268: "nihil creari posset . . . cujus creandi ratio, si tamen ratio recte dicitur, non in Dei Verbo Patri coaeterno coaeterna vita viveret."

16. *ST*, I.4.1 *resp*: "Deus est ipsum esse per se subsistens."

17. *ST* I.115.2 *resp*.

18. Augustine, *div. qu.*, 46, *CCL* 44A:70–73.

19. Augustine, *div. qu.*, 46.2, *CCL* 44A:71: "Si autem rationes eas vocemus, ab interpretandi quidem proprietate discedimus—rationes enim Graece λόγοι appellantur non ideae."

But in this case the term *rationes* means the same thing as *ideae*, which is more literally translated as "forms" (*formae*) or "species" (*species*) in Latin.[20] And so,

> whoever wants to use this word [*rationes*] will not be far from the thing itself. For in fact the original ideas are certain forms or reasons (*rationes*) of things, stable and immutable, which are not themselves formed. And so they are eternal and always bear in themselves their own proper measure, and they are themselves bound together and comprehended by the divine intelligence.[21]

These stable and immutable ideas can be called *rationes*. "And where," he asks, "ought we suppose these rules (*rationes*) to be except in the very mind of the creator?"[22] It is by participating in them that any creature is whatever it is.[23] In the divine mind, these rules do not change, but creatures made according to them do.[24]

Thomas on Augustine on the Divine Ideas

In question 15 of the *Summa Theologiae*, where Thomas treats the divine ideas, he draws directly on Augustine's *De diversis quaestionibus*. The first article of the question asks whether any such ideas exist.[25] Like Augustine, he

---

20. Augustine, *div. qu.*, 46.2, *CCL* 44A:71: "Ideas igitur Latine possumus vel formas vol species dicere, ut verbum e verbo trasferre vedeamur."

21. Augustine, *div. qu.*, 46.2, *CCL* 44A:71: "quisquis hoc vocabulo uti voluerit, a re ipso non abhorrebit. Sunt namque ideae principales quaedam formae vol rationes rerum stabiles atque incommutabiles, quae ipsae formatae non sunt ac per hoc aeternae ac seomper eodem modo ses habentes, quae divina intellegentia continentur."

22. Augustine, *div. qu.*, 46.2, *CCL* 44A:72: "Has autem rationes ubi esse arbitrandum est nisi in ipsa mente creatoris?"

23. Augustine, *div. qu.*, 46.2, *CCL* 44A:73: "Quarum participatione fit ut sit quidquid est, quoquo modo est."

24. Augustine, *div. qu.*, 46.2, *CCL* 44A:71: "Et cùm ipsae neque oriantur neque intereant, secundum eas tamen formari dicitur omne quod oriri et interire potest et omne quod oritur et interit."

25. *ST* I.15.1: "Utrum ideae sint."

connects the Greek *idea* to the Latin *forma*.[26] The forms exist apart from the things themselves, either as their exemplars or as principles of knowledge of those same things.[27] As a principle of knowledge, Thomas means the forms are that by which we know a human is a human or a cat is a cat and so on. It has to do with the abstractive power of the intellect. The form of something can be in the intellect in this way insofar as it is something capable of being known.[28] When Thomas speaks of form in the first sense, in terms of a form's exemplarity, he is speaking of it as principle of action. In this case the form is in the agent in one of two ways, either according to the agent's nature, or, in the case of those capable of intellection, in the intellect.[29] Thomas gives some examples of what he means by the form existing and acting "according to its natural being (*esse*)."[30] This is what happens when "a human comes from a human" in procreation or when "fire produces fire" by putting a lit match to a pile of kindling.[31]

The other way a form may exist as an exemplar in an agent is "according to its intelligible being (*esse*), as in those who act by intellect."[32] This kind of exemplary form is most closely associated with our investigation of the *rationes seminales*. According to Thomas, the exemplary form of a thing exists in an intellectual agent in a way that allows the agent to act in accordance with it. The exemplary form as a principle of action differs from the intelligible form as a principle of knowledge. Key to the treatment of both kinds of exemplary form, *secudum esse naturale* and *secundum esse intelligibile*, is that their

26. *ST* I.15.1 *resp*: "Idea enim Graece, Latine forma dicitur."

27. *ST* I.15.1 *resp*: "Forma autem alicuius rei praeter ipsam existens, ad duo esse potest, vel ut sit exemplar eius cuius dicitur forma; vel ut sit principium cognitionis ipsius."

28. *ST* I.15.1 *resp*: "secundum quod formae cognoscibilium dicuntur esse in cognoscente."

29. *ST* I.15.1 *resp*: "In quibusdam enim agentibus praeexistit forma rei fiendae secundum esse naturale, sicut in his quae agunt per naturam."

30. *ST* I.15.1 *resp*: "In quibusdam enim agentibus praeexistit forma rei fiendae secundum esse naturale."

31. *ST* I.15.1 *resp*: "sicut homo generat hominem, et ignis ignem."

32. *ST* I.15.1 *resp*: "In quibusdam vero secundum esse intelligibile, ut in his quae agunt per intellectum."

presence allows us to say a thing is not brought about by chance.[33] The preceding question of the *Summa Theologiae* dealt with the divine intellect.[34] In question 15, he stipulates that "the world is not made by chance, but by God acting as an intellectual agent."[35] As the idea of a house in the mind of a builder preexists the actual house he builds, so too does the idea of the world in the mind of God preexist the world he brings into being. God makes the world according to the form that exists within the divine mind, he shapes it to its likeness.[36]

Following Augustine's identification of the *rationes* with the *ideae* in *De diversis quaestionibus*, it is reasonable to read Thomas's treatment of form (in the singular) as the world's *ratio*. When I worked through Augustine's use of *ratio* above, I remarked on the distinct use of it as the *creandi ratio*, the rule of things to be created, because of its identification with the second person of the Trinity, the Word through whom all things were made (John 1:3; cf. Col 1:16). In the reply to the third objection in question 15, Thomas supports this point by saying, "according to his essence, God is the likeness of all things. So, an idea in God is nothing other than his essence."[37] Because it is reasonable to appropriate talk of that by which God creates to the person of the Son, it is fair to say there is not much daylight between Thomas and Augustine about

33. *ST* I.15.1 *resp*: "In omnibus enim quae non a casu generantur, necesse est formam esse finem generationis cuiuscumque."

34. *ST* I.14.

35. *ST* I.15.1 *resp*: "Quia igitur mundus non est casu factus, sed est factus a Deo per intellectum agente." In the same sentence, Thomas goes on to say "this will be made clear below (*ut infra patebit*)." The English Dominicans' translation points the reader to *ST* I.46.1, which has quite a bit to say about the world being made, but nothing in particular to say about God making it as an intellectual agent. The Blackfriars translation points the reader instead to *ST* I.19.4, which deals with the divine intellect and will as "the cause of things (*causa rerum*)." Thomas Aquinas, *Summa Theologiae: Knowledge in God (Ia. 14–18)*, trans. Thomas Gornall, vol. 4 (New York: Blackfriars & McGraw-Hill, 1964).

36. *ST* I.15.1 *resp*: "sicut similitudo domus praeexistit in mente aedificatoris. Et haec potest dici idea domus, quia artifex intendit domum assimilare formae quam mente concepit . . . in mente divina sit forma, ad similitudinem cuius mundus est factus."

37. *ST* I.15.1 *ad* 3: "Deus secundum essentiam suam est similitudo omnium rerum. Unde idea in Deo nihil est aliud quam Dei essentia."

the form or idea or *ratio* of the world. The rule of the things to be created just is the Son.

There is an idea of the world, an *idea* or *forma* or *ratio mundi*, in the singular. Are there also ideas in the plural? Thomas argued that any such idea is identical with God's essence, which is unitary.[38] Thomas's chief concerns as he begins the second article of question 15 are the implications of a multiplicity of ideas in the divine nature for the doctrine of divine simplicity. To begin, Thomas shows why it is necessary for God to have the ideas of particular things in mind. The argument moves from a presumption of the good of order to an explanation that such a good can only be had intentionally.[39] God does not will the existence of individual creatures apart from the ordering of the whole. God not only wills to create singulars, he wills to create them in relation to one another and to himself. God intends and wills the order of the universe.[40] The relations of order are a source of goodness. Taken as a whole, the harmony of created things is not just *a* good. Thomas says that, "what is best in existing things is the good of the order of the universe."[41]

In intending to create an ordered world, it is not enough to know things singularly or to know them in general. For Thomas, knowing and intending the order of the universe means knowing and intending the parts and the whole together. It is in this context that Thomas moves the singular *ratio* into the plural *rationes* for the first time. As he says, "The idea (*ratio*) of any

38. *ST* I.15.1 *ad* 3.

39. *ST* I.15.2 *resp*: "Illud autem quod est optimum in rebus existens, est bonum ordinis universi, ut patet per Philosophum in XII Metaphys. Ordo igitur universi est proprie a Deo intentus, et non per accidens proveniens secundum successionem agentium." The *respondeo* of I.15.2 is specifically directed toward "those who have said that God only created the first creature, that the first creature created the second creature, and so on until the whole multitude of things was produced. According to that opinion, God only has an idea of the first created thing" ("quidam dixerunt quod Deus creavit primum creatum tantum, quod creatum creavit secundum creatum, et sic inde quousque producta est tanta rerum multitudo, secundum quam opinionem, Deus non haberet nisi ideam primi creati"). Thomas is pushing back against an emanationist account, and doing so by emphasizing the good of order, which requires God's willing of all the particulars of creation in the sum total of their relations to one another.

40. *ST* I.15.2 *resp*: "Sed si ipse ordo universi est per se creatus ab eo, et intentus ab ipso, necesse est quod habeat ideam ordinis universi."

41. *ST* I.15.2 *resp*: "quod est optimum in rebus existens, est bonum ordinis universi."

whole cannot be had, unless the particular ideas (*rationes*) of those things out of which the whole is constituted are had."[42] He then returns to the image of the builder from the first article to give an example of this principle at work: "just as a builder may not conceive of the image (*speciem*) of a house, unless he were to conceive of the particular idea (*ratio*) of every part of it."[43] For this reason, there must be many ideas in the divine mind. These ideas must include everything that ever has existed, does exist, and will exist, as well as how those things hang together. The "propriae rationes omnium rerum"—the particular ideas or rules of all things—are in the mind of God.[44]

Thomas anticipates an objection on the grounds of divine simplicity to the statement, "And so it follows that in the divine mind there are many ideas."[45] Thomas must deal with the seeming irreconcilability of simplicity and multiplicity in God. His response comes in a two-part movement whereby Thomas first makes a distinction between "what is understood" and "the image by which something is understood," and second shows how this applies in the case of God.[46] This distinction between *quod intelligitur* (what is understood) and *species qua intelligitur* (the image by which something is understood) is a further specification of a distinction he made in the preceding article. That is, the distinction is between an idea as exemplar and an idea as principle of knowledge.[47]

To make this connection with the previous article, Thomas reintroduces the example of a builder. The builder understands what he is going to build; the form of the house is intellected by him.[48] But it is not that the builder knows

42. *ST* I.15.2 *resp*: "Ratio autem alicuius totius haberi non potest, nisi habeantur propriae rationes eorum ex quibus totum constituitur."

43. *ST* I.15.2 *resp*: "sicut aedificator speciem domus concipere non posset, nisi apud ipsum esset propria ratio cuiuslibet partium eius."

44. *ST* I.15.2 *resp*: "Sic igitur oportet quod in mente divina sint propriae rationes omnium rerum. Unde dicit Augustinus, in libro octoginta trium quaest., quod singula propriis rationibus a Deo creata sunt. Unde sequitur quod in mente divina sint plures ideae."

45. *ST* I.15.2 *resp*: "Unde sequitur quod in mente divina sint plures ideae."

46. *ST* I.15.2 *resp*: "si quis consideret ideam operati esse in mente operantis sicut quod intelligitur; non autem sicut species qua intelligitur, quae est forma faciens intellectum in actu."

47. *ST* I.15.1 *resp*: "Forma autem alicuius rei praeter ipsam existens, ad duo esse potest, vel ut sit exemplar eius cuius dicitur forma; vel ut sit principium cognitionis ipsius."

48. *ST* I.15.2 *resp*: "Forma enim domus in mente aedificatoris est aliquid ab eo intellectum."

it by abstracting its form from a particular house. Instead, by understanding the form, idea, or *ratio* of the house the builder is able to make a particular house. The builder builds it by conforming his materials to the rule of the house in his mind.[49] In a similar way, the divine mind understands many things. God understands them not by being formed from without "per plures species"—through many images—but by knowing the exemplary forms of all things that are not God.[50]

Thomas then offers an elegant solution to the question of what the *plures ideae* in the divine mind are. The ideas are identical with God's essence.[51] But they are plural—*ideae* or *formae* or *rationes*—because in knowing his own essence perfectly, God knows himself as participable by creatures.[52] As John Wippel puts it, "According to Aquinas a divine idea is nothing but a given way in which God understands himself as capable of being imitated by a creature. Hence the essence of any existing creature is an expression of a particular way in which the divine idea can be and in fact is imitated."[53] Every creature participates in the divine essence. Each one can and does do so because the exemplar of that creature exists in the divine mind.[54] Creation is the result of God's self-contemplation, his perfect self-knowledge, which

---

49. *ST* I.15.2 *resp*: "ad cuius similitudinem domum in materia format."

50. *ST* I.15.2 *resp*: "Non est autem contra simplicitatem divini intellectus, quod multa intelligat, sed contra simplicitatem eius esset, si per plures species eius intellectus formaretur." In a discussion of the divine ideas and the metaphysics of participation, this leads John Wippel to conclude, "Participation by composition, as it is expressed in the intrinsic structure of any created entity, receives its final explanation in the order of extrinsic causality by leading one to recognize God not only as the first efficient cause but also as the extrinsic formal or exemplar cause of every participant." John F. Wippel, *The Metaphysical Thought of Thomas Aquinas: From Finite Being to Uncreated Being* (Washington, DC: The Catholic University of America Press, 2000), 130. And cf. esp. *ST* I.44.3 *resp*: "Deus est prima causa exemplaris omnium rerum."

51. *ST* I.15.1 *ad* 3.

52. *ST* I.15.2 *resp*: "Potest autem cognosci non solum secundum quod in se est, sed secundum quod est participabilis secundum aliquem modum similitudinis a creaturis."

53. Wippel, *The Metaphysical Thought of Thomas Aquinas*, 130.

54. *ST* I.15.2 *resp*: "Unaquaeque autem creatura habet propriam speciem, secundum quod aliquo modo participat divinae essentiae similitudinem. Sic igitur inquantum Deus cognoscit suam essentiam ut sic imitabilem a tali creatura, cognoscit eam ut propriam rationem et ideam huius creaturae."

enables him to intend and will the existence of everything that is not God in all its multiplicity.

There is deep agreement between Augustine and Thomas on this point. God is multiplicity in simplicity, plurality without composition, many yet one. The similarity in their thought, both the commitment to divine simplicity and to God as the exemplar of all creatures, can be seen by comparing Thomas's discussion in question 15 to Augustine's reflections in book XI of *De civitate Dei*. There Augustine says,

> Now in Holy Scripture, the Spirit of wisdom is called manifold because she has many things within herself. But what she has, this she also is, and so she is the all-one (*omnia unus est*). For wisdom is not many things, but one. In her are boundless things and also for her a certain well-bounded treasury of intelligible things. In that treasury are all the invisible and immutable rules (*rationes*) of even visible and mutable things, which were made by her.[55]

Augustine goes on to use the image of the human maker (*artifex*), comparable to Thomas's image of the human builder (*aedificator*) in question 15. But for Augustine the human *artifex* serves principally as a point of contrast rather than comparison. For Thomas, the *aedificator* and the exemplar form of a house in his mind serve as an analogue for God as creator, whose mind contains the *forma mundi* and the *propriae rationes*. Augustine, always less sanguine than Thomas when it comes to the possibilities of human knowledge, presents the *artifex* as a kind of foil. "God," he says, "made nothing unknowingly, and this cannot rightly be said about any human maker."[56] Still, there's an undeniable relation between human and divine knowledge, and Thomas clearly draws this out in the case of the *aedificator*. In closing this chapter from *De civitate Dei*, Augustine sums up

55. Augustine, *civ.*, 11.10, *CSEL* 40.1:528: "Ceterum dictus est in scripturis sanctis Spiritus sapientiae multiplex, eo quod multa in sese habeat; sed quae habet, haec et est, et ea omnia unus est. Neque enim multae, sed una sapientia est, in qua sunt infiniti quidam eique finiti thensauri rerum intellegibilium, in quibus sunt omnes invisibiles adque incommutabiles rationes rerum etiam visibilium et mutabilium, quae per ipsam factae sunt."

56. Augustine, *civ.*, 11.10, *CSEL* 40.1:528: "Quoniam Deus non aliquid nesciencs fecit, quod nec de quolibet homine artifice recte dici potest."

what will in Thomas come in the form of careful distinctions between the intelligible and exemplar forms. So he says, "this world could not be known by us unless it were, but unless it were known by God, it could not be."[57]

The Seeds of Creation

In attempting to identify what the *rationes seminales* are in Augustine's *De genesi ad litteram* I first clarified the concept of "*ratio*" by looking at the particular uses it is put to in the work. I then showed the connection between one sense of *ratio*, the one most closely associated with Christ as *Logos*, and Augustine's treatment of the divine ideas. Finally, I looked at Thomas's treatment of the divine ideas in the Prima Pars of the *Summa Theologiae*. This led back to Augustine's thoughts on divine simplicity in *De civitate Dei*. At this point, we have a workable concept of "*rationes*." These *rationes* are the exemplar causes of all creatures. They are in the divine mind by virtue of God's perfect self-knowledge, which includes the knowledge of himself as participable.

What remains to be shown is what connection the *rationes ideales* have to the *rationes seminales*, which God creates atemporally in Augustine's interpretation of the creation narrative of Genesis 1. In the last chapter, I argued that Augustine's interpretation of the hexaëmeron provides the contemporary theologian with the resources to engage modern cosmology and evolutionary biology. The commentary in *De Genesi ad litteram*, his mature thoughts on the days of creation, can bear the weight of the changes to human understanding about the cosmos. It can account for the discoveries of contemporary natural science in a way that Aristotelian cosmology cannot. This is not to say those other accounts lack utility or that they were wrong to use the best scientific evidence available. It is to say those accounts are of limited value when trying to grasp the problem of human and nonhuman creaturely death. To do that requires tangling with the unfolding of cosmic and evolutionary history on nearly unimaginable timescales.[58] I have identified the reasons why Augustine's

57. Augustine, *civ.*, 11.10, *CSEL* 44.1:28: "iste mundus nobis notus esse non posset, nisi esset; Deo autem nisi notus esset, esse non posset."

58. It is worth noting that Augustine relates his own theory of creation to what we might call cosmic or evolutionary timescales in book XII of *De civitate Dei*. Augustine is speculating about the timing of God's creation of humans and about the relation of time to eternity. There he explains that, given the difference between time and eternity, it does not matter whether

reading of Genesis is likely to be of use in this endeavor. Now I will turn to the specifics of it.

Key to Augustine's interpretation of Genesis 1 is his understanding that what is indicated by the succession of days is not a temporal sequence of events. Instead, he attributes it to the rhythmic motion of the angelic intellect. The angels contemplate God, and know the things to be made in the Word of God. When God "makes the creature itself in its own kind" the angels then contemplate those creatures by the light of their intellect (evening knowledge). But the created light of the angelic intellect, by virtue of having known those things in the Word of God, knows also to refer what is known back to God. So, the angelic mind turns back to contemplating all things in the mind of God (morning knowledge). This pattern is repeated for all the kinds of things there are, making up the six days of creation.[59]

If the six days of creation in Genesis 1 are atemporal, what does God make when "he makes the creature itself in its own kind?"[60] On Augustine's reading, it is clearly something that can be known by the angelic intellect, but it also cannot be exactly what we mean when we typically think of creation. When we think of things in the created order, we tend to think of particular things existing in space and time—rocks, trees, dogs, humans, planets, galaxies, stars. Augustine does not mean creatures like these. He is describing the conditions of the possibility of these kinds of things existing. In his *Confessiones*, Augustine

---

you think it has been five or six thousand years, sixty thousand years, or even six hundred thousand years multiplied repeatedly "until you reached a number for we have no name." Even then, "it could be asked, why did he not make man before?" This flags two important points. First, it is clear that Augustine does not find imagining the "deep time"—to borrow a phrase of Charles Taylor's—familiar to modern cosmology particularly outlandish or any more difficult to fathom than we do. Second, that focusing just on the temporal sequencing of events misses the point of reflecting on the relation between God's eternality and creaturely temporality. Cf. Augustine, *civ.*, 12.13, *CSEL* 40.1:585–86: "Ac per hoc si non quinque vel ses, verum etiam sexaginta milia sive sescenta, aut sexagiens, aut sescentiens, aut sescentiens miliens decerentur annorum, aut itidem per totidem totiens multiplicaretur haec summa, ubi iam nullum numeri nomen haberemus, ex quo Deus hominem fecit: similiter quaeri posset, quur ante non fecerit."

59. Augustine, *Gn. litt.*, 4.22.39, *PL* 34:312: "cum jam dictum esset, *Et sic factum est*, in suo genere ipsa creatura fit; quae item cum in suo genere facta cognoscitur ab ea luce, quae jam in Verbo Dei faciendam cognoverat, fit tertio vespera: et inde hoc modo caetera usque ad mane post vesperam sexti diei."

60. Augustine, *Gn. litt.*, 4.22.39, *PL* 34:312: "in suo genere ipsa creatura fit."

identifies two things created by God that meet these criteria. The first of these is the angelic creation, formed for and capable of reveling in the contemplation of God's eternity and immutability even though it is itself mutable. The angelic creation is the "heaven" created "In the beginning" (Gen 1:1). The second thing is the "earth" that "was without form and void" (Gen 1:2). This names a created formlessness. Though completely without form, it is still not nothing. From this formlessness God will create another heaven and earth, visible and corporeal.[61]

The created formlessness, from which a formed, visible creation will be made, is not itself knowable. It is not nothing, but it is also not anything in particular. There is not something to know about it. It is certainly not a candidate for what the angels know when God "makes the creature itself in its own kind." Formless matter is not any *kind* of thing at all, and it cannot be known as such. This "unformed matter" (*informis materies*) is not itself subject to time, as it has no order, "nothing subject to the vicissitudes of time."[62] And still, from this "almost nothing" (*paene nihil*) comes everything that will be in the corporeal creation.[63]

As early as his first commentary on Genesis, *De Genesi contra manichaeos*, Augustine was inclined to think of unformed matter using the metaphor of "seed." He refers to the opening line of Genesis, "In the beginning God created the heavens and the earth" (Gen 1:1), as "a kind of seed (*quasi semen*) of heaven

61. Augustine, *conf.*, 12.12.15, *CSEL* 33:319–20: "duo reperio, quae fecisti carentia temporibus, cum tibi neutrum coaeternum sit: unum, quod ita formatum est, ut sine ullo defectu contemplationis, sine ullo intervallo mutationis, quamvis mutabile, tamen non mutatum aeternitate atque inconmutabilitate perfuatur: alterum, quod ita snforme erat, ut ex qua form in quam formom vel motionis vel stationis mutaretur, quo tempori subderetur, non haberet. sed hoc ut informe esst, non reliquisti, quoniam fecisti ante omnem diem in principo caelum et terram, haec duo quae dicebam. terra autem invisibilis erat et inconposita et tenebrae super abyssum. quibus verbis insinuatur informitas, ut gradatim excipiantur, qui omnimodam speviei privationem nec tamen ad nihil perventionem cogitare non possent, unde fieret alterum caelum et terra visibilis atque conposita et aqua speviosa et quiquid deinceps in constitutione huius mundi non sine diebus factum commemoratur, quia talia sunt, ut in eis agantur vicissitudines temporum propter ordinatas commutationes motionum atque formarum."

62. Augustine, *conf.*, 12.15.22, *CSEL* 33:324: "an quia erat informis materies, ubi propter nullam formam nullus ordo erat? ubi autem nullus ordo erat, nulla esse vicissitudo temporum poterat."

63. Augustine, *conf.*, 12.15.22, *CSEL* 33:324: "et tamen hoc paene nihil in quantum non omnino nihil erat, ab illo utique erat, a quo est quidquid est, quod utcumque aliquid est."

and earth, when the matter of heaven and earth was as yet in confusion."[64] This might seem to indicate an inclination in the formless matter itself. But it is not necessary to read Augustine quite that decisively, as if the formlessness would become something as a matter of course, like a seed sown in rich tilth puts down roots. In his commentary against the Manichaeans, he identifies this as a manner of speech employed in Scripture about things which have not yet been done but will be done.[65] It is not because the formless matter is yet anything, but because it is capable of being made "the heavens and the earth" that Augustine makes the comparison to a seed.[66] He repeats this claim in his *De Genesi ad litteram imperfectus liber*. There unformed matter "is called the seed (*semen*) of heaven and earth," but in this later work he adds that in this state it is prepared by God "for receiving suitable forms."[67]

In book XII of *Confessiones*, there is a further development of this position. Angelic creatures and unformed matter are the first two things created, and he gives form to the latter outside of time. Augustine makes this case by distinguishing the different ways one thing can precede another. Precedence can be understood in terms of eternity, time, choice, and origin.[68] He gives examples of each of these. Precedence "in eternity is as God is to all things. In time it is as flower to a fruit. In choice it is as a fruit is to a flower. In origin it is as a sound is to a song."[69] Augustine thinks the middle two, precedence in time and in choice, are easy to understand. When one thing happens before another, it is a matter of temporal precedence. When one thing is preferred to

64. Augustine, *Gn. c. man.*, 1.7.11, *PL* 34:178: "sic dictum est, *In principio fecit Deus coelum et terram*, quasi semen coeli et terrae, cum in confuso adhuc esset coeli et terrae materia."

65. Augustine, *Gn. c. man.*, 1.7.11, *PL* 34:178: "non quia jam factum erat, sed quia certissime futurum erat."

66. Augustine, *Gn. c. man.*, 1.7.11, *PL* 34:178: "non quia jam sunt, sed quia inde futura sunt."

67. Augustine, *Gn. litt. imp.*, 3.10, *CSEL* 28.1:464–65: "ipsa vero materies caelum et terra, veluti semen caeli et terrae appellata sit et caelum et terra quasi confusum atque permixtum ab artifice deo accipiendis formis idoneum."

68. Augustine, *conf.*, 12.29.40, *CSEL* 33:340: "cum vero dicit primo informem, deinde formatam, non est absurdus, si modo est idoneus discernere, quid praecedat aeternitate, quid tempore, quid electione, quid origine."

69. Augustine, *conf.*, 12.29.40, *CSEL* 33:340: "aeternitate, sicut deus omnia; tempore, sicut flos frutum; electione, sicut fructus florem; origine, sicut sonus cantum."

another, it is a matter of the precedence of choice. But imagining the priority of God's eternity to all things that are not God is much more difficult. This is not a temporal sequence but a kind of relation. Before dealing with precedence of origin, I want to make clear the sort of relation God's eternity bears to creation.

God's act of creation is separable from the idea of a beginning in time. The bringing into being and sustaining in being of all that is—the relation the word "creation" names—is distinct from, though connected to, the temporal sequence of events we think of when we think of time. Creation is not a part of the sequence of temporal events. In this way, the word "creation" is distinctively inflected for the Christian. In English "to create" or "creation" can mark a number of activities, all of which seem to indicate the process or act through which something goes from one state of affairs to another different state of affairs. This does not occur without the intervention of a creator. So, a carpenter uses pieces of wood to create a box or a table or a chair or a spoon. This is distinct in two ways from what Christians mean when they say "God creates." First, the human who creates does not bring anything into being the material for which did not already exist. The human creator rearranges things that already exist to bring about a new ordering with some purpose in mind. God creates by bringing into being not just the creature but also the material out of which the creature is made.

The second distinction between human and divine acts of creation is that to say of a human "she creates" or "she is creating a work of art" names a process. The process has a beginning and an end. It makes sense to say "she is going to create," "she is creating," or "she created something." Human creation is temporally indexed. It begins to happen, happens, then stops happening. This is not true of God's act of creation. This is because as God's act, the act of creation is identical with everything else God has and also is. God does not begin to do something, do it, and then stop doing it. For God, to create is to eternally stand in relation to everything God creates. God's act of creation is connected to time without itself being an event in the order of time. Time is itself a creature, and stands within and is part of the created order, intimate to the existence of space and motion. God's act of creation is the presupposition for the existence of anything at all, including time.

The last kind of precedence Augustine distinguishes is that of origin. Using his chosen example of the relation of sound to a song, he shows both the difficulty and usefulness of making this distinction. He explains that it is not as though a sound is made first and then formed into a song, in the way something might be constructed out of raw materials. Sound and song appear simultaneously.[70] And still, the song is made out of the sound. It would not make sense to say the opposite, that a sound could be made out of a song. It is a case of ontological dependence, you can have a sound without a song, but no song may be sung without a sound.[71] Augustine finds this image a useful way of describing how unformed matter is prior to formed matter. No time elapses between the creation of unformed matter and giving it form. This is an important development of Augustine's earlier insight.

Augustine's earlier commentaries on Genesis referred to formless matter as *quasi semen*—a kind of seed. In *Confessiones*, he adjusts that thought slightly. Something already explained in the unfinished literal commentary, unformed matter's readiness to receive forms, gets fuller treatment. So, he explains, "the matter of things is made first, and it is called heaven and earth because from it heaven and earth are made. But it is not made first in time, because time sprouts up (*exserunt*) from the forms of things."[72] The word choice is important. Augustine uses the word *exsero*, which means to stretch out or put forth. The root of this word, *sero*, means to sow or plant. In *Confessiones*, Augustine begins to imagine the forms of things as seeds sown in formless matter. Like seeds sown in fertile soil, they organize what is disorganized. The detritus of organic matter is given shape in new life. The seed grows. It becomes a plant. This idea, of the forms of things as seeds, as opposed to unformed matter itself as *quasi semen*, marks a real and important shift in Augustine's thought. To arrive at this position, he needs the conceptual resources he deploys in *Confessiones*.

70. Augustine, *conf.*, 12.29.40, *CSEL* 33:341: "neque enim priore tempore sonos edimus informes sine cantu et eos posteriore tempore in formam cantici coaptamus aut fingimus, sicut ligna, quibus arca, vel argentum, quo vasculum fabricatur; tales quippe materiae tempore etiam praecedunt formas rerum, quae fiunt ex eis. at in cantu non ita est. cum enim cantatur, auditur sonus eius, non prius informiter sonat et deinde formatur in cantum. quod enim primo utcumque sonuerit, praeterit, nec ex eo quicquam reperies, quod resumptum arte conponas: et ideo cantus in sono suo vertitur, qui sonus eius materies eius est. idem quippe formatur, ut cantus sit."

71. Augustine, *conf.*, 12.29.40, *CSEL* 33:341: "sed prior est origine, quia non cantus formatur, ut sonus sit, sed sonus formatur, ut cantur sit."

72. Augustine, *conf.*, 12.29.40, *CSEL* 33:341–42: "hoc exemplo qui potest intellegat materiam rerum primo factam et appelatam caelum et terram, quia inde facta sunt caelum et terra, nec tempore primo factam, quia formae rerum exserunt tempora."

Distinguishing between priority in origin and priority in time allows him to go on to say both that formless matter is created first and that this does not mean the forms come to be in time. This will prove an exceptionally powerful tool when Augustine puts it to work in *De Genesi ad litteram*. He uses it to explain what it means to say that on the seventh day "the heavens and the earth were finished, and all the host of them" (Gen 2:1) and that time still has not yet begun. To say this, he still needs to further develop his picture of the forms as seeds.

When Are the *Rationes Seminales*?

Frank Robbins's useful dissertation about the commentary tradition on the hexaëmeron summarizes the key points of Augustine's position well. After reviewing Augustine's illustration of precedence of origin found in the relation of sound to song he says,

> The universe thus made by God had in itself, just as the seed potentially contains the tree, not only heaven, earth and the *maxima mundi membra*, but also whatever these have produced, before they arose in periods of time into the form wherein they now exist. This was brought about by the fact that in the beginning God placed forms (*rationes*) in the universe which later produce things in their genera as we know them.[73]

These are the *rationes*, the forms with which unformed matter is inseminated. These are what the angels know when they know the creaturely kinds in themselves. Making sense of these created *rationes* requires keeping one eye fixed on their source in the uncreated *rationes* and the *creandi ratio*, who is the Word of God. But the created *rationes* are different. They must be in order to affirm, as both Augustine and Thomas do, that the divine ideas are identical with the divine essence. As created things these *rationes* cannot be identical with God. To complete the picture, I will return to my exegesis of Augustine's *De Genesi ad litteram*.

73. Frank Egleston Robbins, *The Hexaemeral Literature: A Study of the Greek and Latin Commentaries on Genesis* (Chicago: The University of Chicago Press, 1912), 67.

In book V, Augustine distinguishes three ways created things can be known. First, it is possible to know them in the Word of God. Knowing them in this way means knowing them according to their "immutable rules" (*rationes incommutabiles*). This corresponds with morning knowledge in the angelic intellect. The second way something may be known is according to the works of God completed in the six days of creation. By this Augustine means according to the created rules, the *rationes seminales*, seeded in formless matter. Knowledge of these corresponds to evening knowledge in the angelic intellect. The third way something may be known is as it is in the order of time. This last way of knowing is what is available to the sensorium. This is the ordinary way corporeal creatures know things in the world. The first two, "are so remote from the senses, and from the usual functioning of human thought" that they have to be believed on divine authority before they can be known. Even then, Augustine claims, we are looking through the mirror darkly and can know them only with God's help.[74]

To sum up, Augustine draws a distinction between God's work in the six days, and God's work in the order of time. He makes it on scriptural grounds, as he sees the necessity of harmonizing seemingly contradictory passages from Scripture. He is especially concerned with the two narratives of creation, which Augustine divides into Genesis 1:1–2:5 and 2:6–3:24.[75] Can the two narratives hang together? If so, how? Augustine tries to resolve these questions by dividing the creation accounts. He locates a suitable point in the first verses of Genesis 2, which read:

> Thus the heavens and the earth were finished, and all the host of them. And on the seventh day God finished his work which he had done, and he rested on the seventh day from all his work which he had done. So God blessed the seventh day and hallowed it, because on it God rested from all his work which he had done in creation.

74. Augustine, *Gn. litt.*, 5.12.28, *PL* 34:331: "Cum ergo aliter se habeant omnium creaturarum rationes incommutabiles in Verbo Dei, aliter illa ejus opera a quibus in die septimo requievit, aliter ista quae ex illis usque nunc operatur; horum trium hoc quod extremum posui, nobis utcumque notum est per corporis sensus, et hujus consuetudinem vitae. Duo vero illa remota a sensibus, et ab usu cogitationis humanae, prius ex divina auctoritate credenda sunt; deinde per haec quae nota sunt, utcumque noscenda, quanto quisque magis minusve potuerit pro suae capacitatis modo, divinitus adjutus internis aeternisque rationibus ut possit."

75. Cf. *Gn. litt.*, 5.6.17–5.7.22.

> These are the generations of the heavens and the earth when they were created. In the day that the LORD God made the earth and the heavens, when no plant of the field was yet in the earth and no herb of the field had yet sprung up—for the LORD God had not caused it to rain upon the earth. (Gen 2:1–5)

These verses, Augustine argues, belong to the first narrative of all things being created atemporally. Verses 4 and 5 are there as a sort of hinge between the two narratives. They set apart what is accomplished when God, "who lives in eternity created all things at once" (Ecclus. 18:1, Vulg.).[76] But, Augustine points to the dominical word of John 5:17, which affirms, "My father is working still."[77] What does it mean to say God rests from all his works if he is in fact still working? To reconcile these apparent differences, Augustine makes a distinction between the work of seeding unformed matter with the *rationes* and the ongoing, providential work of governing the cosmos.

He states this distinction elsewhere in book V where he says, "In the first making (*prima conditione*), God worked all creatures in one way, and from those works he rested on the seventh day; in another way, he works at the administration (*administrationem*) of those things, in which he works until now."[78] The relation between these two kinds of divine work is one of dependence. God administers in time those things he created outside of time. This distinction does not name two separate ways God relates to creation. These two terms, making (*conditio*) and administration (*administratio*), are descriptions of creation at two different levels of discourse. It is the same act of creation seen from the perspective of eternity or that of time. What can be described in terms of *administratio* is what can be discerned of the will of

76. Ecclus. 18:1, Vulg.: "qui vivit in aeternum creavit omnia simul."

77. Augustine, *Gn. litt.*, 5.11.27, *PL* 34:331: "Inter illa ergo opera Dei, a quibus requievit in die septimo, et ista quae usque nunc operatur, quemdam Scriptura interponens suae narrationis articulum, commendavit se illa explicasse, et coepit jam ista contexere."

78. Augustine, *Gn. litt.*, 5.11.27, *PL* 34:330: "Sed illud etiam atque etiam consideremus, utrum possit nobis per omnia constare sententia qua dicebamus, aliter operatum Deum omnes creaturas prima conditione, a quibus operibus in die septimo requievit; aliter istam earum administrationem, qua usque nunc operatur." The last clause, "qua usque nunc operatur" is a clear allusion to the relevant passage from John 5:17 quoted above.

God in the outworking of his providence in time. What is described in terms of *conditio*—the *condition* for a temporal outworking of God's providence—is what can be said about God's atemporal creation of all creaturely kinds.

Augustine's preferred image for understanding the relation of these two levels of discourse is by comparing them to seeds. What is sown in the *conditio* sprouts and grows from them in the *administratio*. This is the force of arguing that God rests from *all* his works on the seventh day. Everything is already created and contained *in nuce* when the first narrative ends. Augustine uses the metaphor of a seed growing into a tree in book II of *De Genesi* to explain the kind of integrity the seed has. "For God is the author and maker of actual natures. But whatever each and every thing, by a natural growth, in some way puts forth and unfolds through suitable times, it contained even before as a hidden thing, though not in the aspect or mass of its body, still by the rule of nature" (*ratione naturae*).[79] A nature is not imperfect on account of being at different stages of its development. So a seed, having the integrity of an actual nature, is "where all things which in some way come forth by the advance of time, lie hidden in invisible ways."[80]

This metaphor should not be pushed too far. While Augustine distinguishes between two levels, the order of making (*conditio*) and the order of time (*administratio*), this distinction inclines us to think God's making is subject to time. First he makes it, then it develops. While this is a perfectly normal way of describing temporal things, it cannot be the case that the relation of God to creation is timebound. We need another picture to complement the seed image of *conditio* and *administratio*. Augustine provides one. The picture comes in the discussion of the nature of time in book XI of the *Confessiones*. It is fitting that the image is of a *canticum*, a song, as the song was his chosen metaphor for describing the relation of precedence of unformed to formed matter.

When Augustine describes the process of reciting a song, he begins with an image of the whole. The singer's "expectation is directed toward the whole."[81] Before beginning to recite the verses line by line, the singer holds all

79. Augustine, *Gn. litt.*, 2.15.30, *PL* 34:276: "Ipsarum enim naturarum est Deus auctor et conditor. Omnis autem res quidquid progressu naturali per tempora congrua quodammodo prodit atque explicat, etiam ante continebat occultum, etsi non specie vel mole corporis sui, tamen ratione naturae."

80. Augustine, *Gn. litt.*, 2.15.30, *PL* 34:276: "ubi omnia quae progressu temporis quodammodo procedunt, modis invisibilibus latent."

81. Augustine, *conf.*, 11.28.38, *CSEL* 33:307: "in totum expectatio mea tenditur."

the parts in his mind as lines to be sung. Once the song has begun he is now moving through the song. There is a past, present, and future to it. Now his expectation (*expectatio*) is directed toward the verses yet to come, while his memory (*memoria*) holds those which have passed by. His attention (*attentio*) is on the present, the moment of recitation that moves the verses, words, syllables, and phonemes from the future to past. The whole motion of the song in the mind of the singer is one of shortening remaining expectation and lengthening memory. In the end, expectation will have vanished, and memory alone will remain.[82] This same pattern of movement, from expectation to memory, also applies to "the whole life of a human, of which the parts are all the actions of a human."[83] It applies further to "the whole age of the sons of men, of which the parts are all the lives of humans."[84] Augustine does not himself do so, but we might further extend this image to the whole history of the cosmos.

In *Confessiones*, the song serves as an illustration in the story he has been telling about the temporal order, which is "a kind of distention."[85] For Augustine, the Latin *distentio* connotes not just extension, but a painful stretching out, more like the distended belly of a starving child than a runner limbering up before a race. Andrea Nightingale explains it this way: "At the theological level, Augustine associates psychic distention with sinful dissolution and fragmentation. As O'Daly observes, Augustine links *distentio* with a cluster of verbs that express the human lament over being 'poured forth' and 'torn apart' into multiplicity: *effundo, dissilio, multiplico, gemo, ingemisco.*"[86] Augustine reaffirms his position on the nature of time even more forcefully

82. Augustine, *conf.*, 11.28.38, *CSEL* 33:307–8: "cum autem coepero, quantum ex illa in praeteritum decerpsero, tenditur et memoria mea, atque destenditur vita huius actionis meae in memoriam propter quod dixi et in expectationem propter quod dicturus sum: praesens tamen adest attentio mea, per quam traicitur quod erat futurm, ut fiat praeteritum. quod quanto magis agitur et agitur, tanto breviata expectatione prolongatur memoria, donec tota expectatio consumatur, quum tota ill actio finita transierit in memoriam."

83. Augustine, *conf.*, 11.28.38, *CSEL* 33:308: "hoc in tota vita hominis, cuius partes sunt omnes actiones hominis."

84. Augustine, *conf.*, 11.28.38, *CSEL* 33:308: "hoc in toto saeculo filiorum hominum, cuius partes sunt omnes vitae hominum."

85. Augustine, *conf.*, 11.23.30, *CSEL* 33:301: "video igitur quandam esse distentionem."

86. Andrea Nightingale, "Augustine on Extending Oneself to God through Intention," *Augustinian Studies* 46, no. 2 (2015): 197. In this quotation Nightingale is citing Gerard J. P. O'Daly, "Time as *Distentio* and St. Augustine's Exegesis of *Philippians* 3,12–14," *Revue d'Etudes Augustiniennes et Patristiques* 23, no. 3–4 (1977): 268.

a few chapters on when he says, "it seems to me time is nothing other than distention."[87] A distention of what, though? Augustine asks himself this very question. He hazards an answer, though not a definitive one. He thinks it is most likely the distention, the painful pulling apart, "of the mind itself."[88] I think it is possible to understand this distention in another way.

Augustine is right, the human mind is stretched out from past to future. The objects of our present fly by as they move from expectation to memory. This condition is unique to the rational soul with the capacity to make present the past and the future.[89] But this threefold pattern Augustine describes has its roots in a more fundamental question about the ontological status of the past and future. Are these times such that,

> when the future is made present it comes forth from some hidden place, and then, when the present is made the past, it recedes into some hidden place? For where did those who sang of future things see them if they are not yet? For it is not possible to see that which is not. And those who tell of the past, would certainly not be able to speak truly, if they could not see those things with their mind. If past things were not, there would be no way at all to see them. Therefore the future and the past are.[90]

One solution to this set of questions is the one Augustine has already offered. The past and the future have a kind of existence in the mind of

87. Augustine, *conf.*, 11.26.33, *CSEL* 33:304: "inde mihi visum est nihil esse aliud tempus quam distentionem."

88. Augustine, *conf.*, 11.26.33, *CSEL* 33:304: "sed cuius rei, nescio, et mirum, si non ipsius animi."

89. Augustine, *conf.*, 11.20.26, *CSEL* 33:298: "sunt enim haec in anima tria quaedam et alibi ea non video, praesens de praeteritis memoria, praesens de praesentibus contuitus, praesens de futuris expectatio."

90. Augustine, *conf.*, 11.17.22, *CSEL* 33:295: "an et ipsa sunt, sed ex aliquo procedit occulto, cum ex futuro fit praesens, et in aliquod recedit occultum, cum ex praesenti fit praeteritum? nam ubi ea viderunt qui futura cecinerunt, si nondum sunt? neque enim potest videri id quod non est. et qui narrant praeterita, non utique vera narrarent, si animo illa non cererent: quae si nulla essent, cerni omnino non possent. sunt ergo futura et praeterita."

rational souls who can cast their present gaze into the future in expectation or the past in memory.

But is this enough to satisfy the strong claim Augustine makes: "sunt ergo futura et praeterita" (the future and the past are)? Perhaps it is for the past, memory having at least the benefit of being a kind of record of things that once were. Things are more tenuous when applying this to the future. Augustine knows this, and settles for the mind's *expectatio* being the capacity to predict future events by knowledge of causes and signs.[91] But this is not a candidate for future *knowledge*, it is rather a knowledge of the past and present "quae iam sunt" (the things that already are). In *De Trinitate*, Augustine compares this human ability to predict the future to that of the demons, who because of their subtlety of intellect are able to make it appear as though they can divine the future.[92] This comparison in *De Trinitate* is important, because there Augustine provides two other possible ways of knowing the future.

The first possibility is that future things are announced to humans by the holy angels or that those humans to whom future things been announced have handed on the knowledge to other humans. The second possibility is that knowledge of future things is directly revealed to humans after being drawn up by the Holy Spirit to see "the immediate causes of future things in the very highest height of things."[93] Both of these possibilities are more suited to Augustine's description in book XI of *Confessiones* of those "qui futura cecinerunt" (who sang of future things) than the capacity for prediction shared by humans and demons. The reference to the sung future most readily suggests the prophetic witness of the Psalms, but is general enough to encompass the prophetic genre more broadly. The possibility of prophetic, not just predictive,

---

91. Augustine, *conf.*, 11.18.24, *CSEL* 33:297: "cum ergo videri dicuntur futura, non ipsa, quae nondum sunt, id est quae futura sunt, sed eorum causae vel signa forsitan videntur, quae iam sunt."

92. Augustine, *trin.*, 4.17, *CCL* 50:189: "an vero iam ventura praecesserint et longe visa venientia nuntientur pro acuto sensu videntium, quod cum faciunt aeriae potestates divinare creduntur, tamquam si quisquam de montis vertice aliquem longe videat venientem et proxime in campo habitantibus ante nuntiet."

93. Augustine, *trin.*, 4.17, *CCL* 50:180: "an ipsorum hominum quorundam mentes in tantum euehantur spiritu sancto ut non per angelos sed per se ipsas futurorum instantes causas in ipsa summa rerum arce conspiciant."

knowledge is closer to Augustine's declarative statements about the reality of past and future times.

This position is further borne out by the specific way Augustine talks about the revelation of prophetic knowledge through angelic intermediaries—the first possibility just discussed. In that case humans learn of future things "from the holy angels to whom God has announced them through his word and wisdom *where both future and past things stand*."[94] There is an echo here from book XI of *Confessiones* in the use of the Latin verb *sto*.[95] It is one of a constellation of words Augustine uses in book XI with reference to God, the stable (*stabilis*) one,[96] who makes us solid (*solido*);[97] who will take hold of our heart and fix it in place (*figo*),[98] and upon whom we can take a stand (*insisto*).[99] The fixity of all things, which are standing in God's eternity, provides another way of thinking about the actuality of the past and the future. Not only should we say that they have existence in the human mind, distended though able to remember the past and expect the future. Augustine holds the door open to the reality of all things past, present, and future, in and for God. These things are not distended in time but eternally present to the divine mind. God's thinking and willing the existence of past, present, and future events just is their reality.[100]

Augustine's inclination to cast the reality of things in terms of their existence in the present moment is right. All things are by virtue of existing in the present.[101] And the present in which all things exist is the "today" of God's

---

94. Augustine, *trin.*, 4.17, *CCL* 50:189: "an ab angelis sanctis quibus ea deus per verbum sapientiamque suam indicat ubi et futura et praeterita stant." Emphasis added.

95. Cf. *conf.*, 11.11.13, 11.13.16, 11.24.31, 11.30.40.

96. Augustine, *conf.*, 11.8.10.

97. Augustine, *conf.*, 11.30.40.

98. Augustine, *conf.*, 11.11.13.

99. Augustine, *conf.*, 11.27.34.

100. Augustine, *conf.*, 11.11.13, *CSEL* 33:289–90: "et videat omne praeteritum proelli ex futuro et omne futurum ex praeterito consequi et omne praeteritum ac futurum ab eo, quod semper est praesens, creari et excurrere."

101. Augustine, *conf.*, 11.18.23, *CSEL* 33:296: "ubicumque ergo sunt, quaecumque sunt, non sunt nisi praesentia."

eternity.[102] God's present is both like and utterly unlike the concept of the present Augustine works out in book XI of *Confessiones*. It is like it in that God's present, like our own, has no duration. Our present is the mirror of eternity because it cannot be measured by time.[103] Unlike the human present, God's present does not begin to be or come to an end. It does not move from future into past, but is always present. The distention of the present into a past and a future is what distinguishes time from eternity.[104] To be present in time is to "tend not to be," as Augustine puts it.[105] This is why the only stability to be had is in God, whose eternity is participable by his creatures. Some of these creatures, the holy angels and saints, already partake of it. It is Augustine's hope of resting in this stability, which is not the absence of a present but the fullness of an eternal present, that brings Augustine to meditate further on the image of the song at the close of book XI.

What if, Augustine asks, there were a mind that could know the whole course of time the way Augustine himself knows the whole song before he begins to sing it? Even if we could imagine what this would be like—to know all past, present, and future events as they would unfold—we still would not have imagined what it is for God to know all times.[106] That is because God knows all times without being distended in those times. For "the maker of the universe, the maker of souls and of bodies" is the Lord of time, and of

102. Augustine, *conf.*, 11.13.16, *CSEL* 33:291: "anni tui nec eunt nec veniunt: isti autem nostri eunt et veniunt, ut omnes veniant. anni tui omnes simul stant, quoniam stant, nec euntes a venientibus excluduntur, quia non transeunt: isti autem nostri omnes erunt, cum omnes non erunt. anni tui dies unus, et dies tuus non cotidie, sed hodie, quia hodiernus tuus non cedit crastino; neque enim succedit hesterno. hodiernus tuus aeternitas."

103. Augustine, *conf.*, 11.27.34, *CSEL* 33:304: "praeteriens enim tendebatur in aliquod spatium temporis, quo metiri posset, quoniam praesens nullum habet spatium."

104. Augustine, *conf.*, 11.14.17, *CSEL* 33:292: "praesens autem si semper esset praesens nec in praeteritum transiret, non iam esset tempus, sed aeternitas. si ergo praesens, ut tempus sit, ideo fit, quia in praeteritum transit, quomodo et hoc esse dicimus, cui causa, ut sit, illa est, quia non erit."

105. Augustine, *conf.*, 11.14.17, *CSEL* 33:292: "ut scilicet non vere dicamus tempus esse, nisi quia tendit non esse."

106. Augustine, *conf.*, 11.31.41, *CSEL* 33:309: "certe si est tam grandi scientia et praescientia pollens animus, cui cuncta praeterita et futura it nota sint, sicut mihi unum canticum notissimum, nimium mirabilis est animus iste atque ad horrorem stupendus."

creatures who know things by way of temporal succession.[107] In the final lines of *Confessiones* book XI, Augustine makes a direct address to God. He speaks of the way God knows and makes his creation. What he says bears directly on this investigation's attempt to describe what the *rationes seminales* are. "Therefore just as you knew heaven and earth in the beginning without variation of your knowledge, so too you made heaven and earth in the beginning without distention of your action."[108] What God makes in the *prima conditione* he makes eternally, outside of time. It is also true that God's *administratio* of all times is not temporally indexed in any way, though it is experienced by God's creatures as a succession of time.

One speculative way of sorting out the difference between the *conditio* and the *administratio* of all things is to say that *creatio* marks the relation of creator and creature. *Creatio* is the umbrella term for everything God does to bring creatures into existence and to sustain them in existence. *Creatio* is inclusive of both the *conditio* described by the *factum/a est* of Genesis 1 or the *condita sunt* of Colossians 1:16 and the *administratio* Augustine picks out as the way of describing the way God works until now (John 5:17).[109] *Conditio* refers specifically to the "seeding" of creation. It is a description of the created conditions for the fulfillment of God's will in creating all the things that are. This includes all past, present, and future events. These, as I have argued with Augustine's help, "stand" in God's eternal present. God's being present to them is what gives them their existence. *Administratio*, on the other hand, is a description of the outworking of those created conditions in time. The *conditio* and the *administratio* of God's creative relation to all creatures are interwoven, plaited together. They can be treated as logically distinct, but they are not truly

107. Augustine, *conf.*, 11.31.41, *CSEL* 33:309: "conditor universitatis, conditor animarum et corporum."

108. Augustine, *conf.*, 11.31.41, *CCL* 27:216: "Sicut ergo nosti in principio caelum et terram sine varietate notitiae tuae, ita fecisti in principio caelum et terram sine distentione actionis tuae." Here I have used the *CCL* edition of the text of Augustine's *Confessiones*. The *CSEL* substitutes "*distinctione*" for "*distentione*." There is a manuscript tradition supporting both variants, and there are good theological reasons to say both that there is no distinction and no distention in God's act of creation. However, given that the principal focus of the argument in book XI has to do with the relation of time to eternity, and that Augustine identifies the nature of time specifically with distention, I have opted for the *CCL*'s "*distentione*."

109. Augustine, *Gn. litt.*, 5.11.27, *PL* 34:330: "qua usque nunc operatur."

separable. The *conditio* is the condition for the possibility of the *administratio*, and the *administratio* is precisely of the *conditio*. The *conditio* contains all the possibilities for God's administrative work. It is not that God could not act otherwise than he has and does. But given the suppositional necessity of God having willed the *conditio* of creation eternally, it makes little sense to say that the outworking of it in his *administratio* would differ from God's unitary will.

If it is the case that the *conditio* and the *administratio* are in fact two descriptions of God's creative work, this distinction must be brought to bear on talk of the creation and duration of the *rationes seminales*. This way of speaking about the created order disciplines the metaphor of the seeds. Instead of thinking of those seeds simply as things planted that develop in time, we need to take into account that their creator is not subject to time. A description of the unfolding of creation in the order of time, the *administratio*, only makes sense from a creaturely perspective. The *administratio* offers a view of the creator–creature relation under the aspect of temporality. I will now offer a provisional description of that same relation under the aspect of eternity, in terms of the *conditio*. Like Augustine, I recognize at the outset that such speculations sit near the edges, and bump up against the borders, of language. But, as Wittgenstein observes, "These bumps allow us to understand the value of the discovery."[110] The following attempt at a speculative solution to the question, "What are the *rationes seminales*?" proceeds on the basis of what's already been said, extending it in likely and useful directions.

What Are the *Rationes Seminales*?

The *rationes seminales* have active powers. In this way the comparison to seeds is quite useful. Given the right conditions—good soil, water, sunlight—a seed germinates and will grow into a plant. Similarly, the *rationes seminales* have in themselves whatever they will be in time. Michael McKeough convincingly argues for the active powers of the *rationes seminales* in a dissertation on the subject.[111] Drawing on evidence in the writings of both Augustine

110. Wittgenstein, *Philosophical Investigations*, §119: "Sie, die Beulen, lassen uns den Wert jener Entdeckung erkennen."

111. Michael J. McKeough, *The Meaning of the Rationes Seminales in St. Augustine* (Washington, DC: Catholic University of America, 1926).

and Thomas, McKeough rejects the idea that the *rationes seminales* are passive.[112] He refutes the position that, in addition to the natural capacities of the seed-like rules implanted in unformed matter, the existence in time of all actual creatures depends upon a special intervention of God.[113] A survey of *De Genesi ad litteram* shows that whatever the *rationes seminales* are for Augustine, it would be incorrect to call them merely passive.[114] They cannot be if, as Augustine says, the creation of the six days just is the creation of all things that will unfold in time. The contrary view rests on the mistaken presupposition that in addition to creating and sustaining the cosmos it is also necessary for God to continually fiddle with what he creates. The faulty presupposition amounts to anthropomorphizing God by imagining God's omnipotence as something that interferes with the natural order of created things rather than being the condition for their possibility. This view lacks a sufficient account of secondary causality, whereby God as primary cause wields his creatures by giving them to be the kinds of things they are. Herbert McCabe expresses this point with characteristic clarity when he says,

> It is clear that God cannot *interfere* in the universe, not because he has not the power, but because, so to speak, he has too much; to interfere you have to be an alternative to, or alongside what you are interfering with. If God is the cause of everything, there is nothing he is alongside. . . . [And so] every action in the world is an action

---

112. McKeough, *The Meaning of the Rationes Seminales in St. Augustine*, 35–46.

113. This reading of Augustine on the *rationes seminales* is presented in Henry Woods, *Augustine and Evolution: A Study in the Saint's "De Genesi Ad Litteram" and "De Trinitate"* (New York: Universal Knowledge Foundation, 1924; repr., Eugene, OR: Wipf & Stock, 2009). In it Woods argues against Augustine's account of creation being deployed to support Darwinian evolution.

114. Cf. *inter alia*, Augustine, *Gn. litt.*, 5.4.11, *PL* 34:325: "Causaliter ergo tunc dictum est produxisse terram herbam et lignum, id est producendi accepisse virtutem"; *Gn. litt.*, 6.10.17, *PL* 34:346: "In quibus omnibus ea jam facta modos et actus sui temporis acceperunt, quae ex occultis atque invisibilibus rationibus, quae in creatura causaliter latent, in manifestas formas naturasque prodierunt"; *Gn. litt.*, 8.3.6, *PL* 34:374–75: "quia tunc scilicet, quod scriptum est, ea produxisse terram, causaliter factum erat in terra; hoc est, quia tunc ea producendi virtutem latenter acceperat, qua virtute fit ut etiam nunc talia terra progignat in manifesto atque in tempore suo."

> of God; not because it is not an action of a creature but because it is by God's action that the creature is *itself* and has its *own* activity.[115]

When created, the *rationes seminales* have the capacity to become whatever they will be in the order of time. These powers only express themselves at particular times and under particular conditions, but they are present and capable of development without an additional, miraculous nudge from their author.

The *rationes seminales* are also passive. While these seed-like rules of the *conditio* govern the possibilities of the *administratio* and its unfolding in time, Augustine also thinks there is a certain indeterminacy about them. Discussing the creation of humans in the two accounts given in the first and second chapters of Genesis, Augustine explains how he would answer if asked how humans were made in the first narrative, in the hexaëmeron. To this he replies, "Invisibly, potentially, and causally, in the way future things not finished things are made."[116] This statement is a perfect example of how the distinction between *conditio* and *administratio* is useful, but I will return to that later. Right now I want to emphasize Augustine's description of being made potentially (*potentialiter*). It is true that the *rationes seminales*, given the right conditions, will develop in particular ways. It is also true that the conditions play an important role in how that development occurs. To return to the image of a seed, plants grow differently in hard rocky soil than in rich loam. The Bonsai groomer works with the active powers of the plant to realize the possibility of a stunted yet beautiful tree. The *rationes seminales*, likewise, have the potential to develop variously in the order of time.

Augustine illustrates the passive possibilities of the *rationes seminales* when he explains how it is possible to imagine the causal, potential creation in the *conditio* such that creatures come to be in the *administratio* either through a process of growth and maturation or by an immediate and special creation. His argument is biblical. He maintains both that the earth puts forth grasses and trees as a result of the unfolding of the *rationes seminales*. At the same

---

115. Herbert McCabe, "Creation," in *God Matters* (London: Geoffrey Chapman, 1987; repr., London: Continuum International, 2012), 6–7.

116. Augustine, *Gn. litt.*, 6.6.10, *PL* 34:343: "Invisibiliter, potentialiter, causaliter, quomodo fiunt futura non facta."

time, Augustine needs to account for the distinctiveness of the special creation of Adam.[117] But he does not want to say that in creating Adam God was doing something altogether new. Rather, the *rationes seminales* in the *conditio* contain both the possibility of development over time and the possibility of being brought about by God's purposive and miraculous action. In this way Augustine manages to account for the existence of miracles, not as an overturning of the natural order of things but as an actualization of what exists only potentially in the *rationes seminales*. God is the one who makes nature and in this way determines what belongs to it. Most importantly for our broader search for the origins of death, this idea of the seed-like rules' potentiality is extensible to include possibilities that are not in fact actualized. As Augustine says of the making of Adam, "it is clear, therefore, that he was not to be made man contrary to what was in that first making (*prima conditione*) of causes; because there it was determined that he could be made in that way, although not that he must necessarily be made in that way."[118] The way the *rationes seminales* unfold "was not in the making of creation, but in the pleasure of the creator, whose will is the necessity of things."[119] The determinative necessity governing the *conditio* and its *administratio* is the will of God. While the *rationes seminales* have powers and potencies of their own, which might cause them to develop in various ways, those powers and potencies are given and governed by the divine will. In order to understand what this means and what it does not it is necessary to have a strong account of the efficacy of secondary causes. These do not undermine, but have their efficacy from, the will of God as primary cause.[120]

---

117. Augustine, *Gn. litt.*, 6.14.25, *PL* 34:349: "Quaeri autem merito potest, causales illae rationes, quas mundo indidit, cum primum simul omnia creavit, quomodo sint institutae: utrum ut, quemadmodum videmus cuncta nascentia vel fruticum vel animalium in suis conformationibus atque incrementis, sua pro diversitate generum diversa spatia peragerent temporum? an ut, quemadmodum creditur factus Adam sine ullo progressu incrementorum virili aetate, continuo conformarentur?"

118. Augustine, *Gn. litt.*, 6.15.26, *PL* 34:350: "manifestum est etiam sic non factum esse hominem contra quam erat in illa prima conditione causarum; quia ibi erat etiam sic fieri posse, quamvis non ibi erat ita fieri necesse esse."

119. Augustine, *Gn. litt.*, 6.15.25, *PL* 34:350: "non erat in conditione creaturae, sed in placito Creatoris, cujus voluntas rerum necessitas est."

120. This is just the account Augustine gives just two chapters onward at *Gn. litt.*, 6.17.28, *PL* 34:350: "Hoc enim necessario futurum est quod ille vult, et ea vere futura sunt quae ille praescivit. Nam multa secundum inferiores causas futura sunt; sed si ita sunt et in praescientia

With an account of the *rationes seminales* as both active and passive, I now want to turn back to Augustine's description of them existing, "invisibly, potentially, and causally, in the way future things not finished things are made."[121] Here we can see again the limits of human language's capacity to describe a making that is outside of all time. What does Augustine mean when he says Adam is made, "quomodo fiunt futura non facta"? Another way to translate this is to say, "they are made the way future things not made things are made." This translation is useful because it highlights what is being said here as nonsense.[122] That is, we have no idea what it means to say something is not made the way made things are made but the way future things are made. As nonsense, this sentence is useful in that it highlights what we are inclined to say about God creating everything that is at once, from nothing. We are inclined to think of the act of creation as if it were a kind of making. But it is also clear that it is nothing like making something. It is like making future things, not made things.

But the fact that this sentence has no determinative meaning is not to say that Augustine does not mean anything by writing it. Cora Diamond, describing how to understand those who utter nonsense explains, "To want to understand the person who talks nonsense is to want to enter imaginatively the taking of that nonsense for sense."[123] One way of entering imaginatively into Augustine's utterance is to be willing to make the logical cut I have used to distinguish the *conditio* from the *administratio*. This distinction names two

Dei, vere futura sunt: si autem ibi aliter sunt, ita potius futura sunt, sicut ibi sunt, ubi qui praescit, falli non potest."

121. Augustine, *Gn. litt.*, 6.6.10, *PL* 34:343: "Invisibiliter, potentialiter, causaliter, quomodo fiunt futura non facta."

122. I am using "nonsense" here in a technical sense, as deployed by the so-called "resolute readers" of Ludwig Wittgenstein. By calling this sentence of Augustine's nonsense, I mean to highlight that this sentence does not have a determinate meaning, a sense in which it ought to be taken. As Cora Diamond argues in an essay meant to explain this view of nonsense, "for Wittgenstein there is *no* kind of nonsense which is nonsense on account of what the terms composing it mean—there is as it were no 'positive' nonsense. *Anything* that is nonsense is so merely because some determination of meaning has *not* been made; it is not nonsense as a logical result of determinations that *have* been made." Cora Diamond, "What Nonsense Might Be," in *The Realistic Spirit* (Cambridge, MA: The MIT Press, 1991), 106.

123. Cora Diamond, "Ethics, Imagination and the Method of Wittgenstein's *Tractatus*," in *The New Wittgenstein*, ed. Alice Crary and Rupert Read (London: Routledge, 2000), 157.

levels of description of God's relation to the whole of creation. This distinction is suggested by Augustine's thoughts, but it is clear that I am extending rather than describing his position. I will now defend this extension on the basis of distinctions in our everyday language and of the language used in Scripture.

The only way timebound creatures have of discussing future things is as things that are not yet. That is how our language works. Imagine I said to you, "I am at the store," when I clearly am not, and you said in reply, "No, you are not, you are in the library." To say in reply, "Oh, no, you have misunderstood, I am at the store tomorrow," would be a case of miscommunication. I might not know how to use the verb "to be" properly, or I might be insane. In either case, what I have said does not work in English. Your instinct would be to either correct me or to get me professional help, depending on how you adjudged the nature of my mistake. But this odd pattern of speech is the same one deployed by Jesus Christ in the eighth chapter of the Gospel of John. There Jesus speaks in the temple in Jerusalem saying, "Your father Abraham rejoiced that he was to see my day; he saw it and was glad" (John 8:56). To this he receives an incredulous reply: "You are not yet fifty years old, and have you seen Abraham?" (John 8:57). Jesus's answer to their question is, "Truly, truly, I say to you, before Abraham was, I am" (John 8:58). This "I am" is a clear echo of the divine name given to Moses in Exodus 3:14, "I am who I am."

God's "I am," whether from the burning bush or the mouth of Jesus Christ, has classically been taken to indicate God's peculiar mode of being. God's essence is not something distinct from God's existence. The same cannot be said about creatures, who have their existence not as an essential property but as a gift from God. This "I am" also supports what I said above about the relation of time and eternity. There is no past or future for God—God is not temporally indexed in any way. Paul Griffiths takes these words of God in John and Exodus as evidence of something further. If God is eternal, and God's acts are indistinguishable from what and who God is, then those acts are also eternal. If this is so, it is also true that with respect to the incarnation, God acts atemporally such that, "the second person of the Trinity is eternally conjoined with a particular human nature, thus constituting the person Jesus Christ. That person, an indissoluble union of human and divine, is eternal."[124] This conclusion follows from God being the one who *is*,

124. Paul J. Griffiths, *Decreation: The Last Things of All Creatures* (Waco: Baylor University Press, 2014), 77.

and is so in the eternal present tense. Griffiths goes on to give an account of creaturely four-dimensionalism which can be taken to undergird some of my forthcoming speculations.[125]

The upshot of these speculations about God's "I am" is that these words should not be understood with reference to time. It does not make sense to speak that way. "Before Abraham was, I am" (John 8:58) is another bit of nonsense, precisely because it has no determinate meaning. What it is meant to do is allow us to enter imaginatively into what it is *to be* under the aspect of eternity. Augustine's investigations of time and eternity in *Confessiones* book XI serve a similar purpose, and though he himself might not have argued for a four-dimensionalist view of time, the building blocks are all there. Past, present, and future times stand in God's own eternity. They have their reality from the one whose essence is identical with his existence. Attempts to speak of how that might be leave us grasping for words. Like laying hold of a lattice of spiderweb, the structure of our thought collapses as soon as we make contact.

Pressing the imagination to consider "how future things not made things are made" by the one who eternally *is* in his own divine present, it is possible to glimpse the *rationes seminales* under the aspect of the *conditio*. Augustine calls the creation described in the six days total and complete. Everything is made all at once, invisibly, potentially, causally. What is completed in the six days is then described as unfolding or unfurling in time. Those seed-like rules take shape in time by becoming whatever it is they were, are, and will be. But if God's action in creation is eternal and we take the *conditio* to be a description of that relation, then it does not make sense to say the seed-like rules are sown *in the past*. To say so would be to confuse the two levels of discourse. When referring to the seed-like rules under the aspect of the *administratio*, it would make sense to speak this way. The unrolling of the ages takes place because the *rationes seminales* "were made, so to speak, in the roots of time."[126] But those same rules of speech prevent tensed talk of the *rationes seminales* in the *conditio*.

The act of creation from the perspective of the *conditio* is God's bringing into being of the total set of all creaturely relations—spatial, temporal,

125. Griffiths, *Decreation*, cf. esp. 81–87.

126. Augustine, *Gn. litt.*, 5.4.11, *PL* 34:325: "In ea quippe jam tanquam in radicibus, ut ita dixerim, temporum facta erant, quae per tempora futura erant."

intellectual, and intentional.[127] At the heart of these relations is the one *ratio*, the *Logos*, the Son, incarnate in the person of Jesus Christ. The divine ideas in the mind of God consist of God's own knowledge of the infinite number of ways in which he is participable. In a similar way, the *rationes seminales*, taking root in unformed matter outside of all time, are the actualization of the infinite set of relations of all things that are not God to Jesus Christ, the *ratio* of the cosmos made flesh. God qua divine is the exemplar cause of all possible things—every way that any cosmos might exist. God incarnate is the exemplar cause of all actual things—every way that this cosmos, the one reconciled by the blood of his cross, does exist. This is another way of saying with Paul in Colossians, "He is the image of the invisible God, the first-born of all creation; for in him all things were created, in heaven and on earth, visible and invisible, whether thrones or dominions or principalities or authorities—all things were created through him and for him. He is before all things, and in him all things hold together" (Col 1:15–17). In the *conditio*, all things hold together in Jesus Christ, perfectly and atemporally. As Augustine says, there is nothing else to be created after the six days. And yet, God is working until now, under the aspect of the *administratio* (John 5:17).

If this view is right, then the *administratio* is the distension of the *conditio*, the relations of all creatures to the flesh of Christ. In the stretching out of the *rationes seminales*, the whole panoply of their active and passive capacities in the past, present, and future is on display. Another way to think about the unrolling of past and future times from Jesus Christ is to return to the metaphor of the seed. Most of what I have said about seeds has focused on their ability to sprout upwards, out of the soil. But the growth of a seed is bidirectional. Plants put down roots while they develop and grow above ground. The distention of the *rationes seminales* is like this. These seeds put down roots in the past and come into bloom in the future. Time and space and the whole of the created order contained by them grow out of the *ratio seminalis* who was conceived by the power of the Holy Spirit. The far-reaching, racinated tendrils terminate at the beginning of time, the highest branches mark time's end. All flow from one source and stand in relation to the person of the God-man.

This is a speculative suggestion that builds on Augustine's uses of the word *ratio*, Augustine's and Thomas's thoughts on the divine ideas, and Augustine's own speculations about the nature of time. I have also attempted to clarify

127. Griffiths, *Decreation*, 76.

the distinction between creation considered under two different aspects. The doctrinal archive of the Church's teaching on the subject of creation offers a number of terms to describe God's creating and sustaining action. By deploying these terms in the way I have, I am offering a lexical toolkit for theologizing about creation from the point of view of eternity and from the point of view of time. Augustine's own thought tends in this distinction. Parsing Augustine's usages in the way I have suggested makes his own insights clearer. I now intend to put this toolkit to work. In the chapters that follow, I will explain how sin, evil, and death enter the world given the assumption that the *rationes seminales* are the sum total of the relations creatures bear to the flesh of Christ.

CHAPTER THREE

What Demons Are and How They Fell

IN THIS CHAPTER I will deal with the origins of nonhuman creaturely death considered under the aspect of the *conditio*. In order to do that, I need to say something more about the relationships that are constitutive of creatures. I will then consider how the intentional relations of rational creatures to God affect not only those relations but also the relations of everything else, creature to creature and creature to God. To make my case about the origins of death, I will focus on the relations the reprobate angels bear to God and on what effect those relations have on everything else that exists.

Not every possibility contained in the creation of all things in the *conditio* is actualized. The *conditio* is a description of creation under the aspect of eternity. It names the all-at-once creation of everything that is. This description is not temporally indexed because time is one of the things created and so subject to atemporal description. The seed-like rules (*rationes seminales*) that norm creation are the sum total of the spatial, temporal, intellectual, and intentional relations of all things to the person of Jesus Christ. God incarnate is the *ratio seminalis*, the rule of the whole created order, who makes actual some of the infinite set of possible ways the divine nature is participable by creatures. In addition to the set of relations all things bear to the incarnate Lord, every individual creature stands in some combination of relations to every other creature. Every rock, for example, stands in a set of spatiotemporal relations to every other rock. Every human stands in a set of intellectual and intentional relations to every angel. These relations include the dispositions of ignorance and indifference as much as knowledge and delight.

This second tier of relations between creatures depends on the first tier of relations all things bear to Jesus Christ. The first-tier relations create the possibility of the second, but both belong to the order of the cosmos. One way to say what a creature is is to give an account of its relations to other creatures and to God. This view is attractive for a number of reasons. One of them is that it is analogous to speaking, "about the Trinity that God is."[1] God is not something separate from who God is as Father, Son, and Holy Spirit. God qua God *just is* the sum total of the relations between the three divine persons.[2] It also means that there are relations some creatures are capable of having but do not have. This might be because other creatures have them (e.g., two stones cannot have the same set of spatiotemporal relations because they cannot occupy the same place at the same time). It might also occur because the way the total set of relations are constituted prevents some kinds of relations from occurring (e.g., angelic creatures are constitutionally capable of loving God, but the fallen angels are not able to actualize this capacity).

In order to understand how the relation the reprobate angels bear to God affects all other creatures it is first necessary to understand what the angelic fall is. The account I give is broadly Augustinian. That is, I continue to rely heavily on Augustine's angelology, particularly his insistence that the rebel angels fall atemporally. For Augustine, this argument is scriptural. His reflections on the angelic fall's atemporality come from his reading of John's Gospel. In the eighth chapter Jesus says of the devil, "He was a murderer from the beginning, and does not stand in the truth, because there is no truth in him" (John 8:44, NRSV). Augustine's reading of this verse must

1. Augustine, *trin.*, 1.4.7, *CCL* 50:34–35: "de Trinitate quae deus est."

2. John Zizioulas makes this point elegantly in his *Being as Communion: Studies in Personhood and the Church* (New York: St. Vladimir's Seminary Press, 1985), cf. esp. 36–41. The only problem with his approach is his failure to recognize that the "Western position" he pans and attributes to Augustine, is not in fact Augustine's position. In *De trinitate*, Augustine's equation of *Deus* with *Trinitas* emphasizes the point Zizioulas makes when he says: "Consequently, the ontological 'principle' of God is traced back, once again, to the person. Thus when we say that God 'is,' we do not bind the personal freedom of God—the being of God is not an ontological 'necessity' or a simple 'reality' for God—but we ascribe the being of God to his personal freedom. In a more analytical way this means that God, as Father and not as substance, perpetually confirms through 'being' His *free* will to exist. And it is precisely His trinitarian existence that constitutes this confirmation: the Father out of love—that is, freely—begets the Son and brings forth the Spirit." *Being as Communion*, 41. The space between Augustine and Zizioulas does not have to do with the former's emphasis on "being" as the substance of God as opposed to the latter's on personhood. *Being as Communion*, 41n35. The difference rests on the insistence upon the Father's *monarchia*, as when Zizioulas says "Thus God as person—as the hypostasis of the Father—makes the one divine substance to be that which it is: the one God." *Being as Communion*, 41. Augustine's trinitarian logic stands opposed to this assertion, not that of the primacy of personhood.

avoid Manichaean dualism. Augustine cannot have a devil that acts as an independent principle of activity, nor can he offer an account of the devil that God creates to be or do evil. To avoid these pitfalls, as I will explain further on, Augustine offers a privative account of evil. Augustine diffuses the possible tensions in John 8:44 by locating the fall of angelic creatures outside all time.

Scriptural Evidence for the Angelic Fall

Before offering any particular account of the fall of the angels, I want to look at the sources for thinking about the nature of the demons and their separation from God. The scriptural warrant for an angelic fall is varied but consistent. There is a line in salvation history beginning in Genesis that runs through Revelation referring to spiritual creatures, present and active in the lives of humans. Some of these creatures are evidently corrupt, engaged in open conflict with God's purposes. In Genesis 3, there is the deceitful serpent, which the Christian tradition has nearly unanimously interpreted as the presence of Satan in the Garden of Eden. On this scriptural basis we can claim that nonhuman, rational creatures exist. There is at least one nonhuman creature with the capacities of intellect and will present in the earliest chapters of Scripture.[3] This creature acts to precipitate Adam and Eve's fall by enticing them to disobey God's commandment not to eat of the tree of knowledge of good and evil (Gen 2:17). Not only can this creature act willfully, this creature can act in a way worthy of punishment, evilly (Gen 3:14–15).

There is more information about angels in the book of Job. The angels were there when God "laid the foundation of the earth" (Job 38:4). Where were you, God asks Job, "when the morning stars sang together, and all the sons of God shouted for joy?" (Job 38:7). The angels are there from the beginning, but it is also clear that some did not persist in their singing and joyful shouting. Apart from the presence of Satan in the first chapters (Job 1:6–12, 2:1–8), we also hear in the words of Eliphaz, "Even in his servants he puts not trust, and his angels he charges with error" (Job 4:18). While we should be cautious in accepting the word of Eliphaz, both Gregory the Great and Thomas Aquinas

3. Angels make frequent appearances in Genesis. I will not attempt to recount them all, but they are alluded to in the story of Noah (Gen 6), and they appear explicitly and implicitly throughout the Abraham cycle (cf. Gen 16, 18, 19, 21, 32).

understand his comments to articulate an important insight about angelic nature. As Gregory puts it, angels, unlike God, are subject to change, "For if the substance of the angels were incompatible with movement from mutability, being well made by its author it would never have fallen in the reprobate spirits from the blessedness of its high state. But marvelously, almighty God made the nature of the highest spirits good, but mutable."[4] Thomas likewise says that it is Catholic doctrine that angels are created good and that some "fell through their own fault."[5] The Latin of the Vulgate, reflected in both Gregory's and Thomas's text, is even stronger in its assertion than the RSV. Job reads "et in angelis suis repperit pravitatem" (Job 4:18, Vulg.). It is not just error that is found in the angels but *pravitas*—depravity or evil. Although the morning stars sang together, the tune grows discordant when God discovers *pravitas* in some of them.

The reference to the singing of the morning stars calls to mind Isaiah 14, where there is another reference to the angelic fall. The use of the name Lucifer in reference to the devil comes from this text. In the Vulgate the text of Isaiah 14:12 says, "quomodo cecidisti de caelo lucifer qui mane oriebaris," which I translate as, "How did you fall from heaven, Lucifer, who rose in the morning?" Jerome's exegesis of this passage is fascinating and contains some notes on the translation choices of Aquila Ponticus. In Hebrew, says Jerome, the word for *lucifer*—Latin for the morning star, Venus—is *elil*. Aquila's translation of Isaiah 14:12 renders the reference to Lucifer as "the lamenting (*ululantem*) son of the dawn."[6] Jerome appreciates the onomatopoetic symmetry of the Hebrew and the Latin in *elil* and *ululare*. And so he runs with this translation, tying the morning star, *lucifer*, to Satan. He says, "For he indeed ought to lament and wail, who on account of his pride was hurled down from heaven and ground

4. Gregory the Great, *mor.*, 5.38.68, *CCL* 143:267–68: "Nam si angelorum substantia a mutabilitatis motu fuisset aliena, bene ab auctore condita, nequaquam in reprobis spiritibus a beatitudinis suae arce cecidisset. Mire autem omnipotens Deus naturam summorum spirituum bonam, sed mutabilem condidit."

5. Thomas Aquinas, *super Iob*, ch. 4, lect. 3: "quae quidem sententia secundum doctrinam catholicae fidei plana est: tenet enim fides catholica omnes angelos bonos fuisse creatos, quorum quidam per propriam culpam ceciderunt a rectitudinis statu."

6. Jerome, *in Esaiam*, 6.14.12, *CCL* 73:240: "Pro Lucifero qui Hebraice dicitur Elil, Aquila transtulit: Ululantem aurorae filium."

into the earth."[7] Augustine likewise interprets Isaiah 14:12 to refer to "the devil figured under the person of the prince of Bablyon."[8]

Jerome ties his interpretation into New Testament thought about the devil and his fall. He shows that Isaiah is dealing with the same fall recounted by Jesus himself. Jerome quotes Luke 10:18, "And so the Savior says to his disciples: *I saw Satan falling from heaven like lightning.* Not only *I see* but *I saw* when he fell. . . . He is the prince of the age, who rose among the other stars in the morning, and by his own fault from the morning star (*lucifero*) was made the evening star (*vesper*), not rising but setting."[9] The terrible beauty of this passage is made only more profound when we remember that *lucifer* and *vesper* are both names for the planet Venus, just as Satan is the same angelic person who rose in light and fell into darkness.

The New Testament is full of references to demons beyond Jesus's account of the fall of Satan in Luke 10. To make clear that Scripture warrants thinking not just of an individual rebel angel but a demonic host, I will draw attention to a few key passages. The different versions of Gerasene demoniac pericope in the gospels of Matthew (Matt 8:28–34), Mark (Mark 5:1–20), and Luke (Luke 8:26–39) illustrate the point. In them we learn two things about the demons. The first is that the demons know who Jesus is. They identify him as "Son of the Most High God" (Mark 5:7, Luke 8:28; cf. Matt 8:29). The knowledge of the demons in these narratives stands in contrast to the ignorance of Jesus's disciples, who in the preceding pericope are confounded by the identity of the man they are following. "Who then is this, that even wind and sea obey him?" they ask one another (Mark 4:41; cf. Luke 8:25). There is no similar hesitancy on the part of the demons. Fear rather than awe grips them. "Do not torment me," they cry (Mark 5:7, Luke 8:28). They know the Son of God has power over them. In Matthew's gospel this torment is coupled with knowledge of the

7. Jerome, *in Esaiam*, 6.14.12, *CCL* 73:240: "Vere enim ululare debuit et eiulare, qui propter superbiam suam de coelo in terram praecipitatus est atque contritus."

8. Augustine, *civ.*, 11.15, *CSEL* 40.1:534: "sub figurata persona principis Babyloniae diabolum."

9. Jerome, *in Esaiam*, 6.14.12, *CCL* 73:240: "Unde et Salvator ad discipulos loquitur: Videbam Satanam quasi fulgur de coelo cadentem. Non modo video, sed prius videbam quando corruit. . . . Iste est princeps saeculi, qui inter stellas caeteras mane oriebatur, et suo vitio de lucifero vesper effectus est, et non oriens, sed occidens."

future as well as the present, when they ask, "Have you come here to torment us before the time?" (Matt 8:29).

The second thing these passages show is that Jesus is confronted with not one but many demonic persons. Each of the synoptics demonstrates this, though with different emphases. In Matthew, Jesus is faced with "two demoniacs" (Matt 8:28). There is no indication in the text that there are more or fewer than one demon per possessed person. Turning to Luke, this event takes on a slightly different hue. In his version of the story, there is only one possessed man. Jesus asks him, "What is your name?" to which he responds, "Legion" (Luke 8:30). Luke offers the reader an explanatory gloss. The demoniac responds, "Legion," because, "many demons had entered him" (Luke 8:30). In this version of the story there are good textual reasons to think that many demons have taken a single human captive by residing in him.

Mark's account of this incident says more. When Christ asks, "What is your name?" he receives a confusing reply: "My name is Legion; for we are many" (Mark 5:9). The demons reply in both the singular and the plural—"my name is" and "we are." There is something individual and something corporate about fallen angels. Unlike Luke, who interprets the name, Legion, for his reader, in Mark the demons themselves provide the explanation. This language should resonate with the reader as an inversion of Paul's explanation of the corporate nature of life in Christ in First Corinthians. There Paul says, "For just as the body is one and has many members, and all the members of the body, though many, are one body, so it is with Christ" (1 Cor 12:12). Mark's demons present a devilish simulacrum of the body of Christ. Commenting on the passage from First Corinthians, Augustine makes a similar observation about the corporate nature of the fallen angels. "In the same way the body of the devil—that is, the multitude of the impious and most of all those who fall from Christ or from the Church as from heaven—whose head is the devil, is called the devil. And many things are said figuratively in that very body which do not so much fit the head as they do the body and members."[10] Demons are

10. Augustine, *Gn. litt.*, 11.24.31, *PL* 34:442: "eo modo etiam corpus diaboli, cui caput est diabolus, id est ipsa impiorum multitudo, maximeque eorum qui a Christo vel de Ecclesia sicut de coelo decidunt, dicitur diabolus, et in ipsum corpus figurate multa dicuntur, quae non tam capiti quam corpori membrisque conveniant." On the body of the devil cf. also *Gn. litt.*, 11.22.29, 11.25.32.

not only multiple, they are united in a way that it makes sense to refer to them together in the singular and the plural.

The last piece of scriptural evidence I will examine comes from Revelation 12, which strengthens the corporate image of the demons. This chapter from Revelation provides the most vivid and detailed description of the angelic fall in Scripture. But the narrative is not straightforward. It is best read as a cosmic drama played out on two levels, in heaven and on earth. It begins with "a great portent" (Rev 12:1). A woman appearing in heaven, "clothed with the sun," is preparing to give birth (Rev 12:1–2). "A great red dragon" sets upon the woman, ready to devour the child upon delivery (Rev 12:3–4). The child is saved and "caught up to God and to his throne" while the woman flees "into the wilderness" (Rev 12:5–6). After this, a war in heaven ensues between "Michael and his angels" and "the dragon and his angels" (Rev 12:7). The dragon, "that ancient serpent, who is called the Devil and Satan," is defeated and "thrown down to the earth, and his angels were thrown with him" (Rev 12:9). Being cast down, the dragon continues his fight not against Michael and his angels but against "the woman who had borne the male child" and "the rest of her offspring" (Rev 12:13, 17). I am going to point out three features of this text. First, I will look at the two levels of this drama. Second, to elaborate on the corporate nature of the demons, I will offer a reading of the dragon's tail sweeping the stars from the sky. Third, I will touch on what it means to say of the demons, "there was no longer any place for them in heaven" (Rev 12:8), and what this means for the earth to which they have been cast down.

A possible reading of Revelation 12 takes it as a single narrative that occurs in two different settings: heaven and earth. The scene opens with the announcement of the two great portents "in heaven" (Rev 12:1, 3), the woman clothed with the sun and crowned with stars along with the seven-headed, ten-horned serpent. The war between Michael and Satan also plays out "in heaven" (Rev 12:7), and from heaven the demons are cast out (Rev 12:8–9). On this reading, the heavenly narrative ends after the twelfth verse, and Revelation 12:13–17 picks up where 12:6 leaves off.

Another interpretive option is to read the whole text as a two-level drama. This strategy has some advantages over a single narrative switching from a heavenly to a terrestrial backdrop. This reading works best when linked with the two ways of describing creation, considered from the perspective of the *conditio* and the *administratio*. Taking it like this makes a cut at the transition from the twelfth to the thirteenth verse. Everything before that cut belongs to the description of creation under the aspect of eternity, in the *conditio*. The events described there are not best understood as a temporal sequence. On this view, Revelation 12:1–12 is a description of the cosmos considered as a whole, created good but also the site of an epic battle. After the cut, verse 13 begins to describe those events under the aspect of time. They point to a sequential unfolding of discrete happenings in the temporal order, in the *administratio*.

Alcuin of York's *Commentariorum in Apocalypsin* inclines in this direction. What we have of his commentary ends after five books, midway through chapter twelve, right where I suggest the division of the two-level drama should be made. Two things he says in this commentary are suggestive. First he says, "The woman clothed with the sun is the Blessed Virgin Mary, covered by the power of the Most High, and in her a type is also understood, that is the Church."[11] His interpretation emphasizes the Church signified by the Virgin Mary rather than the Virgin Mary herself. But his thoughts on this first verse comport well with Pope Pius XII's recognition in *Munificentissimus Deus* that in these words there is scriptural warrant for the doctrine of Mary's Assumption into heaven and crowning in glory.[12]

Alcuin's commentary contains another detail that prompts the reader to think about the relation between time and eternity. He says, "Through the moon, which wanes by increments of time, the mutability of time is expressed, which the Church—because it despises it—presses down as if beneath her feet."[13] This fits with the idea that the unfurling of things in the *administratio*, under the aspect of time, is something painful, a distention. The Church, with her emphasis on things eternal, including the consummation of all things eschatologically, tramples upon mutability. She puts it under foot. This trampling of the moon and mutability brings to mind another classical image of Mary found in devotional statuary and paintings, crushing the head of a serpent under foot. These images are a visual form of scriptural interpretation, which recognizes Mary as the fulfilment of God's words in Genesis 3:15 in the

11. Alcuin of York, *in Apoc.*, 5.12, *PL* 100:1152d: "Mulier amicta sole beata virgo Maria est, obumbrata Altissimi virtute, in qua etiam genus, id est Ecclesia, intelligitur."

12. Pius XII, *Munificentissimus Deus*, §§27–28, http://w2.vatican.va/content/pius-xii/la/apost_constitutions/documents/hf_p-xii_apc_19501101_munificentissimus-deus.html.

13. Alcuin of York, *in Apoc.*, 5.12, *PL* 100:1152d: "Per lunam vero, quae per incrementa temporum deficit, mutabilitas temporis exprimitur, quam Ecclesia quia despicit quasi sub pedibus premit."

Vulgate, "ipsa conteret caput tuum"—"she shall crush your head." The words in Genesis come as a promise of ongoing conflict between Satan, under the guise of a serpent, and Eve's offspring. This makes it immediately relevant to the reading of Revelation 12, which is a description of pitched battle between a woman and a giant serpent.

Aside from noting that Mary's feet are suitable for crushing both the devil and the changeableness of time, these observations illuminate some aspects of the two-level drama of Revelation 12. The first is that Mary has a key role in the life of the cosmos. The centrality of Mary comes to the fore in her confrontation with the Satan and his angels. This confrontation takes place because she bears in her womb and gives her flesh to the one who is the life of the world. In the next chapter I will examine how this perspective relates to a theologoumenon which links the fall of the angels with the incarnation. For now it is enough to say that Mary in her own person and as a type of the Church is at war with the demons. That war plays out in heaven and on earth. The cosmic nature of Mary's war under the aspect of the *conditio* has its counterpart in the *administratio*.

The battle fought in time is found in the narrative of Revelation 12 from verse 13 onward. The "dragon" (*draco*), once thrown down from heaven, pursues the woman and her offspring precisely as a "serpent" (*serpens*), humanity's ancient enemy (Rev 12:13–15; cf. Gen 3:15). More clearly than in the first twelve verses, the woman here typifies the Church on pilgrimage in this world. She is pursued to the ends of the earth by an enemy who targets those "who keep the commandments of God and bear testimony to Jesus" (Rev 12:17). But a strong separation between Mariology and ecclesiology would be a mistake. The flesh of Jesus, which unites the Church as the mystical body of Christ, is taken from Mary. Those "who bear testimony to Jesus" in the face of demonic onslaught do so fortified by that flesh present in the Eucharist.

Next we need to look at the tail of the dragon, which "swept down a third of the stars of heaven" (Rev 12:4). As I have already shown, Scripture sometimes refers to the angels as stars (Job 38:7, Isa 14:12). It is reasonable to think this reference has to do with Satan's role in the fall of some of the host of heaven. This is the view of Thomas Aquinas, who thinks it probable that Satan was the highest of all the angels before his fall and that his fall caused the fall of the lower angels.[14] In article 8 of question 63 in the Prima Pars of the *Summa Theologiae*, Thomas cites Revelation 12:4 as an authority to support

14. Cf. *ST*, I.63.7–8.

the claim that Satan causes the other angels to fall.[15] The highest angel's sin does not force the others to sin, but it was a "kind of exhortation, leading them into" sin.[16] Because the other angels follow Satan they are made his subjects. Thomas argues this point with Scripture, citing Matthew 25:41, where Jesus refers to "the devil and *his* angels."[17] This is the same pattern of speech deployed in Revelation 12:7, where the angels are divided into two groups, "Michael and his angels" who are fighting "the dragon and *his* angels."

This further supports the view that demons exist corporately as well as individually as I argued using Mark's account of the Gerasene demoniac and Augustine's reading of First Corinthians. Thomas's interpretation shows that the demons' subjection to Satan fits their sin. Thomas considers it likely that Satan was the highest angel, and so he concludes that, "it was not contrary to the demons' pride that they willed to be under an inferior [Satan rather than God] . . . especially because even then, in the order of nature, they were subject to the highest angel."[18] The turn away from God occurs first in Satan and second in the rest of the fallen angels, but this is not a first and second in the order of time. Satan's sin is causally but not temporally prior to the other angels' sin. For Thomas, this makes sense to say because angels are intellectual substances not weighed down by a perishable body (Wis 9:15). It is possible to affirm both that "the demons sinned all at once" and that "the sin of one could be the cause of the others sinning."[19] Unlike humans, angels do not need time to make choices. While human reason acts discursively, deliberatively, angelic reason grasps and chooses instantaneously, intuitively. Thomas compares this to the way even humans are able to seize upon first principles.[20]

15. *ST*, I.63.8, *sed contra.*

16. *ST*, I.63.8 *resp*: "peccatum primi angeli fuit aliis causa peccandi, non quidem cogens, sed quadam quasi exhortatione inducens."

17. *ST*, I.63.8 *resp.*

18. *ST*, I.63.8 *ad* 2: "Sic igitur non fuit contra superbiam daemonum quod subesse inferiori voluerunt . . . praesertim quia supremo angelo naturae ordine etiam tunc subiecti erant."

19. *ST*, I.63.8 *ad* 1: "licet simul daemones peccaverint, tamen peccatum unius potuit esse aliis causa peccandi."

20. *ST*, I.63.8 *ad* 1: "Angelus enim non indiget ad eligendum vel exhortandum vel etiam consentiendum, temporis mora; sicut homo, qui deliberatione indiget ad eligendum et ad consentiendum, et locutione vocali ad exhortandum, quorum utumque tempore agitur. Manifestum

In turning immediately and subordinating themselves to Satan, the demons band together to form a body united under the headship of Satan as *princeps.*

Before turning my attention to the Church's doctrinal resources on the fall of the angels, I will examine the defeat of the demons and their being cast down when "there was no longer any place for them in heaven" (Rev 12:8). Not only are the angels who turn away from God defeated, this defeat signals the loss of their proper place. Angels are made according to the divine *ratio*, the *Logos*. This *ratio* does not simply belong to this or that individual creature. It is best understood with reference to all creatures considered as an ordered whole.[21] For this reason, we should not underestimate the calamitous effects of the angelic fall. Angels belong in heaven. When some of them fall away such that there is no longer any place in heaven for them, it disrupts the ordering of the whole. For this reason, both Augustine and Anselm, among others, speculate that the number of lost angels will be made up by humans reconciled in Christ.[22] There is a keen sense that vacating certain places in the celestial hierarchy means damage for the cosmos. For Anselm and Augustine, in order for the cosmos to be properly ruled—brought back into alignment with the *ratio* of its maker—the emptiness left by the angelic fall needs to be filled back up.

Speculations on humans repopulating the angelic hierarchies aside, the important point for my argument is that angelic disobedience involves disorder. Like a soldier abandoning his post, when there is no longer any place in heaven for some of the angels, a duty that ought to be carried out is left undone. But it is more than abandonment, as Revelation 12 points out. The fallen angels are not just deserters, but turncoats. A battle with its origins outside time has effects in the temporal order. The devil's ongoing war with the Church in time is characterized precisely by its rejection of divine rule. His enemies are those "who keep the commandments of God and bear testimony

---

est autem quod etiam homo simul dum aliquid iam corde concepit, in eodem instanti incipit loqui. Et in ultimo instant locutionis, in quo aliquis sensum loquentis capit, potest assentire ei quod dicitur, ut patet maxime in primis conceptionibus, quas quisque probat auditas."

21. In the last chapter I dealt with Thomas on the ordered whole in *ST*, I.15.2 *resp*: "Illud autem quod est optimum in rebus existens, est bonum ordinis universi."

22. Augustine, *civ.*, 22.1, *CSEL* 40.2:583: "qui de mortali progenie merito iusteque damnata tantum populum gratia sua colligit, ut inde subpleat et instauret partem, quae lapsa est angelorum." Cf. Anselm, *Cur Deus Homo*, 1.17–18, *PL* 158:382A-389B.

to Jesus" (Rev 12:17), who is the rule of the cosmos. The role angels do and should play in the cosmos as the variegated expression of God's gift of self is rejected by the demons. For this reason, the battle is most pitched where the demons encounter those who bear witness to the ruler of the cosmos, whose rule they seek to undermine by their turn.

The Doctrine of the Angelic Fall

The Church has offered some definitive interpretation of the biblical witness of the existence of nonhuman, rational creatures, some of whom are at war with God. One of the earliest authoritative statements about fallen angels recognizes the stakes involved. Pope Leo I, in the letter *Quam Laudabiliter* to Bishop Turribus of Astorga, puts it this way: "The true faith confesses the good substance of all creatures—whether spiritual or corporeal—and that there is no nature of evil, because God, who is the maker of the universe, made nothing not good. So even the devil would be good, if he had remained in the good which he was made."[23] Leo recognizes that the existence of evil, incorporeal beings presents a prima facie challenge to the Christian doctrine of creation by an omnibenevolent deity. The existence of any evil, corporeal or spiritual, poses such a challenge. The note Leo rings here sounds continually in the Church's teaching on angels and demons. God, being all good, only creates good things. There is no nature of evil.

In this letter, Leo is responding to the contrary claim, attributed to the Priscillianists, who say, "that the devil never was good, nor was his nature the work of God, but that he emerged out of the chaos and darkness because surely he has no author, but is himself the principle and substance of all evil."[24] Evil, according to the Priscillianists, *is* something. The devil is that something's source. Before refuting it, it is important to see why the position in this passage

23. Leo I, *Quam Laudibiliter*, *DS* §286: "fides vera . . . omnium creaturarum sive spiritualium sive corporalium bonam confiteatur substantiam, et mali nullam esse naturam: quia Deus, qui universitatis est conditor, nihil non bonum fecit. Unde et diabolus bonus esset, si in eo quod factus est permaneret."

24. Leo I, *Quam Laudibiliter*, *DS* §286: "quod diabolus numquam fuerit bonus, nec natura eius opificium Dei sit, sed eum ex chao et tenebris emersisse: quia scilicet nullum sui habeat auctorem, sed omnis mali ipse sit principium atque substantia."

is an attractive one that recurs throughout Church history. It appears to have great explanatory power. In it, the problem of evil is not resolved but dissolved without remainder. Evil, on this account, is definitively not from God. It originates in an opposing force, whose characteristic marks are chaos and darkness. This comports well with the image of a cosmic war, the battle for souls and *imperium* over creation. Surfacing time and again, versions of this heresy claim adherents for a reason. Augustine himself was held captive by the glamor of the Manichaean worldview.

But the attractiveness of this view and what it seems to explain cannot survive contact with the Christian doctrine of creation from nothing, *ex nihilo*. The cost of dissolving the problem of evil is too high. To give evil substantial, independent existence that stands apart from God's creative act robs God of his lordship. If evil is *something* rather than a *lack* of something it either has its source elsewhere than God, who is all good and creates only good creatures. Or even worse, God is not wholly good, and the substantial darkness present in the created order mirrors an uncreated darkness the divine nature. In the first case, God is not the source of all that is. In the second case, though all come from God, that source is corrupt, shot through with a darkness that expresses itself in a broken creation. Neither of these views is compatible with Christian orthodoxy.

Leo's letter is a doctrinal development that makes explicit what is implicit in Scripture and the creedal affirmations of the first three ecumenical councils. God is the creator of all things. There is "one God, the Father almighty, creator of heaven and earth, of all things visible and invisible."[25] The first possibility proposed by the Priscillianists and the Manichaeans and later the Cathars, of an evil *tertium quid* apart from God and his creatures, is excluded. Further, the Augustinian tenor of Leo's contribution to Church doctrine on this point is evident in his asseverations, "there is no nature of evil" and God "made nothing not good." To make clear the source of Leo's thought, I will turn briefly to book VII of Augustine's *Confessiones* to highlight the pattern of questioning that leads to these answers. Leo's ability to teach it as the doctrine of the Church depends upon this pattern of reasoning. But there is another reason to look closely at Augustine's questions and answers. Augustine's

---

25. The Niceno-Constantinopolitan Creed, *DS* §150: "Credo in unum Deum, Patrem omnipotentem, factorem caeli et terrae, visibilium omnium et invisibilium."

thoughts on these matters in *Confessiones* also show that the contrary view is something that must be surmounted, not just rejected. His recognition of the temptation to see the world as a struggle between a substantial goodness and a substantial evil allows him to move beyond this perspective.

Augustine on the Problem of Evil

Moving beyond the Manichaean worldview cannot entail a simple rejection, any more than dissolving the problem of evil counts as an answer to it. What Augustine provides instead is a refashioning of a dualistic metaphysics into something Christian. To deny the hold that the conflict between light and darkness has on the imagination would be to ignore its obvious explanatory power and fail to make sense of the Scripture's use of those images. Taking these images seriously is the only way to grasp the nature of Augustine's rejection of the school of Mani. Augustine understood the problem evil poses and the desire to explain it with dualism. Because he was taken with the Manichaeans and had inhabited their imaginative world he was prepared to offer a rebuttal that involved pushing his speculations to the brink.

In book VII of the *Confessiones*, Augustine examines two ways of offering a substantive account of evil. He weaves together his discussion of both ways, so part of the task is to untangle them. I have already argued briefly that the Nicene-Constantinopolitan Creed rules out a *tertium quid* standing apart from God and his creatures, I will first look at the way Augustine deals with the second possibility, that God is evil or corruptible. The questions he asks and answers are just as interesting for their epistemological commitments as they are for their conclusions. After examining these commitments and conclusions, I will return to Augustine's treatment of the idea of evil as an independent substance and show how his critique results in the view that evil originates in the will of rational creatures. This volitional account of evil's origin allows Augustine to maintain many of the insights of his Manichaean past by appropriating them into a new kind of dualism. Rather than a dualism of substance, Augustine presents his readers with a dualism of the will. Augustine's account of the turning will as the source of evil is essential to grasp what Leo I says in *Quam Laudabiliter*. Further, we need it to make sense of Augustine's account of the angelic fall, which Serge-Thomas Bonino has argued is the starting place for all theological speculation on the topic.[26]

At the start of book VII, Augustine lays out the problem. He is not sure how to think of God in terms other than corporeal: "I could not conceive (*cogitare*) of any substance except such as is normally seen by these eyes."[27] He is lost, and it does not yet occur to him that there is another way of understanding what Christians mean by "God."[28] Though just a man, he "tried to conceive" (*conabar cogitare*) of the "highest and sole and true God," but continued to fall short.[29] Unable to think of God as something other than an object in the world, Augustine is driven to confusion. If God is not the source of all existing things but instead one of those things, then it is possible for him to be in conflict with other existing things. And being in conflict with other existing things, it is possible for God to suffer change. But, Augustine says, "I believed (*credebam*) with my whole heart you to be incorruptible and inviolable and immutable, because not knowing (*nesciens*) why or how I saw clearly and was certain what can be corrupted is worse than what cannot, and what cannot be violated I put unhesitatingly above violable things, and what suffers no change is better than what can change."[30] Augustine believes, he says, but does not know why or how. He makes a distinction between two kinds of knowledge. Relating these two ways of knowing and bringing them into alignment is

26. Serge-Thomas Bonino, *Les anges et les démons: quatorze leçons de théologie* (Paris: Éditions Parole et Silence, 2007), 201: "Soulignons simplement que saint Augustin, même s'il a beaucoup hésité sur le scénario exact de l'histoire angélique, a donné à la réflexion théologique sur la chute du diable sa forme quasi-définitive."

27. Augustine, *conf.*, 7.1.1, *CSEL* 33:140: "qui cogitare aliquid substantiae nisi tale non poteram, quale per hos oculos videri solet."

28. Augustine, *conf.*, 7.1.1, *CSEL* 33:140: "quid te aliud cogitarem non occurrebat."

29. Augustine, *conf.*, 7.1.1, *CSEL* 33:140: "et conabar cogitare te homo et talis homo, summum et solum et verum deum."

30. Augustine, *conf.*, 7.1.1, *CSEL* 33:140–41: "et te incorruptibilem et inviolabilem et incommutabilem totis medullis credebam, quia nesciens, unde et quomodo, plane tamen videbam et certus eram id, quod corrumpi potest, deterius esse quam id quod non potest, et quod violari non potest, incunctanter praeponebam violabili, et quod nullam patitur mutationem, melius esse quam id quod mutari potest."

integral to Augustine's overcoming a corporeal image of God, which leads to his rejection of the idea that God could be admixed with the evil of corruption.

The two ways of knowing Augustine juxtaposes are cogitative, scientific knowledge and authoritative, volitional knowledge. Augustine identifies the first kind with thinking verbs. He flags this with "cogitare" and "nesciens." With these thinking verbs, Augustine highlights his inability to "think" an incorporeal substance—"cogitare aliquid substantiae nisi tale non poteram, quale per hos oculos videri solet." And he believes because he does not understand—"credebam, quia nesciens." But lacking penetrative, cognitive command of his subject does not prevent Augustine from knowing something about it. The second kind of knowledge Augustine describes rests on an act of will—belief—rather than intellect. He believes with his whole heart—"totis medullis credebam." And though you might think this would lead him to be less sure of this kind of knowledge, that is not the case. Lacking discursive knowledge of God, he still claims to see clearly and with certainty—"plane tamen videbam et certus eram."

He is certain but he does not understand. What are we to make of this? What is clear from the text is that he places these two ways of knowing in opposition to one another. His volitional knowledge, born of belief, runs up against his discursive knowledge. "My heart cried out violently against all my mental images and by this one blow tried to drive the spiraling roar of impure thoughts away from my mind's eye. And hardly was it dispersed, when, in the blink of an eye, here it was gathered back up again, and it pressed in upon my vision and darkened it."[31] His firm belief beats back the bodily phantasms of intellectual habit, the well-trod paths of Augustine's Manichaean materialism, only to just as quickly find itself playing defense to a resurgent swirling mass of confused thoughts. The cry of his heart—"clamabat violenter cor meum"—is in conflict with his mind's eye—"acie menti meae."

This text brings to mind the familiar aphorism from Blaise Pascal's *Pensées*, "The heart has its reasons, that reason knows not."[32] A related

---

31. Augustine, *conf.*, 7.1.1, *CSEL* 33:141: "clamabat violenter cor meum aversus omnia phantasmata mea et hoc uno ictu conabar abigere circumvolantem turbam immunditiae ab acie menti meae: et vix dimota in ictu oculi ecce conglobata rursus aderat et inruebat in aspectum meum et obnubilabat eum."

32. Blaise Pascal, *Pensées*, ed. Michel Le Guern (Paris: Gallimard, 2004), §397: "Le cœur a ses raisons, que la raison ne connaît point."

comment of Pascal's on the reasons of the heart bears even more precisely on Augustine's situation. Pascal says, "We know the truth, not only through reason, but even through the heart. It is by this latter kind that we know first principles, and it is in vain that reasoning, which plays no part, tries to oppose them."[33] Pascal offers some examples of first principles known in this way: space, time, movement, number. They are not less certain because they belong to the heart's knowledge.[34] The skeptics who claim the incertitude of all knowledge on account of our reliance on these reasons are confused when they point out the inability to prove them rationally. This does not constitute an inability to know, but shows the weakness of human reason.[35] They, the skeptics, have got it the wrong way round. Our knowledge of first principles, known *par le cœur*, "is as firm as any that our reasoning gives to us, and it is upon this knowledge of the heart and of instinct that reason supports itself and there that it bases all its discourse."[36] The heart does not depend first upon the reason for its knowledge, instead reason needs the knowledge of the heart to do its work. It would therefore be as ridiculous for reason to demand rational proofs of the heart before consenting to first principles as it would be for the heart to demand a feeling or sentiment for the conclusions of reason's own operations.[37] Pascal observes, in conclusion, that the inability of the heart to offer a rational demonstration of what it knows, "should therefore only serve

---

33. Pascal, *Pensées*, §101: "Nous connaissons la vérité, non seulement par la raison, mais encore par le cœur. C'est de cette dernière sorte que nous connaisson les premiers principes, et c'est en vain que le raisonnement, qui n'y a point de part, essaie de les combattre."

34. Pascal, *Pensées*, §101: "Car la connaissance des premiers principes, comme qu'il y a espace, temps, mouvement, nombres, <est> aussi ferme qu'aucune de celles que nos raisonnements nous donnent."

35. Pascal, *Pensées*, §101: "Nous savons que nous ne rêvons point, quelque impuissance où nous soyons de le prouver par raison; cette impuissance ne conclut autre chose que la faiblesse de notre raison, mais non pas l'incertitude de toutes nos connaissance, comme ils [pyrrhoniens] prétendent."

36. Pascal, *Pensées*, §101: "<est> aussi ferme qu'aucune de celles que nos raisonnements nous donnent, et c'est sur ces connaissances du cœur et de l'instinct qu'il faut que la raison s'appuie et qu'elle y fonde tout son discours."

37. Pascal, *Pensées*, §101: "Et il est aussi inutile et aussi ridicule que la raison demande au cœur des preuves de ses premiers principes pour vouloir y consentir, qu'il serait ridicule que le cœur demandât à la raison un sentiment de toutes les propositions qu'elle démontre pour vouloir les recevoir."

to humble reason, which would like to judge everything, but not to oppose our certainty as if only reason were capable of instructing us."[38] The position that heart and reason both offer certainty, but by different paths, is an Augustinian conviction which Pascal commends with characteristic clarity.

Armed with this respect for the heart's knowledge and a humbled reason, I now turn to Augustine's *De utilitate credendi*. In this early treatise, Augustine is attempting to convince an old friend of his, Honoratus, that the Manichaeans (like Pascal's skeptics) have made the mistake of thinking reason ought "juger de tout." The Manichaeans "promise they will offer a rational account of the most obscure things to those whom they attract. And for that reason especially they accuse the Catholic [Church], that whoever comes to her is enjoined to believe. They, however, pride themselves that they do not impose the yoke of believing, but instead open a fount of teaching."[39] The claim the Manichaeans are making, to offer reasons apart from any belief is misguided and false. It is false because by pursuing true religion, one has already conceded to believe there is one. More than that, "No one doubts him who seeks the true religion either to believe there is an immortal soul—for which that religion is a boon—or even that he wants to find precisely that belief in that same religion."[40] To be in pursuit of the true religion is to believe there is some point to it. Augustine identifies two: the belief in an immortal soul or the desire for that belief.

Jason BeDuhn does not find Augustine's overall epistemological stance particularly convincing. Although he is mistaken about this, BeDuhn does an excellent job summing up what Augustine thinks is at stake in the priority of belief in matters of religion. "The Manichaeans," he explains,

> leaped over the necessary preliminaries, and offered access to truth at the beginning, rather than at the end, of personal reform. In this

38. Pascal, *Pensées*, §101: "Cette impuissance ne doit donc servir qu'à humilier la raison, qui voudrait juger de tout, mais non pas à combattre notre certitude comme s'il n'y avait que la raison capable de nous instruire."

39. Augustine, *util. cred.*, 9.21, *CSEL* 25.1:26: "quod illis, qui ad eam veniunt, praecipitur, ut credant, se autem non iugum credendi inponere, sed docendi fontem aperire gloriantur."

40. Augustine, *util. cred.*, 7.14, *CSEL* 25.1:19: "nemo dubitat eum, qui veram religionem requirat, aut iam credere inmortalem esse animam, cui prosit illa religio, aut etiam id ipsum in eadem religione velle invenire." Cf. *util. cred.*, 14.30.

> way, Augustine claimed, their followers were fooled into thinking that they had arrived before they had even begun. They reversed the proper order of progress; first must come the moral and intellectual disciplining by which people learned to give up "love of anything besides God and the soul."[41]

Promising their adherents good reasons, the Manichaeans render true understanding unattainable. Offering not only the adept but also the beginner access to their "fount of teaching" they have consigned all to eat solid food for which they are not ready (1 Cor 3:2). Worse still, with their attractive veneer, preying upon the vanity of the multitudes, "they ingratiate themselves by employing the name of reason."[42] Without any regard for their capacity, the crowds to whom the Manichaeans have pandered, "seize upon the poisons of the deceivers."[43] Augustine's counterpoint, and a common theme in his early anti-Manichaean writings, is to hold up belief as the basis of a great deal of human knowledge. It is the foundation of all interpersonal relationships and life together in human society.[44] There is no way to make a friend or know who your parents are without belief.[45] This gives us more reason, not less, to put trust in authority when the stakes are highest.[46]

Augustine's *De utilitate credendi* provides its reader with a taxonomy of human knowledge. Three kinds of knowing—to understand, to believe, and

---

41. Jason David BeDuhn, *Augustine's Manichaean Dilemma: Making a "Catholic" Self, 388–401 ce*, vol. 2 (Philadelphia: University of Pennsylvania Press, 2013), 95, quoting Augustine, *util. cred.*, 16.34.

42. Augustine, *util. cred.*, 9.21, *CSEL* 25.1:26: "sed ut aliquam concilient multitudinem nomine rationis."

43. Augustine, *util. cred.*, 9.21, *CSEL* 25.1:26: "inruit in venena fallentium."

44. Augustine, *util. cred.*, 12.26, *CSEL* 25.1:34: "multa possunt adferri, quibus ostendatur nihil omnino humanae societatis incolume remanere, si nihil credere statuerimus, quod non possumus tenere perceptum."

45. Cf. *util. cred.*, 10.23, 12.26.

46. Augustine, *util. cred.*, 12.27, *CSEL* 25.1:35: "nam et res humanae promptiores ad dinoscendum sunt quam divinae et in quibuscumque sanctioribus et praestantioribus, quo maius eis obsequium cultumque debemus, eo sceleratius periculosiusque peccatur."

to opine—border one another in the human mind.[47] This is a hierarchical ordering. For Augustine, to understand is better than to believe, which is itself better than to opine. That Augustine describes them as bordering one another—"velut finitima sibimet"—is not incidental. He sees that these three states of mind are intimate with one another, and he spends a chapter tracing their interrelations. To understand (*intellegere*), he explains, is reserved only for those things which are known with scientific precision. You can only properly understand what you can also offer a demonstration of. This kind of knowledge Augustine describes using the verb *scire*. He gives a negative example of it in his accompanying description of what it is to believe (*credere*). "For," he says, "I believe (*credo*) the most wicked conspirators to have been killed at one time by the virtue of Cicero. And yet not only do I not know (*nescio*) it, but I even know with certainty (*certo scio*) there is no way for me to be able to know (*scire*)."[48] Augustine sets a high bar when it comes to understanding. This kind of knowing belongs to things demonstrably true, which he shows to include his knowledge of the impossibility of knowing (in this strong sense) matters of historical record. What we can know about Cicero or any other person from history is properly called belief, not scientific knowledge. On the other hand, what we can know about our knowledge—that is, whether it is belief or understanding—is something we can know with the level of precision required to say *intellego* or *scio*.[49]

---

47. Augustine, *util. cred.*, 11.25, *CSEL* 25.1:31: "tria sunt item velut finitima sibimet in animis hominum distinctione dignissima: intellegere, credere, opinari."

48. Augustine, *util. cred.*, 11.25, *CSEL* 25.1:32: "credo enim sceleratissimos coniuratos virtute Ciceronis quondam interfectos: atqui id non solum nescio, sed etiam nullo pacto me scire posse certo scio."

49. I use "knowledge" to describe what we know by belief and what we know by understanding for two reasons. First, it is clear that English usage favors "know" in both these cases. Consider this example: Suppose I learn the periodic table of elements, along with the atomic number of each individual element. If someone were to ask me whether I "knew" the atomic number of each element, my answer would be an unequivocal yes. It is also clear that this kind of knowledge would not rise to the level of knowledge required by Augustine's taxonomy to say *intellego* or *scio*. It would not, because my knowledge of atomic numbers would not be rooted in my understanding why it is correct to say the atomic number of strontium is 38. I could not offer a demonstration of my knowledge, but it would still be right to say, "I know the atomic weight of strontium is 38." My knowledge of strontium, like Augustine's of history, is a matter of belief. But in English it would be strange to use the verb "believe" instead of "know." That is because in English we regularly refer to both as "knowledge." The second reason for maintaining the usage of knowledge in both cases is that it hews close to Pascal's

It is clear that Augustine gives belief a much wider scope than we might expect. Belief is not a thing we do only sometimes concerning relatively uncertain phenomena. Believing accounts for most of the things we know, the field of things knowable with scientific precision is relatively small, and the chance that we would take the time to learn them all is smaller still. But it would be wrong to think you could not know something simply because you lacked *scientific* knowledge of it. Part of the epistemic stance Augustine labels "to believe" involves knowing what you do and do not know and how you know it. As we saw in the example of our knowledge of Cicero, belief involves understanding. In that case it was understanding that we do not have scientific knowledge about the facts. Provided that you understand that you do not know (*nescire*) it, there is no problem having the epistemic stance of belief toward it.[50] This is not an excuse to hold any beliefs whatsoever. Augustine explains that believing unworthy things about God or being too quick to believe unworthy things of your fellow humans is blameworthy.[51] Belief qua belief is not a problem, though it may be put to problematic uses.

One of the problematic uses of belief is having an opinion. The trouble with opinion is you believe you know what you do not or cannot know. This makes *opinari* the worst possible epistemological position in which to find yourself. Whereas *intellegere* means to know by reason and *credere* to know by authority, *opinari* is not properly to know at all but to be in error.[52] But Augustine has something fascinating to say about the role belief plays in both understanding and opining: "Everyone who understands also believes, and everyone who opines believes, but not everyone who believes understands, and no one who opines understands."[53] This can be glossed in two directions

---

use of *connaître* to refer to what's known *par la raison* and *par la cœur*. For Pascal, the reason's knowledge and the heart's knowledge are clearly both ways of knowing the truth, each with its own standards of proof. These map nicely onto Augustine's division of *intellegere* and *credere*.

50. Augustine, *util. cred.*, 11.25, *CSEL* 25.1:32: "in ceteris vero rebus si quis quid credit, si se id nesire intellegat, nulla culpa est."

51. Augustine, *util. cred.*, 11.25, *CSEL* 25.1:32: "credere autem tunc est culpandum, cum vel de deo indignum aliquid creditur vel de homine facile creditur."

52. Augustine, *util. cred.*, 11.25, *CSEL* 25.1:32: "quod intellegimus igitur, debemus rationi, quod credimus, auctoritati, quod opinamur, errori."

53. Augustine, *util. cred.*, 11.25, *CSEL* 25.1:32: "intellegens omnis etiam credit, credit omnis et qui opinatur; non omnis qui credit intellegit; nullus qui opinature intellegit."

to sum up Augustine's basic epistemological position. The first direction deals with the belief involved in opining. When you opine, you believe yourself to understand when you do not. In doing so you not only fail to understand, but make it impossible to understand were an occasion for learning to present itself.[54] In the other direction, Augustine explains, understanding does not do away with belief—"everyone who understands also believes." What does he mean by this? Surely, once you have understood, once you know in the strong sense of *scire*, the need for belief is adumbrated. Augustine does not think so, and it is important to see why.

There are two reasons Augustine does not think understanding does away with belief. The first has to do with the possibility of knowledge in general. The second has to do with the possibility of religious knowledge in particular. I will deal with religious knowledge first. Augustine's *De utilitate credendi* is about the pursuit of the true religion. He writes it to a friend of his who, like Augustine, was taken in by the Manichaeans' promises to reveal religious truth by way of reason alone. The aim of the work is to show the rash and sacrilegious character of Manichaean critiques of Catholic belief. Catholics, Augustine contends, follow the authority of the Church. By believing that authority, they are made ready—"strengthened and prepared"—to receive truth from God.[55] Belief is beneficial, even if you are unable to understand, "For, as I see it, to believe before reason—that is, when you are not capable of perceiving the reasons—and to cultivate the mind by that faith for the seeds of truth to be received, is not only very healthy, but indeed without it health cannot return to sick minds."[56] To believe is to prepare the way for understanding the truth. Belief tills the soil of the mind when believers are "moved by authority so that [their] life and character might first be purged and in that way be made fit

54. Augustine, *util. cred.*, 11.25, *CSEL* 25.1:32: "opinari autem duas ob res turpissimum est: quod et discere non potest, qui sibi iam se scire persuasit, si modo illud disci potest, et per se ipsa temeritas non bene adfecti animi signum est."

55. Augustine, *util. cred.*, 1.2, *CSEL* 25.1:4: "Est igitur propositum, ut probem tibi, si possum quod Manichaei sacrilege ac temere invehantur in eos qui catholicae fidei auctoritatem sequentes, antequam illud verum, quod pura mente conspicitur, intueri queant, credendo praemuniuntur et inluminaturo praeparantur deo."

56. Augustine, *util. cred.*, 14.31, *CSEL* 25.1:38: "nam ego credere ante rationem, cum percipiendae rationi non sis idoneus, et ipsa fide animum excolere excipiendis seminibus veritatis non solum saluberrimum iudico, sed tale omnino, sine quo aegris animis salus redire non possit."

for the reasons to be received."[57] In a reversal of Manichaean ambition which promised to all, even the unprepared, a rational account of the truth of religion, Augustine prioritizes the remaking of the person. Belief will continue to play an important role in understanding this side of the eschaton because the remaking of the human person that will make it so that "I may know as I also have been known" ("cognoscam sicut et cognitus sum") (1 Cor 13:12, Vulg.) will only be complete when we see God "face to face" (1 Cor 13:12).

A mind stuck in its loves of things other than God cannot "cleave to the truth" and so remains incapable of understanding in the area of religion.[58] But Augustine's account of belief also applies more generally to the possibility of knowledge. I have already pointed out his observation that friendship and many of the social truths we hold most dear depend upon belief.[59] The a fortiori argument for belief's necessity in matters of religion has the force it does because it builds upon this basic fact about human knowledge. Dig deep enough and you discover that what we know about God and one another sooner or later rests on a foundation of belief. Here Pascal's insights on first principles illuminate what Augustine means when he says, "everyone who understands also believes." The heart's reasons, by which we know the truth—"nous connaissons la vérité"—give us the first principles upon which all other knowledge rests.[60] To grow in understanding first requires belief, this volitional move of the heart. First principles are not themselves susceptible to rational explanation. As you grow in understanding it becomes possible to give a rational account of some things once held simply on authority. But the basic structure of human thought rests upon those principles for which no further explanation can be offered. So, for Augustine, belief remains essential in matters religious and mundane.

The structure of human thought as Augustine describes it corresponds well with Pascal's distinction between the truth known by reason and by the heart. This is clear when Augustine describes how authority takes hold of

57. Augustine, *util. cred.*, 15.33, *CSEL* 25.1:42: "commotorum auctoritate hominum prius vita moresque purgarentur et ita rationi accipiendae habiles fierent."

58. Augustine, *util. cred.*, 16.34, *CSEL* 25.1:43: "sed id nunc agitur, ut sapientes esse possimus, id est inhaerere veritati: quod profecto sordidus animus non potest."

59. Cf. *util. cred.*, 12.26.

60. Pascal, *Pensées*, §§397, 101.

those drawn to believe. The Church's authority to teach impresses itself upon the seeker of religious truth on the basis of miracles, the blood of the martyrs, the lives of the saints, and even the fact of sheer numbers.[61] That a great mass of people look to her as an authority is itself a kind of evidence for it being so. But these are not truths demonstrable by reason. And even if we do want to consider them all, taken together, as a sort of proof for the Church's authority, their scope is limited. As Pascal puts it, "Faith is different than proof. The one is human, the other is a gift of God. *The just man lives by faith.* It is this faith that God himself puts in the heart, for which proof is often the instrument, *faith comes from hearing*, but this faith is in the heart, and it makes one say not 'I know' (*scio*), but 'I believe' (*credo*)."[62]

Applying Augustine's taxonomy of human knowledge to the progress he makes in book VII of *Confessiones*, his initial juxtaposition of the thinking verbs *cogitare* and *nescire* with the believing verb *credere* makes more sense.[63] While Augustine has not yet arrived at the epistemic stance of understanding, he does believe. The opening chapter of book VII highlights how these remain at odds for a time, warring against one another. Augustine must wait for the reasons of his heart, "que Dieu lui-même met dans le cœur,"[64] to remake his understanding from the ground up. As Stanley Hauerwas has rightly claimed,

> We can only act within the world we can envision, and we can envision the world rightly only as we are trained to see. We do not come to see merely by looking, but must develop disciplined skills through initiation into that community that attempts to live faithful to the story of God. Furthermore, we cannot see the world rightly unless we are changed, for as sinners we do not desire to see truthfully.[65]

61. Augustine, *util. cred.*, 16.34, 17.35, 7.15–16.

62. Pascal, *Pensées*, §5: "La foi est différente de la preuve: l'une est humaine, l'autre est un don de Dieu. *Justus ex fide vivit.* C'est de cette foi que Dieu lui-même met dans le cœur, dont la preuve est souvent l'instrument, *fides ex auditu*, mais cette foi est dans le cœur et fait dire non *scio*, mais *credo*."

63. Augustine, *conf.*, 7.1.1.

64. Pascal, *Pensées*, §5.

65. Stanley Hauerwas, *The Peaceable Kingdom: A Primer in Christian Ethics* (Notre Dame: University of Notre Dame Press, 1983), 29–30.

This is an Augustinian insight which runs counter to the Manichaean impulse to prioritize ratiocination over formation. The act of knowing, in the sense of *intellegere*, requires training. In Augustine's case, it requires *re*training an intellect formed by his previous Manichaean convictions. He sees God and the world in the false categories given by his former teachers. Book VII narrates Augustine's learning to see, and so to understand, the world in a way that comports with the reasons of his heart.

This is why Augustine never offers an argument for the goodness of God. To do so would be to treat it as something that could be argued for rather than the premise from which all faithful argumentation flows. Instead, what we find are the roots of what is often called Anselm's ontological argument. Note how Augustine's version of this line of thought proceeds:

> I had already discovered the incorruptible to be better than the corruptible, and for that reason I confessed you, whatever you are, to be incorruptible. Neither was there, nor will there ever be, any soul able to think something better than you, who are the highest and best good. When, however, the incorruptible is ranked most truly and certainly ahead of the corruptible, as I had already ranked it, were you not incorruptible I would have been able to touch something in thought that was better than my God.[66]

There is no effort to prove or defend God's goodness. It is clear he considers it to be fundamental. His observations about the nature of things must be brought into alignment with this basic truth. What is inconceivable to him is the idea that he would be able to imagine something better than God, but he still has not arrived at understanding of how or why this is the case.

Augustine is not offering his readers a defense of God's goodness *in spite* of the fact of evil in the world. God's goodness is a given that rests on the certainty of his belief. Instead of thinking that Augustine's argument in book

66. Augustine, *conf.*, 7.4.6, *CSEL* 33:145: "ut iam inverneram melius esse incorruptibile quam corruptibile, et ideo te, quidquid esses, esse incorruptibilem confitebar. neque enim ulla anima umpquam potuit poterituе cogitare aliquid, quod sit te melius, qui summum et optimum bonum es."

VII in *Confessiones* is a theodicy, I want to relate what he says to D. Z. Phillips's thoughts on the problem of evil. For Phillips, Scripture gives us "a conception of human life."[67] To believe in God "is to embrace that whole way of looking at the world."[68] On this account it would be foolhardy to attempt to defend God's goodness in general terms. The believer recognizes that there is no way of speaking of "good" that could oppose it to what God is and does. Belief in the goodness of God "is not a belief 'built up' out of standards prior to it. It is offered as a system of reference in itself, one that is not a hypothesis about the world, but an element, a light, that is constitutive of a vision of the world. It offers a spirit in which to see the world, and believers call that spirit, God."[69] Speaking of God's goodness in this way prevents the instrumentalist and consequentialist mistakes pervading the work of theodicy.[70] Those mistakes originate in the prior mistake of imagining God's goodness could be judged by a standard external to God.

One source of this confusion comes from treating the covenant with God as a temporal as opposed to an eternal reality. God is not, Phillips insists, "a member of our moral community."[71] Our dealings with God are not quid pro quo. To think of them that way is to imagine God responding to our petitions and rewarding our behavior as if God were another creature alongside us, from whom we could legitimately stand in expectation of receiving what is our due according to the terms of the covenant. To treat the covenant as temporal is to treat it as a contract, something we might have with another human but not with the creator of the cosmos. Against this view, Phillips offers the idea of an eternal covenant. "An eternal covenant offers *a conception of human life*, such that *anything* that may happen within it is understood in a certain way. *What happens in history will be the occasion for such an understanding, but not the criterion of it.* In this way, what happens in history can still be of eternal

67. D. Z. Phillips, *The Problem of Evil & the Problem of God* (Minneapolis: Fortress Press, 2005), 254. Phillips is developing a comment of Simone Weil's "The Gospel contains a conception of human life, not a theology." Quoted in Phillips, *The Problem of Evil & the Problem of God*, 139.

68. Phillips, *The Problem of Evil & the Problem of God*, 135.

69. Phillips, *The Problem of Evil & the Problem of God*, 139.

70. Phillips, *The Problem of Evil & the Problem of God*, 139. Cf. *inter alia*, 40, 59.

71. Phillips, *The Problem of Evil & the Problem of God*, 40.

significance."[72] Another way to put this is to say, "To believe in a Creator *is* to believe in the givenness of life as a grace."[73] Like Hauerwas, Phillips insists that the gospel offers a way of seeing and understanding the world. History matters, but not in the way a theodicist thinks it does. The history of God's relations with his creatures cannot be used either to defend or impugn God's character because the criteria for such an evaluation are lacking. Attempting to do so is to fundamentally misunderstand the kind of relation God bears to creation.

This perspective on the creator–creature relation is shared by Augustine in an early anti-Manichaean work, *De Genesi contra Manichaeos*. In it, Augustine shows how the question, "Why did it please God to make heaven and earth?" is malformed if what you are after in asking it are reasons God himself would be answerable to.[74] Augustine's way of dealing with this question shows two things clearly. First, God's goodness is not something, as Phillips said, "built up out of standards prior to it." Second, because God is not answerable to reasons outside himself, God cannot be a "member of our moral community." God is the ground upon which all moral considerations rest and from which they take their measure. Augustine's response to those who ask, "Why did it please God to make heaven and earth?" captures this well.

> They seek to know the will of God, when the will of God is the cause of everything there is. For if the will of God has a cause, there is something that comes before the will of God, which is impious to believe. Therefore, to someone who says: "Why did God make heaven and earth?" You ought to respond, "Because he willed it." For the will of God is the cause of heaven and earth, and for that reason the will of God is greater than heaven and earth. However, someone who says: "Why did God *will* to make heaven and earth?" is searching for something greater than the will of God, but nothing greater can be found. He, therefore, should restrain his human thoughtlessness, and not seek what is not, as then he might not find what is. And if anyone desires to know the will of God, let him be a friend to God. Because

72. Phillips, *The Problem of Evil & the Problem of God*, 162. Emphasis original.

73. Phillips, *The Problem of Evil & the Problem of God*, 183. Emphasis original.

74. Augustine, *Gn. c. Man.*, 1.2.4, *PL* 34:175: "Quid placuit Deo facere coelum et terram?"

> if he were to want to know the will of a human to whom he was not a friend, everyone would deride his impudence and stupidity.[75]

Augustine turns his reader's attention to the theme of friendship in a way similar to *De utilitate credendi*. Augustine does not say it is impossible to know why God made heaven and earth. He says it is impudent and stupid (because impossible) to do so by searching for reasons that are not God's own, reasons which are identical with the divine nature. This is a way of saying, "God's nature is the grammar of God's will."[76] And the only way to learn God's nature is to become friends with God. Like any friendship, this depends upon belief.

With this in mind, Augustine's assertion in book VII of *Confessiones* that were God a corruptible substance he would not be God comes into focus.[77] This is because trusting God to be the *summum bonum*, and knowing corruptibility to be inferior to incorruptibility, there is no way for him to attribute corruption to God. To do so would be to imagine God's will to be one thing and his power to accomplish it to be something else. Augustine lays out what the grammar of God's will demands we say. The first point already established is that God is good. But when "good" is predicated of God, it is not done evaluatively. We do not refer to God as good in the same way we do of a good meal, or a good book, or even a good man. The goodness of all particulars have their goodness from God. God's goodness does not depend on anything apart from God in the way the goodness of created things does. God is the selfsame

75. Augustine, *Gn. c. Man.*, 1.2.4, *PL* 34:175: "Causas enim voluntatis Dei scire quaerunt, cum voluntas Dei omnium quae sunt, ipsa sit causa. Si enim habet causam voluntas Dei, est aliquid quod antecedat voluntatem Dei, quod nefas est credere. Qui ergo dicit, Quare fecit Deus coelum et terram? respondendum est ei, Quia voluit. Voluntas enim Dei causa est coeli et terrae, et ideo major est voluntas Dei quam coelum et terra. Qui autem dicit, Quare voluit facere coelum et terram? majus aliquid quaerit quam est voluntas Dei: nihil autem majus inveniri potest. Compescat ergo se humana temeritas, et id quod non est non quaerat, ne id quod est non inveniat. Et si voluntatem Dei nosse quisquam desiderat, fiat amicus Deo: quia si voluntatem hominis nosse quisquam vellet, cujus amicus non esset, omnes ejus impudentiam ac stultitiam deriderent."

76. Phillips, *The Problem of Evil*, 114.

77. Augustine, *conf.*, 7.4.6, *CSEL* 33:146: "et ut quid multa dicimus, cur non sit coruptibilis substantia, quae deus est, quando, si hoc esset, non esset deus?"

good that God wills.[78] It would be wrong to say that Augustine's conviction that God wills for himself the very good that he is tells us something about what God is like. To do so would be to mistake the work "good" is doing for an evaluative claim. What we have here is instead a grammatical remark that bears a resemblance to Wittgenstein's remarks in the *Philosophical Investigations* about the standard meter in Paris.

The standard meter (before it was redefined with reference to the speed of light) was a metal bar kept and measured under certain conditions. As the name suggests, the standard meter was the norm against which mensurated things were whatever length they were. It would be a mistake, Wittgenstein explains, to say the standard meter was a meter long. The criteria for such an evaluation were lacking, since the standard meter's length *was* the criterion. What this marks is the standard meter's "peculiar role in the game of measuring with a metre-rule."[79] We can say something analogous about the statement "God is good" and the very goodness God wills. This does not tell us that God is really, really good. Instead, it tells us something about the nature of God, what God is, not what God is like.[80] As Romano Guardini, in line with Phillips, Wittgenstein, and Augustine says, "God is good, He is goodness itself. Goodness is not a measuring rod applicable to everything, including God Himself: it is but another name for God Himself."[81] When Augustine says God's will and power are identical with God, he is offering grammatical guidelines about what can and cannot be said about God.[82]

Augustine claims God is good in such a way as to be the measure of all goodness, and that he wills it indefectibly because his will and power are identical with it. There is no way to get behind God's reasons. Just as he asserted in *De Genesi contra Manichaeos*, as Augustine grows in friendship with God, his

78. Augustine, *conf.*, 7.4.6, *CSEL* 33:145: "ipse est deus, et quod sibi vult, bonum est et ipse est idem bonum."

79. Wittgenstein, *Philosophical Investigations*, §50.

80. Wittgenstein, *Philosophical Investigations*, §373: "Grammar tells what kind of object anything is. (Theology as grammar.)."

81. Romano Guardini, *The Last Things: Death, Purification, Resurrection, Judgment, and Eternity*, trans. Charlotte Forsyth and Grace Branham (Richmond, VA: Preservation Books, 2019), 37.

82. Augustine, *conf.*, 7.4.6, *CSEL* 33:146: "voluntas enim et potentia dei deus ipse est."

grasp of God's reasons grow too. When Augustine sees the immutable light of God with the eye of his soul he says, "It was superior, because it made me, and I was inferior, because made by it. He who knows the truth knows it, and he who knows it knows eternity. Love knows it."[83] Augustine repeatedly deploys a thinking verb, *novit*. To know that you are made, that your life is from another, is to know truth and eternity. You come to know the truth about yourself, you are a creature, and the truth about God, it is God who created you. You also come to know that the one who created you is good, and so you too are good.

It is also apparent to Augustine that being a creature, though good, means not existing in the same manner as God. It is when Augustine hears God's "I am who I am" (Exod 3:14) that he comes to grasp this.[84] In grasping it, he realizes that he had things the wrong way round. "And I heard, as something is heard in the heart, and there was absolutely no way I could doubt. It would have been easier for me to doubt my own life than for there to be no truth, the truth which is seen and understood through the things that are made."[85] It is not God's goodness that is rendered doubtful by evil in the world, but my own. This passage is something of a climax for book VII. When he arrives here, Augustine has answered the first question I put to him about the goodness of God in the face of evils in the world. It is impossible to think of God as corruptible, susceptible to evil, not fully and completely good. To think it is not to be thinking of the God Christians confess. It is instead to imagine, as Augustine could not help but do at first, God as something alongside creatures, part of the furniture of the cosmos. And importantly, it is only by believing the truth, which he comes to through the authority of the Catholic Church, that he begins to understand. He can only learn to see and understand the world he believes is there.

With these key assumptions about the divine nature in place, I now turn back to the other way of thinking about evil, as a substance with an existence independent of God. Augustine's thoughts turn in this direction immediately

---

83. Augustine, *conf.*, 7.10.16, *CSEL* 33:157: "[erat] superior, quia ipsa fecit me, et ego inferior, quia factus ab ea. qui novit veritatem, novit eam, et qui novit eam, novit aeternitatem. caritas novit eam."

84. Augustine, *conf.*, 7.10.16, *CSEL* 33:158: "et clamasti de longinquo: ego sum qui sum."

85. Augustine, *conf.*, 7.10.16, *CSEL* 33:158: "et audivi, sicut auditur in corde, et non erat prorsus, unde dubitarem faciliusque dubitarem vivere me quam non esse veritatem, quae per ea, quae facta sunt, intellecta conspicitur."

after he recognizes the true significance of the creator–creature distinction. He admits that his Manichaean sympathies were born of a desire not to do an injustice to God by attributing evil or corruptibility to him. This is why he came to think there were two substances, one good and one evil.[86] After passing through the iteration I just examined, conceiving of God as spatially infinite, Augustine says, "I awoke in you and saw you to be infinite in another way, and that vision did not come from the flesh."[87] In this process of ascent, he comes to realize that God made all things good and nothing exists that God did not make.[88] Evil is not something in its own right, but a corruption of a created good. On Augustine's own terms, what he says about this is not a theodical account that explains God's goodness in the face of recognizable evils. His thoughts are descriptive, showing that God does not create the recognizable evils of the world, qua evil, because qua evil they are not anything at all. Evil names the absence of something that ought to be there.

Augustine also directs our attention to the problem of the *iniquitas* of rational creatures. I will translate *iniquitas* as "instability" rather than something more straightforward like "iniquity." "Instability" captures a valence that is lost with "iniquity." This is because the badness of *iniquitas* comes from imbalance, unevenness, or disorder. When Augustine looks at the disorder of voluntary agents, he sees an instability which makes them "apt for the lower parts of creation insofar as they are dissimilar" to God and "apt for the higher parts of creation as they become more like" God.[89] The source of this instability is the turning away from the supremely stable one. Doing so, creatures unbalance themselves by directing their attention and love toward things that are not God.[90] This instability is not the *result*

86. Augustine, *conf.*, 7.14.20, *CSEL* 33:160: "et inde ierat in opinionem duarum substantiarum."

87. Augustine, *conf.*, 7.14.20, *CSEL* 33:160: "et evigilavi in te et vidi te infinitum aliter, et visus iste non a carne trahebatur."

88. Augustine, *conf.*, 7.12.18, *CSEL* 33:159: "itaque vidi et manifestatum est mihi, quia omnia bona tu fecisti et prorsus nullae substantiae sunt, quas tu non fecisti."

89. Augustine, *conf.*, 7.16.22, *CSEL* 33:161: "apta inferioribus creaturae tuae partibus, quibus et ipsi iniqui apti sunt, quanto dissimiliores sunt tibi, apti autem superioribus, quanto similiores fiunt tibi."

90. Augustine, *conf.*, 7.16.22, *CSEL* 33:161: "et quaesivi, quid esset iniquitas, et non inveni substantiam, sed a summa substantia, te deo, detortae in infima voluntatis perversitatem proicientis intima sua et tumescentis foras."

of the turning away, as if turning away from God had as its consequence an instability. For Augustine, this instability *is* the "contorted perversity of the will."[91] Degrees of perversity exist along a continuum of similarity and dissimilarity to God.

The recognition that evil is nothing in itself and that the imbalance of voluntary agents is evil's cause, leads Augustine to a classic and important axiom of Christian thought: everything that is, insofar as it is, is good. Put another way, evil is strictly privative. "All things that are corrupted are deprived of a good."[92] Were they so corrupted that they lacked all goods what would be left would not be the substance of evil but nothing at all. "And so," Augustine says, "whatever things are (*sunt*), are good (*bona sunt*), and that evil—whose source I sought—is not a substance, because if it were a substance it would be good."[93] All this lies in the background of Leo's assertion in *Quam Laudibiliter* that "there is no nature of evil, because God, who is the maker of the universe, made nothing not good."[94] This bedrock assumption is central to any Christian theology of creation. To suppose otherwise is already to have courted the idea that there is something other than God and his creatures or that God is corruptible. With these positions sufficiently interpreted and supported, I now turn back to the doctrinal witness of the Church's Magisterium before showing at last what difference this all makes for the origins of death.

The Doctrine of the Angelic Fall, Continued

Leo's basic metaphysical claim about the nature of the demons is that they were originally good. How could they not be, if the alternative is to be nothing at all? This succeeds as a strategy for showing the compatibility of the presence of evil with a God who creates nothing but good creatures. But in another sense, this has only pushed the most important question back a level. The problem

91. Augustine, *conf.*, 7.16.22, *CSEL* 33:161: "detortae in infima voluntatis perversitatem."

92. Augustine, *conf.*, 7.12.18, *CSEL* 33:158: "omnia, quae corrumpuntur, privantur bono."

93. Augustine, *conf.*, 7.12.18, *CSEL* 33:159: "ergo quaecumque sunt, bona sunt, malumque illud, quod quaerebam unde esset, non est substantia, quia, si substantia esset, bonum esset."

94. Leo I, *Quam Laudibiliter*, *DS* §286: "et mali nullam esse naturam: quia Deus, qui universitatis est conditor, nihil non bonum fecit."

has never really been the existence of evil per se. The problem always was God's permission of it. There is nothing inherently contradictory in the presence of privative evil in a cosmos created by an all good God. Not, at least, the kind of contradiction that comes from affirming substantial evil or a corrupt creator of everything that is. Without simply adverting to the mysteriousness of God's permission of evil, it is important to note that this mystery is epistemically primitive. Nothing offered in the way of doctrinal formulations or theological speculations is meant to get behind it—as if the correct response to divine mystery were to solve it. But mysteriousness does not mean unintelligibility. Attending to the evil of the angelic fall will clarify some features of angelic nature. From there, I will turn to a description of the effects this fall has on the created order as a whole.

There is a final, doctrinal point to highlight about the nature of demons before looking at some theological treatments of them. The point remains rooted in the metaphysics of participation and the privative account of evil already given. It deals with the question of how privative evil comes about in the case of angelic creatures. The point can be summarized this way: angelic beings fall by an exercise of will. Turning back briefly to Leo's *Quam Laudibiliter* we already find the beginnings of this formulation. It says this of the devil: "But because he used his natural excellence badly 'and did not stand in the truth,' he was not changed into the opposite substance, but departed from the highest good to which he ought to cling, just like those . . . who are damned for their voluntary perversity."[95] The devil is not only not an independently existing principle of evil, but is evil through an exercise of his created power of volition. This point is reaffirmed in the *Statuta Ecclesiae Antiqua* compiled in the fifth century by Gennadius of Marseilles. Prospective bishops were to be asked whether they "believe . . . the devil was made evil not through a natural condition but through choice."[96] The Fourth Lateran Council, this time with the weight of an ecumenical council, affirms, "God certainly created the devil and the other demons good by nature, but they were made evil by

95. Leo I, *Quam Laudibiliter*, *DS* §286: "Sed quia naturali excellentia male usus est 'et in veritate non stetit' [Io 8:44], non in contrarium transiit substantiam, sed a summo bono, cui debuit adhaerere, descivit, sicut ipsi . . . pro sua voluntaria perversitate damnantur."

96. Gennadius of Marseille, *Statuta Ecclesiae Antiqua*, *DS* §325: "credat . . . si diabolus non per condicionem, sed per arbitrium factus sit malus."

themselves."[97] Here it is no longer the devil mentioned in the singular, but all the demons who are said to be created good and yet to fall. In each of these instances, the doctrinal pronouncements come in the context of affirmations of God as creator of all things. At Fourth Lateran, the force of this is even greater, coming on the heels of the first conciliar specification of God as the one who creates "at once" and "from nothing."[98]

This teaching, that the demons are angels who fell as a result of their own volition, is critical for understanding the origins of evil. As I have argued, the existence of a good God is not something to be argued for, but assumed. This is a first principle of Christian theological reflection upon creation and the evils found there. Kenneth Schmitz, in his 1982 Aquinas Lecture, argued that reasoning upon the given of God's goodness in a way that takes evil seriously results in "a paradox that is a ground for hope" as "it should be recognized that there could be no evil in a universe created by an absolutely benevolent love, *if* its creatures did not possess their own integrity, and were not bent upon realizing their own possibilities, including for some of them their free possibilities."[99] This claim is not defending God in the face of evil but stating an entailment of the fact of evil. At the same time, it tells us nothing definitive about why there is evil because evil cannot be necessary for the actualization of creaturely freedom. So even though the presence of evil is a negative proof of creaturely freedom, this does not make the presence of evil any more explicable.

What do I mean when I say evil is not necessary for the actualization of creaturely freedom? The answer is an extension of a point I made in chapter 2 concerning secondary causality and God's noninterference in the created order. To recapitulate, I drew on Herbert McCabe's thoughts on creation to explain why it is impossible for God to interfere in his creation. It is impossible because God is the active cause of everything that is not God, including all our creaturely powers. In other words, our creaturely

97. Fourth Lateran Council, *DS* §800: "Diabolus enim et alii daemones a Deo quidem natura creati sunt boni, sed ipsi per se facti sunt mali."

98. Fourth Lateran Council, *DS* §800: "qui sua omnipotenti vitute simul ab initio temporis utramque de nihilo condidit creaturam, spiritualem et coroporalem."

99. Kenneth L. Schmitz, *The Gift: Creation* (Milwaukee: Marquette University Press, 1982), 91.

freedom is a capacity given and actualized by God's agency. It is given not in such a way that it is not our own. It is our own because it has been given to us to be our own.[100] This is a fundamental truth about being a creature. To want a freedom that is not given, not utterly dependent on God's free gift of it, is to desire to be God. It is for this reason McCabe can say, in another essay, "There can be no doubt, then, that had he wished to do so God could always have prevented me from sinning—without, of course, in any way interfering with my freedom."[101] Freedom itself being given by God, it would be no interference were God to give along with it the actualization of it toward exclusively good ends. This would be a great gift, to have not only freedom but the desire and motivation to direct it properly always and everywhere.

But this is not the only kind of creatures God has willed to create. Ones, I mean, that only and always employ their freedom toward good ends. The particular kind of creaturely integrity that marks all humans (save two) and the fallen angels is one in which free creaturely *actualities* include sin. About this Schmitz says, we find that God "freely determines to create a creature of a certain sort with integrity and freely determines to respect that integrity. In creating creatures who have freedom, he even determines to respect the capacity to flaw the original gift."[102] I have to stress, again with McCabe, "that there is no question of God *having* to permit me to sin in order to leave me with my freedom. *That* kind of argument belongs to a theory that freedom makes me independent of God. In fact God could have made a world in which nobody ever sinned at all and everyone was perfectly free."[103] Schmitz is right when he insists creaturely freedom includes the "capacity to flaw the original gift," *and* in saying that we have evidence of this freedom from the fact of evil. But McCabe is also right that this capacity need never be realized in order for there to be authentic freedom. The holy angels, Mary, and Jesus Christ are clear evidence that this is the case.

---

100. McCabe, "Creation," 6–7.

101. Herbert McCabe, "Evil," in *God Matters* (London: Geoffrey Chapman, 1987; repr., London: Continuum International, 2012), 37.

102. Schmitz, *The Gift*, 96.

103. McCabe, "Evil," 37. Emphasis original.

Now, aided by Herbert McCabe, Paul Griffiths, Thomas Aquinas, and Augustine, I intend to plait together the threads I have spun so far into cord capable of supporting the view that attributes the origins of death to the angelic fall. This will involve pulling in what we have learned about the nature of angels and demons from Scripture and the tradition to support a theological exposition and interpretation of some key texts. What we can glean from these texts inclines in a definite direction concerning the consequences of the angelic fall. Consequences that include the origins of death.

Natural and Voluntary Evils

The first thing to lay out here is a serious disagreement about the status of so-called "natural evils" in the created order. Calling something a natural evil distinguishes it from the evils brought about by the voluntary actions of rational agents. The distinction is useful in that it helps to sort and separate the evils that occur in creatures due to their being what they are from those caused by creatures failing to be what they are. I will illustrate this view of natural evil using one of Thomas Aquinas's preferred examples, then clarify it by looking to Herbert McCabe's treatment of it. Following that, I will examine what Paul Griffiths has to say about the very idea of natural evils. The overarching point of this discussion is to determine at what level of discourse the concept "natural evil" has purchase. Does natural evil obtain absolutely, as a necessary feature of the cosmos? Or does it pick out something useful for us to distinguish in the cosmos as it stands, but which does not rise to the level of a necessary feature of the created order? Knowing which is the case clarifies what is at stake in the description of the effects of the angelic fall that is the subject of this section.

First, Thomas on natural evil. In question 49 of the Prima Pars of the *Summa Theologiae*, Thomas distinguishes between evils caused by voluntary and natural things. The latter, he explains, come from things producing an effect similar to themselves.[104] Thomas uses the example of fire burning a piece of wood. As fire (the agent) produces fire (the effect), it consumes the wood. This is bad (evil) for the wood because as the fire continues to burn the wood is corrupted until the wood is reduced to smoke and ash and ceases to be wood

104. *ST*, 1.49.1 *ad* 3: "malum habet causam deficientem aliter in rebus voluntariis, et naturalibus. Agens enim naturale producit effectum suum talem quale ipsum est."

at all.[105] This is how natural evils work. They are produced by creatures being the kinds of things they are. Fire burns, ice freezes, and by extension, bacteria infect, and lions kill and eat lambs. The effects, a tree burnt, the small bird that drops "frozen dead from a bough,"[106] a person infected with meningitis, and the lamb dead and consumed are all, on this account, natural evils.

Natural evils differ from voluntary evils. The defect or privation that occurs in the case of natural evils is caused by the creature being the kind of thing it is. The good of the fire causes a privation of the good of the tree. In the case of voluntary evils, the privation is caused by and in the agent itself, the result of a deficient will. The will is deficient, Thomas says, "insofar as it does not actually subject itself to its rule" (*suae regulae*).[107] For voluntary evils, privation does not lie in the effect. Although an act of voluntary evil may have bad (privative) effects, this is not what makes it a voluntary evil. Actions produced by an agent's defective will are evil because, as Thomas suggests, the agent is not properly ordered to its rule (*suae regulae*). The defective will *itself* is not blameworthy—"non est culpa"—but blame follows from acting with a disordered will—"sequitur culpa ex hoc."[108]

Herbert McCabe takes up this distinction between natural and voluntary evil. He is committed to drawing a hard line with it, as doing so allows us to speak intelligibly about nonhuman creaturely death before human sin. He is arguing against a view that attributes all death, human and nonhuman alike, to Original Sin. Here is what he says:

> Let us look first at the evil suffered in the world. Let us be clear that by no stretch of the imagination can this be attributed to the viciousness of men and women, or hardly any of it can. For millions upon millions of years before the human race even appeared, dinosaurs were

---

105. *ST,* 1.49.1 *resp*: "Sicut ergo, quanto ignis fuerit perfectior in virtute, tanto perfectius imprimit formam suam, ita etiam tanto perfectius corrumpit contrarium, unde malum et corruptio aeris et aquae, est ex perfectione ignis."

106. D. H. Lawrence, "Self-Pity," in *The Complete Poems of D. H. Lawrence* (Ware, UK: Wordsworth Editions, 1994), 382.

107. *ST,* 1.49.1 *ad* 3: "Sed in rebus voluntariis, defectus actionis a voluntate actu deficiente procedit, inquantum non subiicit se actu suae regulae."

108. *ST,* 1.49.1 *ad* 3: "Qui tamen defectus non est culpa, sed sequitur culpa ex hoc quod cum tali defectu operatur."

> setting upon each other or upon harmless plants and chewing them up, undoubtedly inflicting evil on them; a plant that has been chewed by a dinosaur is nothing like as good a plant as it was before. The lamb that is attacked by a lion speedily becomes a very defective lamb.[109]

This is a good corrective to a certain kind of Christian thinking. This is the kind of Christian thinking I criticized in chapter 1, which privileges its own interpretations of Scripture to the point of affirming it in the face of certain evidence to the contrary. McCabe does two things in this extract. He at once denies young earth creationism and affirms the presence of death well before the existence of humans in the order of time. The distinction between natural and voluntary evil allows him to do this.

Since natural evils arise from the competition of created goods with their own integrity and ends, it's possible to affirm both that God creates all things good and very good and that the existence of those created goods entails certain evils. It therefore makes sense to say, as McCabe does, "Thus if God is to make a lion, and a good lion, he cannot but allow for the defect of the lamb, that is the kind of things that lions and lambs are. It is no reflection on God's omnipotence that he cannot make good lions without allowing for damaged lambs."[110] This observation is right. It belongs to what we mean by "lion" that "eats lambs" is a suitable predicate. Were you to insist lions were at one time vegetarians but only became carnivorous as a result of the human fall, you would be insisting lions were not lions.

On the other hand, following this observation, McCabe goes on to say something unwarranted. He does this when he attempts to extend his observations about lions into the realm of metaphysics. He insists not just that what we mean by lions is something that eats lambs, but further "that you cannot make material things that develop in time without allowing for the fact that in perfecting themselves they will damage other material things."[111] This is an unhelpful extension of the concept of natural evil. McCabe is here subliming what he says about natural evil out of a context in which it has a use and applying it to materiality in general. He claims asking after the source of a

109. McCabe, "Evil," 31.

110. McCabe, "Evil," 31.

111. McCabe, "Evil," 31.

lion's lethality ends with us "thinking that it would be better not to have any material world at all."[112] It seems to me better to think of this as an instance of language "idling."[113]

Thomas Aquinas's treatment of suppositional necessity in the *Summa Contra Gentiles* helps to illustrate what I mean. In the second book of that work, Thomas uses the example of animal death to explore the relation between suppositional and absolute necessity. There he says, "For nothing at all keeps principles from being produced not from necessity, for which—when put in place—a certain effect follows necessarily. Just as the death of this animal has an absolute necessity on account of this, that it is at present made up of contraries. Although it was not absolutely necessary the animal be made up of contraries."[114] What exactly Thomas thinks an animal not composed of contraries might be is unclear. I take Thomas to be imagining an order to the material world as a whole which would not involve its being composed of contraries. Not being composed of contraries—in an Aristotelian conception of physics—would mean you would have corporeal creatures not susceptible to dissolution or corruption. And apparently he can imagine a way in which it would still be intelligible to call these creatures animals. While this is obviously not the case for the material world as it stands at present, this state of affairs is the result of a suppositional not an absolute necessity.

Thomas's insistence that being composed of contraries is not itself an absolutely necessary precondition for the existence of animals does not mesh well with McCabe's account. McCabe is opposed to the very idea of a material cosmos that does not involve corruptible bodies and natural evils. He goes so far as to say, "A world without any defects suffered . . . would be a world without any natural order in it."[115] It would in fact be "a world without *any* natural causes, entirely consisting of miracles" and so "would not be a natural

112. McCabe, "Evil," 32.

113. Wittgenstein, *Philosophical Investigations*, §132.

114. Thomas Aquinas, *SCG*, 2.30.7: "Nihil enim prohibet aliqua principia non ex necessitate produci, quibus tamen positis, de necessitate sequitur talis effectus: sicut mors animalis huius absolutam necessitatem habet propter hoc quod iam ex contrariis est compositum, quamvis ipsum ex contrariis componi non fuisset necessarium absolute."

115. McCabe, "Evil," 33.

material world at all."[116] It will not take us too far afield to point out the major problems this poses for eschatological thinking and for the Thomistic dictum, "grace does not destroy nature, but perfects it."[117] McCabe might wish to demur and say he is speaking of the natural material world, while matter caught up supernaturally into God's own life in the eschaton will not be that kind of thing at all. Are we to think, then, that the supernatural elevation of resurrected flesh will preclude its having a natural order? What, precisely, would the subject of that elevation be?

It is better to say Thomas's imagination is simply more developed than modern cosmological sensibilities are likely to allow. Thomas clearly does take there to be things that are both material and in no way subject to defect. These are the heavenly bodies. Heavenly bodies are not subject to corruption because they are not composed of contraries and their matter is entirely attuned to the reception of their form.[118] Now, Thomas is wrong in the particular case. Heavenly bodies are not the kinds of things he thought they were. They are subject to change and corruption in the same way sublunary things are. But this does not eclipse the value of his insight on this point. Thomas has the ability to imagine, in a way we cannot (easily anyway), what it would mean to talk about bodily creatures immune from corruption. This is something we are all called to do when we meditate on the resurrected and ascended flesh of Jesus Christ and the assumed flesh of Mary. We are called to do it, that is, if we think these bodies are immune from corruption and that they are so not *un*naturally but *super*naturally. Jesus and Mary have, and—*deo volente*—we will have, human, viz. material, bodies perfected by grace. "Seminatur in corruptione, surget in incorruptione" (1 Cor 15:42 Vulg.).

McCabe unnecessarily equates materiality with the necessary sufferance of natural evil. Thomas's cosmology allows for incorruptible, material things, but his cosmology is factually incorrect. Does this mean we are bidden to

---

116. McCabe, "Evil," 33.

117. *ST* 1.1.8. *ad* 2: "gratia non tollat naturam, sed perficiat."

118. Thomas Aquinas, *pot.*, 5.1 *resp*: "Si quae autem formae sunt non in materia, ut sunt substantiae intellectuales, vel in materia nullo modo indisposita ad formam, ut est in corporibus caelestibus, in quibus non sunt contrariae dispositiones." Cf. *ST*, 1.58.1 *resp*: "corpora superiora, scilicet caelestia, non habent potentiam ad esse, quae non sit completa per actum."

incline toward McCabe's view of things? No, not entirely. Consider instead the view of things proposed by Paul Griffiths in *Intellectual Appetite*.

> The corporeal world is out of joint, not as it should be; that is why the ensemble of causal connections that constitutes its activity is so often destructive to beings like us, and indeed to the harmony of the whole. Earthquakes, and tsunamis, and plagues are, at least in part, the world not working as it should. We tend to call such things "natural disasters," but this is misleading. They are not natural if by that is meant that they belong to the world as it should be, the world as it was brought into being by its creator. Rather, they are anti-natural, instances of the chaos that disorder the world's nature rather than of the order that constitutes its beautiful harmony.[119]

This is a different world than the one McCabe offers. Griffiths paints with a darker brush. His somber hues resolve into an image where so-called natural evils are in fact marks of a deep and abiding disorder. Griffiths does not limit this disorder to evils affecting humans.

> The lacks to which the world is subject, the vitiation of its created goodness, are evident most clearly in death, violence, and pain, which are not part of the divine gift but are instead clear signs of its corruption. And those signs are everywhere. The nonhuman animate world is an ocean of blood flowing from violent death; and the human world differs from it in this only in the scale of the violence and the ingenuity of its performance, in both of which our world far exceeds the nonhuman one.[120]

Griffiths's account requires an act of imagination similar to Thomas's. This is more challenging than it might seem. Not only because there is no object for comparison—it is not clear what the world would be like without these

---

119. Paul J. Griffiths, *Intellectual Appetite: A Theological Grammar* (Washington, DC: The Catholic University of America Press, 2009), 47–48.

120. Griffiths, *Intellectual Appetite*, 43.

"clear signs of its corruption"—but also because to hold this view requires us to utter something intelligible about the origin of that "ocean of blood."

How can we claim the deaths of all nonhuman creatures are the result of ontological disorder when the origins of life and death on earth precede the origins of human life by three-and-a-half billion years? This offers some prima facie evidence in favor of McCabe's view on the natural evil of death resulting from the competition among good creatures. But an entailment of this view might leave us uneasy. Thomas used the example of fire and what it consumes to describe natural evil. Are we prepared to extend the use of this concept to all instances of nonhuman creaturely death? What would that look like? Perhaps something like this. You might want to say there is no reason at all to think the fire consuming the stick differs in any meaningful way from the death of your dog after contracting rabies. As the fire destroys the stick by propagating itself, so too the rabies virus your dog. The destruction of nervous function, encephalic swelling, eventual paralysis, and death are just the epidemiological equivalent of a stack of dry tinder going up in smoke.

This way of thinking about the deaths of plants and animals has its advantages. On this view, it is relatively easy to assimilate the facts of the known world to a neat division into natural and voluntary evil. It still would not be necessary to extend the concept of natural evil metaphysically to include materiality in general. You would do just fine to stick with mundane cases. Dinosaurs eating plants, dinosaurs eating other dinosaurs, water and wind weathering a mountain, the campfire burning a dead branch, the forest fire consuming a live tree, and your dog dying from disease are all instances of the same kind of thing. Created goods bump into one another, come into conflict, and one comes out ahead. But what if we are disinclined to accept that the deaths of plants and animals are the same sort of thing as the Colorado River carving the Grand Canyon? Griffiths is so disinclined, as am I. At the same time, it is clear the concept of natural evil has a place in our discourse. It *is* distinct from voluntary evil, and in important ways.

What I am naming in these two different worlds is a disagreement in judgment. The difference between these linguistic and moral universes is profound and will have serious implications for the doctrine of sin accompanying each one.[121] What is needed to pull off Griffiths's account are reasons that can

121. Wittgenstein, *Philosophical Investigations*, §242: "It is not only agreement in definitions, but also (odd as it may sound) agreement in judgements that is required for communication by means of language."

account for the cosmos being deeply fractured in this way. The reasons offered need to manage that while also maintaining a place for a distinction between natural and voluntary evil.

What Happens When the Angels Fall

So far in this chapter, I have cobbled together some of the scriptural and doctrinal evidence pointing to the existence and nature of fallen angelic creatures. It is time to fit those creatures and their fall into an account of evil and disorder and death. To do this, I turn back to Augustine. In chapter 1, I treated the creation of the angels. In Augustine's *De Genesi ad litteram* their creation is traceable to Genesis 1:3, with God's utterance, "Let there be light." That light is the enlightenment of intellectual creation, the created form of God's uncreated light.[122] What I did not treat in the first chapter was Augustine's account of the angelic fall. For that we need to turn to *De civitate Dei*.

In *De civitate Dei* Augustine says many things about angelic nature that are also said in *De Genesi ad litteram*. In the former work, however, he offers an interpretation of Genesis 1:4 that extends the use of referring to the angels as "light." When Scripture says, "God separated the light from the darkness" (Gen 1:4) this is describing God's separation of the holy from the impure angels.[123] God alone can make this division because his foreknowledge includes the demons' sin of pride.[124] The fallen angels are good by nature and evil by will. God's division of light and darkness is between those angels who remain true to their good nature, gazing upon the light of truth, and those who turn away from that light to make themselves darkness.[125] There is a strong anti-Manichaean thrust here. He manages this by showing that his account is a way of saying, "the devil sinned from the beginning" (1 John 3:8) and "he was

122. Augustine, *Gn. litt.*, 4.22.39.

123. Augustine, *civ.*, 11.19, *CSEL* 40.1:538: "non mihi videtur ab operibus Dei absurda sententia, si, cum lux prima illa facta est, angeli creati intellegentur, inter sanctos angelos et immundos fuisse discretum, ubi dictum est: Et divisit Deus inter lucem et tenebras; et vocavit Deus lucem diem et tenebras vocavit noctum."

124. Augustine, *civ.*, 11.19, *CSEL* 40.1:538–39: "Solus quippe ille ista discernere potuit, quui potuit etiam priusquam caderent praescire casuros et privatos lumine veritatis in tenebrosa superbia remansuros."

125. Augustine, *civ.*, 11.19, *CSEL* 40.1:539: "ipse dividere potuit, cui etiam futurum non naturae, sed voluntatis malum occultum aut incertum esse non potuit."

a murderer from the beginning and did not stand in the truth" (John 8:44), without lapsing into the Manichaean error of assuming evil has a nature.[126]

Augustine works it out by showing the passages that seem to indicate the devil's very nature is sinful have been misunderstood. For "if sin is natural, it is in no way sin."[127] Instead we need to take the "beginning" to refer to the start of his sin, not the start of his existence.[128] But there is a problem here, at least an apparent one, if you compare what Augustine has to say about the beginning of the devil's sin in chapter 15 of book XI with what he says on the same subject in chapter 13. In chapters 13 and 15 Augustine uses the words "since he was created" ("ex quo creatus est") to describe the devil's sin.[129] In both places he is commenting on 1 John 3:8, "The devil sinned from the beginning." But while in chapter 15, Augustine says the devil, "should not be thought to have sinned from the beginning, that is, since he was created, but from the beginning of his sin," in chapter 13 he says the opposite.[130] "The devil sinned from the beginning, that is, since he was created he rejected justice."[131] How can both of these statements be true at once? The answer lies in the mode of angelic creation and existence.

God's creative work occurs outside of all time. Time comes into existence with the movement of creatures through space. Eternity is not a time-when, and we should not think of eternity as a whole lot of time, even an infinite stretch. In book XII of *De civitate Dei* Augustine reiterates this point. What he says there is crucial for resolving the apparent contradiction of the two

126. Augustine, *civ.*, 11.13, *CSEL* 40.1:532: "Ab initio diabolus peccat" and "Ille homicida erat ab initio et in veritate non stetit."

127. Augustine, *civ.*, 11.15, *CSEL* 40.1:534: "Ab initio diabolus peccat, non intellegunt, si natura talis est, nullo modo esse peccatum."

128. Augustine, *civ.*, 11.15, *CSEL* 40.1:534: "non ab initio, ex quo creatus est, peccare putandus est, sed ab initio peccati, quod ab ipsius superbia coeperit esse peccatum."

129. Cf. *civ.*, 11.13, 15, *CSEL* 40.1:532, 534: "Ab initio diabolus peccat, hoc est, ex quo creatus est, iustitiam recusavit"; "non ab initio, ex quo creatus est, peccare putandus est, sed ab initio peccati."

130. Augustine, *civ.*, 11.15, *CSEL* 40.1:534: "non ab initio, ex quo creatus est, peccare putandus est, sed ab initio peccati."

131. Augustine, *civ.*, 11.13, *CSEL* 40.1:532: "Ab initio diabolus peccat, hoc est, ex quo creatus est, iustitiam recusavit."

instances of "ex quo creatus est" I just juxtaposed. The angels have always existed, he says. That is, "they have been in all time, as they were created before all time; if at least, time began with the heavens, and the angels already were before the heavens."[132] This does not make the angels coeternal with God, but it does mean there is no *time* when the angels are not.[133] This mode of being, present to all times because created from nothing before all times, helps make sense of why Augustine needs to utter both that the devil did and did not sin "ex quo creatus est." Just as I showed the fall of Satan could be causally but not temporally prior to the fall of the rest of the reprobate angels, so too it makes sense to say the angels are created prior to their fall. In this way, it resembles my discussion of priority in origin and priority in time from chapter 2. God's creative act occurs in eternity, the angels are created before all time, and likewise the fall of the devil and his angels happens before any time has elapsed.

For this reason it makes sense to say both the devil and his angels did and did not sin "ex quo creatus est." They did so because their fall occurs atemporally. There is no time-when of the angelic fall. They did not because God creates only good things. The demons are not evil from their creation forward, but from their sin forward. Because our "before" and "after" talk are indexed to time, it is difficult to see what this comes to. But a crucial entailment of this position, if we follow Augustine concerning the atemporal creation and fall of angelic creatures, is that there is never a time when the created order is undamaged by sin. As I have argued, Augustine's Manichaean dualism is overcome by finding a new place for that dualism. Instead of a cosmos composed of warring principles, good and evil, light combatting the darkness, we find a dualism rooted in the will of rational creatures. Good creatures pervert themselves by turning away from the one who made them and become darkness by lacking the good of being oriented toward, cleaved to—Augustine likes to say—God. The upshot is that angelic creation is and is fallen "ante omnia tempora," which means the created order with which we have to do is always shot through with darkness. This provides a different starting place for examining the relationship between voluntary and natural evils.

---

132. Augustine, *civ.*, 12.16, *CSEL* 40.1:592: "isti omne tempore fuerunt, ut etiam ante omnia tempora facti sint; si tamen a caelo coepta sunt tempora, et illi iam erant ante caelum."

133. Augustine, *civ.*, 12.16, *CSEL* 40.1:594: "verum tamen non de ipso genitam, sed ab ipso de nihilo factam nec ei coaeternam: erat quippe ante illam, quamvis nullo tempore sine illa."

But what difference does it make if the angels are fallen before there is a place for discussing the unfurling of the *rationes seminales* in the order of time? What difference does angelic sin make for the development of the cosmos in time? As I argued, the *rationes seminales* name the set of relations of created things to the person of Jesus Christ. Bracketing until the next chapter how it is the angels can be said to bear relations to Jesus Christ atemporally, let us assume their fall puts them in bad stead with the incarnate Lord. Their fear at his coming and mention of future torment in the story of the Gerasene demoniac show this amply enough. We have reason to suspect the relations of the fallen angels to Christ are disordered. This disorder has cascading effects on creation as a whole. This is because creatures are not only related to the person of Jesus Christ but to one another. And the relations of angelic creatures to the material world are very important indeed.

Thomas Aquinas's extended treatment of angels in the Prima Pars of the *Summa Theologiae* bears out these observations about the impacts of the angelic fall. He thinks angels exercise a presidential role over both celestial and sublunary bodies.[134] This fits into Thomas's more general observations about creaturely hierarchies, that within the ordered whole of creation it is proper for superior things to govern the actions of inferior things. Unlike Aristotle, he thinks the governance of spiritual substances (i.e., angels) is exercised not only at a distance, giving the heavens their motion, but also immediately. His disagreement with Aristotle is over the philosopher's naturalism. Whereas Aristotle thinks the movements of inferior bodies are strictly natural, flowing from the superior motions of heavenly and finally of spiritual substances, Thomas thinks "many things are done in inferior bodies in addition to the natural actions of bodies, for which the powers of the celestial bodies do not suffice."[135] Thomas is insisting on God's providential governance of and miraculous action in the created order. More than that, he is insisting on the angels' ministerial role in this regard. The angels are spiritual creatures who nonetheless have jobs to do in the material world and who can act in it to accomplish God's will.

---

134. *ST* 1.110.1 *ad* 2: "necesse est ponere quod angeli habeant immediatam praesidentiam non solum supra caelestia corpora, sed etiam supra corpora inferiora."

135. *ST* 1.110.1 *ad* 2: "multa in corporibus inferioribus fieri praeter naturales actiones corporum, ad quae non sufficiunt virtutes caelestium corporum."

This position, that the angels have a role to play in the governance of the material world, has a long pedigree. Thomas cites Augustine's *De Trinitate* and Gregory the Great's *Dialogorum libri quatuor* in the *sed contra* of the first article of question 110.[136] He also points us to Augustine's *De diversis quaestionibus* where Augustine very explicitly presents a vision of angelic power appointed by God for the governance of the material cosmos.[137] Augustine goes so far as to say, "each and every visible thing in this world has an angelic power set over it."[138] He affirms this position in *De genesi ad litteram*, when he discusses the activity of the angels. "Through [the activity of the angels] all the kinds of things, and most especially humans, are looked after, seen to, by the providence of God."[139] They are able to act in this way because bodily things have been subjected to the authority of the angels.[140] Thomas also finds support for this view in John of Damascus's *De fide orthodoxa* and Origen's *Numeros homilia*.[141] And while it is unclear whether Damascene would have received it from Origen directly or via Gregory of Nyssa, the idea is also clearly on display in Nyssen's *Λογοε Κατηχτικοε*, where he explains that God assigned angelic powers roles in the administration of the universe.[142] The position that angels can and do effect the material cosmos, that part of their God-ordained role is carrying out his providential care for creation, is an early and continuous stream of thought in angelology.

When discussing the question of how material bodies are moved by the angelic will, Thomas cites Augustine. The *sed contra* of article 3 in question 110

---

136. *ST* 1.110.1 *sed contra*.

137. *ST* 1.110.1 *ad* 3.

138. Augustine, *div. qu.*, 79.1, *CCL* 44A:225: "unaquaeque res visibilis in hoc mundo habet postestatem angelicam sibi praepositam."

139. Augustine, *Gn. litt.*, 8.25.47, *PL* 34:391: "per quam universarum rerum generibus, maximeque humano providentia Dei prospicitur."

140. Augustine, *Gn. litt.*, 8.25.47, *PL* 34:391: "ipsa extrinsecus adjuvat, et per illa visa quae similia sunt corporalibus, et per ipsa corpora quae angelicae subjacent potestati."

141. *ST* 1.110.1 *ad* 3.

142. Grégoire de Nysse, *Discours Catéchétique*, trans. Raymond Winling, vol. 453, Sources Chrétiennes (Paris: Les Éditions du Cerf, 2000), §6, p. 175. *PG* 45:28: "La création intelligible existait antérieurement à l'autre et chacune des puissances angéliques se vit assigner, par l'autorité qui dirige toutes choses, une part d'activité en vue de l'organisation de l'univers."

says, "that angels employ bodily seeds (*semina corporalia*) to produce certain effects."[143] Thomas refers his reader to book III of Augustine's *De Trinitate*. In *De Trinitate*, Augustine does not call the things moved by angelic willing "bodily seeds." Instead he says, "You see, in all things which are born bodily and visibly certain hidden seeds (*occulta quaedam semina*) lie in the corporeal elements of this world."[144] As this discussion continues, Augustine makes a necessary distinction. While God administers his creatures internally, as their first cause, it is also the case that creatures are administered externally, by other created powers as secondary causes.[145] Angels can act in this capacity because "they know the seeds of things which are hidden to us."[146] They are able to act upon the seeds and, "scatter them in a hidden manner."[147] These seeds are the *rationes seminales* discussed in *De Genesi ad litteram*, which I treated at length in the second chapter.[148] In the ninth book of *De Genesi* Augustine makes the same point found here in third book of *De Trinitate*. The *rationes seminales* are the means by which angels carry out their administrative duties.[149] When Thomas refers to the *semina corporalia* in articles 3 and 4 of question 110, we should understand him to be referring to the seed-like rules which relate

---

143. *ST* 1.110.3 *sed contra*: "quod angeli adhibent semina corporalia ad aliquos effectus producendos."

144. Augustine, *trin.*, 3.8.13, *CCL* 50:140: "Omnium quippe rerum queae corporaliter visibiliterque nascuntur occulta quaedam semina in istis corporeis mundi huisus elementis latent."

145. Augustine, *trin.*, 3.9.16, *CCL* 50:143: "Aliud est enim ex intimo ac summo causarum cardine condere atque administrare creaturam, quod qui facit solus creator est deus; aliud autem pro distributis ab illo viribus et facultatibus aliquam operationem forinsecus admovere ut tunc vel tunc sic vel sic exeat quod creatur."

146. Augustine, *trin.*, 3.8.13, *CCL* 50:141: "pro subtilitate sui sensus et corporis semina rerum istarum nobis occultiora noverunt."

147. Augustine, *trin.*, 3.8.13, *CCL* 50:141: "ea per congruas temperationes elementorum latenter spargunt."

148. On the relationship of the *rationes seminales* in *De Trinitate* and their discussion in *De Genesi ad litteram*, cf. McKeough, *The Meaning of the Rationes Seminales in St. Augustine*, 39–43.

149. Augustine, *Gn. litt.*, 9.15.28, *PL* 34:404: "Voluntas vero angelica obedienter Deo subdita, ejusque exsecuta jussionem, naturalibus motibus de rebus subjectis tanquam materiam ministrare, ut secundum illas principales in Verbo Dei non creatas, vel secundum illas in primis sex dierum operibus causaliter creatas rationes aliquid in tempore creetur, more agricolandi vel medendi potest."

the whole of the created order to the person of Christ. Following Augustine, Thomas says, it is by acting on these seeds "that spiritual powers are able to bring about those things which happen visibly in this world."[150]

The case I have been making in these first three chapters has been leading up to this. Angelic creatures have a place in the administration of the created order and they carry this out by acting on the *rationes seminales*. This much is clearly affirmed by the tradition of reflection on the nature and mission of the angels. Some angelic creatures have fallen, and this fall occurs before (or as) time starts ticking. The effects of this fall are significant for our thinking about creation as a whole. We might say, with Augustine, creation as a whole is both good and fallen *ex quo creatus est*. We can say this because it belongs to the proper ordering of the cosmos that angelic creatures administer it, and some of these creatures have abandoned their mission. A reasonable conclusion of this line of argument is that certain creaturely possibilities lying dormant in the *rationes seminales* are foreclosed, the conditions for their actualization failing to obtain precisely because of the disorder caused by angelic sin. One of these possibilities is that imagined by Thomas in the *Summa Contra Gentiles*, when he speaks of animals not being composed of contraries and so not subject to corruption. Angelic sin, by disordering the cosmos and foreclosing certain latent potentialities in the *rationes seminales*, introduces corruption and death into the cosmos. This offers an important way of affirming, "through the devil's envy death entered the world" (Wis 2:24). Death in creation both is and is not *ex quo creatus est*. The relations of all things to God are created good and are so from before all time. They are also damaged by the angelic fall and so broken from before all time. Just as there is no time-when of the angelic fall, there is no time-when of the origin of death. It makes sense to speak of death as unnatural. And yet, it makes no sense to try to pinpoint "when" the break with nature occurred. These are the consequences of the demons being cast out of heaven. They are not playing their role, gazing upon the face of their creator and enacting his eternal plans in the temporal order. Instead, no longer participating in God's eternity, they are thoroughly timebound. Having forsaken their duties, they actively work to frustrate God's designs by acting in time.

The fall of the angels is an instance of voluntary evil perpetrated by rational creatures before all time, and it has severely damaged God's good

150. *ST* 1.110.4 *ad* 3: "quod spirituales potestates possunt facere ea quae visibiliter fiunt in hoc mundo, abhibendo coporalia semina per motum localem."

cosmos. This is true, at least, under the aspect of the *administratio*. I have yet to offer a complete account of the role this damage plays under the aspect of the *conditio*. Also, given the position I have staked out with respect to creaturely freedom, it is still the case that I need to offer some account of God's permission of this first evil. I am going to hold off on these tasks until the next chapter. Here I am content to have offered a perspective on the nature of demons that allows us at once to affirm, "God did not make death and he does not delight in the death of the living" (Wis 1:13), while also maintaining a distinction between natural and voluntary evils—even if calling the former "natural" tends to introduce some confusion over its ontological status. Further, it makes sense, given the view I have proposed, to say, "the generative forces of the world are wholesome, and there is no destructive poison in them" (Wis 1:14). It makes sense because in creating the cosmos God establishes all things in right relation to the person of Jesus Christ by way of the *rationes seminales*. When some of the angels fall, the relations those angels bear to the incarnate Lord are disrupted. These disruptions play out in the order of time. By extension, the relations between creatures are also thrown into disarray. It is not a total lack of order—fallen creation is not utter chaos—but in some sense we can say the world is not as it should be. Perhaps better, we might say that it is not as it will be eschatologically.

Given this conclusion, there is a final piece of the doctrinal witness about the demons which needs attention. As I have argued, the fallen angels are a kind of corporate body with Satan at its head. The scriptural and doctrinal witness bears this out. Satan's body is a devilish simulacrum of Christ's body, the Church. Being subject to the head of this body, part of Lucifer's demonic burlesque of the heavenly kingdom, is what it means to be under the dominion of the devil. The principal marks of this dominion are sin and death. This dominion is strongly attested by the Church's Magisterium beginning at the Council of Florence where, in the Bull *Cantate Domino*, we are told men and women are "liberated from the dominion of the devil . . . through faith of the mediator of God and humans, Jesus Christ."[151] This view is taken up again at the Council of Trent in its decrees on Original Sin, Justification, and

151. Council of Florence, *Cantate Domino*, *DS* §1347: "neminem umquam ex viro feminaque concepturm a diboli dominatu fuisse liberatum, nisi per fidem mediatoris Dei et hominum Iesu Christi."

Penance—captivity, the devil's power, and bondage to sin and death are the refrain.[152] But it is in the Second Vatican Council's *Gaudium et Spes* that the cosmic scope of the devil's dominion is clearly recognized. It says,

> For an arduous struggle against the powers of darkness pervades the whole of human history. The struggle began from the origin of the world, and will persist until the last day, by the Lord's telling. Man, thrust into this battle, ought continually to struggle that he might cling to the good. Nor is he able to obtain integrity in himself without great labors, being aided by the grace of God.[153]

In this account, the struggle against the powers of darkness precedes human history. Humans enter a drama already raging, we are "inserted" (*insertus*) into a battle, the roots of which lie in the origins of the world. Humans are taken captive in this cosmic war by way of Original Sin, about which I will say more in chapter 5. The powers of darkness are the "body of death" (Rom 7:24), the corporate, demonic body, which holds us in bondage. It is a body warring against the Church and the holy angels (Rev 12:7–9, 17), and it is from that body we are set free by Christ (Rom 7:25).

This is one important way of talking about the power that holds us captive before we are freed by the grace Christ makes available to us in his passion, death, and resurrection. What is included in the "us" of my last sentence is what this chapter is all about. Griffiths's thoughts on death and natural evil offer a maximalist view of how we might interpret it. Death, destruction, violence, even when they can be meaningfully spoken of as natural evils, are primordially the result of voluntary evil. The fall of the angels precipitates the unfurling of creation in time as a place of conflict, a vast charnel house whose brokenness frequently obscures and sometimes entirely occludes our ability to see it as God's good creation. The whole of the cosmos, shot through

152. *DS* §§1511, 1521, and 1668.

153. Second Vatican Council, *Gaudium et Spes*, §37, *DS* §4337: "Universam enim hominum historiam ardua colluctatio contra potestates tenebrarum pervadit, quae inde ab origine mundi incepta, usque ad ultimum diem, dicente Domino, perseverabit. In hanc pugnam insertus, homo ut bono adhaereat iugiter certare debet, nec sinie magnis laboribus, Dei gratia adiuvante, in seipso unitatem obtinere valet."

with darkness *ex quo creatus est*, "has been groaning in travail together" (Rom 8:22). And it is not just humans who have been enslaved to the powers of sin and death, who are in bondage to the devil and his angels. "Creation itself was subjected to futility" (Rom 8:20) and Jesus Christ's reconciling work extends to the whole of it, "because the creation itself will be set free from its bondage to decay and obtain the glorious liberty of the children of God" (Rom 8:21).

What I have said in this chapter makes clear the importance of reflecting on the nature of angels, the sin of the demons, and how this meaningfully contributes to our talk about evil and death. It demonstrates how it is possible to speak of the created order as both good and fallen from before all time. On this view, certain problems about pinpointing the origins of death are shown to be confusions about what can and cannot be said about the relations between time and eternity, creature and creator. If this reading is right, not only do the problems surrounding the origins of death begin to fade, the supposed conflicts between theology and evolutionary biology and modern cosmology should seem much less interesting. We have a way of saying "the wages of sin is death" (Rom 6:23) which allows us to include nonhuman creaturely death as a part of this paradigm. It gives us a way of accounting for the visceral sense that things are not as they should be when the lion tears at and consumes the flesh of a still living gazelle, or when we walk along the White Cliffs of Dover and realize we are standing atop a mountain of death, the discarded skeletons of prehistoric algae.

The next two chapters of this work will continue to build upon this framework. I will examine the implications of my speculations on the effects of the angelic fall in three different ways. The first way, in chapter 4, will involve peering a bit deeper into the origins of angelic sin. This will mean panning out to examine the created order under the aspect of eternity. The goal will be to get clear on what it means for us to say that the world is not as it should be and whether this can be meaningfully said of the *conditio* at all. The second way, in chapter 5, will involve shifting aspects back to the *administratio* to look closely at how the *rationes seminales* unfurl in time that is always already damaged. There I will also show how what I have said so far does and does not apply to human creatures. That is, given what has been said about angelic sin, there is work yet to do in order to place and describe the consequences of human sin.

CHAPTER FOUR

Literary Myths of the Angelic Fall

AFTER PUSHING BACK against a certain construal of the problem of evil and insisting creaturely freedom is in no way dependent upon God allowing sin, it is clear that further treatment of the question of evil is necessary. My principal interlocutors up to this point have been theological and philosophical thinkers. I want to extend the conclusions arrived at so far by examining literary portrayals of evil and evil's origins in the angelic fall. One of the presuppositions of this chapter is that turning to literature is not only warranted but often necessary in theological work. This chapter will not attempt to resolve the *mysterium iniquitatis* in general or the problem of angelic evil in particular. It will try to shed some much-needed light on both of these mysteries. In doing so, I will, "Tell all the truth but tell it slant."[1]

Donald MacKinnon presents his thoughts on the need to engage literature—specifically tragedy—in his essay "Atonement and Tragedy." For MacKinnon, theology and philosophy treat moral evil but fail to reckon adequately its depths. This is not, I take it, because what philosophy and theology say about evil is not true, but because it is often unclear what that truth comes to. The picture we are left with is an abstract one. This is useful to a point. It helps us get the grammar of evil right—no small feat—but it does not always help us go on. The conceptual treatment of evil shows that the problem never was a logical problem but a moral one. What remains to be seen is how to live in the world I have described. This is why I am turning to literature, to picture the kinds of responses available to creatures inhabiting a broken cosmos.

Tragedy deals with evil in a concrete way. It shows us things about evil that are easily overlooked. In tragedy, MacKinnon says,

> there is a presence to the reality of moral evil, to the ways in which its power is experienced as a destructive force which makes the writings

1. Emily Dickinson, "Tell All Truth but Tell It Slant — (1263)," Poetry Foundation, https://www.poetryfoundation.org/poems/56824/tell-all-the-truth-but-tell-it-slant-1263.

> of most philosophers and theologians seem somehow trivial.... Even if we are tempted to write them off as works of imagination, the imagination displayed in them is one powerful in the disclosure of what is; it is not the servant of idealist fantasy in the way in which we must surely judge that the comfortable musings of theologians and metaphysicians often are.[2]

This picture, of imaginative work deployed to counteract idealist fantasy, is compelling. I am counting on the literary works I engage to put flesh on the bones of the "comfortable musings" of the last chapter. At the same time, I do not see these two modes of engaging evil as contradictory or incompatible. I am arguing here for the possibility of each mode serving the other. "Conceptual abstraction" might be a less pejorative way to describe what MacKinnon dubs "idealist fantasy." If the work of the last chapter was that—conceptual abstraction—this chapter traffics in concrete particulars. But I will do so with the grammar established by examining the problem in the abstract. There are limits to this approach. It risks reducing the literary witness to data points in an argument. I have tried to avoid that kind of reduction by allowing what these texts teach about responding to and acknowledging evils to interrogate the grammatical argument and put it to the test.

In this chapter I draw on three principal literary sources, each of which helps me answer the question, "How do we go on speaking in a damaged world?" The chapter is built around two characters from Shakespeare's *Troilus and Cressida*. Both characters, Ulysses and Troilus, serve as types to highlight two kinds of responses to evil. I match these characters with a reading of another text. The position voiced by Ulysses, especially his concern over the disordered cosmos in his "Degree Speech," receives an answer from J. R. R. Tolkien's creation myth in *The Silmarillion*. Troilus, and his fetishization of "constancy," meets his match in the Satan of John Milton's *Paradise Lost*. This chapter shifts the discourse from reflections made *sub specie aeternitatis* to those made about the order of time and flux. My observations will move from what I have called Augustine's concern for the *conditio* into his concern

2. Donald M. MacKinnon, "Atonement and Tragedy," in *Borderlands of Theology and Other Essays*, ed. George W. Roberts and Donovan E. Smucker (Philadelphia: J. B. Lippincott Company, 1968), 101.

for the *administratio*. This chapter ought to position me to undertake the remainder of the investigation in the next chapter under the aspect of the *administratio*. Having offered a theoretical account of sin's and death's origins and a literary account of responses to it, it will be time to deal with the deaths of creatures. Actual nonhuman and human death, and death's relation to the evolutionary account of the origins of life, are the subject of the next and final chapter.

Ulysses and the Drive for Order

In the first act of *Troilus and Cressida*,[3] Ulysses is in council with the other Greek leaders during the Trojan War. They are conferencing with Agamemnon over the continued failure to bring the conflict to decisive issue. Agamemnon wants to know, "What grief hath set these jaundies o'er your cheeks?" (1.3.2). How is it, he wonders, that his captains fail to realize what kind of thing their ongoing war is? Above all, Agamemnon argues, what the Greeks have in Troy is a chance to prove their mettle—the "fineness" of their "metal" (1.3.22)—in the midst of trials. He asks,

> *Why then, you princes,*
> *Do you with cheeks abash'd behold our works,*
> *And call them shames which are indeed nought else*
> *But the protractive trials of great Jove*
> *To find persistive constancy in men?*
> *(1.3.17–21)*

"Constancy" and its failures are central themes of the play. Agamemnon sees the war as a test which will show who proves resolute in the face of uncertainty. He is concerned to find whether, when all is said and done, "Distinction, with a broad and powerful fan" (1.3.27) will have winnowed all away to nothing, or whether we will find upon the threshing room floor "what hath mass or matter, by itself / Lies rich in virtue and unmingled" (1.3.29–30). But Ulysses is not content with this explanation for the

3. All citations from Shakespeare's plays are taken from William Shakespeare, *The Riverside Shakespeare*, 2nd ed. (New York: Houghton Mifflin Company, 1997). I give all citations to the text in-line, using three Arabic numerals that indicate, in order, act, scene, and line numbers.

Greeks' continued failure to take the city. He offers a different diagnosis in his "Degree Speech."

Nothing prevents the conquest of Troy but internal strife among the Greeks themselves. But for that, Ulysses claims, "Troy, yet upon his bases, had been down, / And the great Hector's sword had lack'd a master" (1.3.75–76). The Greek failure has a specific pathogenesis—disease is another of the play's major themes—"The specialty of rule hath been neglected" (1.3.78). Order, the ruled whole, has been lost because individuals have forgotten their place. The differences of degree between men have been shrouded in confusion, and chaos abounds. There is little chance Agamemnon's "Distinction"—another word specifying degree—or her winnowing fan will be able to tell the wheat from the chaff. The whole cosmos, Ulysses argues, depends on degree,

> *The heavens themselves, the planets, and this centre*
> *Observe degree, priority, and place,*
> *Insisture, course, proportion, season, form,*
> *Office, and custom, in all line of order . . .*
> *But when the planets*
> *In evil mixture to disorder wander,*
> *What plagues and what portents, what mutiny!*
> *What raging of the sea, shaking of the earth!*
> *Commotion in the winds! frights, changes, horrors*
> *Divert and crack, rend and deracinate*
> *The unity and married calm of states*
> *Quite from their fixture!*
> *(1.3.85–88, 94–101)*

He offers a macrocosmic view. All things have a place, a fit, a rule to keep in the ordered cosmos. We might wonder at and press Ulysses on the inclusion of "office" and "custom" as rightly applied to the heavens. Are these hints of an overblown fulmination or a sly attempt to sneak the present order of society into the very fabric of the cosmos? Whatever the case may be, they give the reader the idea that Ulysses's earnest descriptions of the rightly ordered world do not escape Shakespeare's pen without an ironizing.

Ulysses is right, and we can follow his train of thought. This claim about disorder seems right and appealing. The cosmos is disordered, and that disorder brings "frights, changes, horrors" with it. In this, he is very close to the position sketched in the last chapter. Unruly angelic creatures introduce a deep rent into the fabric of the created world. Abandoning their ministerial role to order creation according to the designs of divine wisdom, they introduce the conditions for the possibility of death and destruction. And those conditions are introduced from the very beginning, *ex quo creatus est*, as Augustine says.[4] We might take Ulysses to be expressing the very same angst in the face of the damaged world that any of us feels when confronted with the death or disease of a loved one, the extinction of a species, or the horrors of war. It is no idle utterance when Agamemnon takes Ulysses to have found, "The nature of the sickness" (1.3.140). What Ulysses sees is the corruption, the rot of the world gone wrong. In this, he is not unlike Thersites, the great proclaimer of the play's "rotten diseases" (5.1.18), who recognizes the world of *Troilus and Cressida* for what it is, a "Sweet sink, sweet sewer" (5.1.75–76).

But there is more to say about Ulysses's speech and the way we left things with the fall of the angels. Ulysses's reaction to the sickness of the world offers one possible way forward. He attempts to locate the root cause of the problem. Agamemnon wants to know, if this is the disease, "What is the remedy?" (1.3.141). In answer, Ulysses launches into a diatribe about "The great Achilles, whom opinion crowns / The sinow and the forehand of our host" (1.3.142–43). Here, Shakespeare's earlier, subtle ironizing of Ulysses's position is more blatantly redeployed. Ulysses is exposed as a bickering, petty, small man. Mixing servile flattery of Agamemnon and his "topless deputation" (1.3.152) with whining over Ajax's and Achilles's failures to take seriously his very important work as a war planner. You can almost hear Ulysses's voice pitching frantically upward as you read his lines,

> *They tax our policy, and call it cowardice,*
> *Count wisdom as no member of the war,*
> *Forestall prescience, and esteem no act*
> *But that of hand. The still and mental parts,*
> *That do contrive how many hands shall strike*
> *When fitness calls them on, and know by measure*

4. Augustine, *civ.*, 11.13, *CSEL* 40.1:532: "Ab initio diabolus peccat, hoc est, ex quo creatus est, iustitiam recusavit."

Of their observant toil the enemies' weight—
Why, this hath not a finger's dignity.
They call this bed-work, mapp'ry, closet-war.
(1.3.197–205)

So run the complaints of every staff officer ever to feel underappreciated by the infantryman. It puts the lie to Ulysses's noble concerns, or it almost does. It is still possible Ulysses will decide to embark on the right course for the wrong reason. But what does he actually do?

After the conversation is interrupted by the arrival of Aeneas bearing Hector's challenge to the Greeks, Ulysses and Nestor scheme together. Achilles, as he has already said, is overproud and thinks he is not beholden to Agamemnon and the rest of the Greeks. His "neglection of degree" (1.3.127) has imperiled their cause. Ulysses's solution? He will knock him down a peg or two. But his plans to do so involve furthering disorder, putting forth Ajax as the Greek's best man, which he knows to be false. As he says,

Therefore 'tis meet Achilles meet not Hector.
Let us like merchants first show foul wares,
And think perchance they'll sell; if not,
The lustre of the better shall exceed.
By showing the worst first.
(1.3.357–61)

In order to make right Achilles's relation to Agamemnon, to restore degree, Ulysses is prepared to introduce more disarray. He does so because he worries Achilles's victory over Hector would only serve to advance the already proud Myrmidon's opinion of himself. All the glory of the win would accrue to Achilles alone. At the same time, if Achilles were to be defeated by Hector, this could only damage the reputation of the Greeks in general.

If he were foil'd,
Why then we do our main opinion crush
In taint of our best man. No, make a lott'ry,
And by device let blockish Ajax draw

The sort to fight with Hector; among ourselves
Give him allowance for the better man
(1.3.371–76)

So much, then, for Ulysses's idealism. As it turns out, he is happy to swap degree for device when it suits his interests. Putting forward Ajax instead of Achilles might conceivably correct one ill, but the sickness and disorder Ulysses has identified runs deeper than Achilles's pride. So deep, in fact, that Ulysses's imagined solution is only further evidence of the problem.

In the end, Agamemnon's observation holds true. "The ample proposition that hope makes / In all designs begun on earth below / Fails in the promis'd largeness" (1.3.3–5). Ulysses's schemes, for all their craftiness, cannot bring about their object. Ulysses has diagnosed the problem rightly but has failed to respond to it correctly. Degree, order, rule, these are all important concepts. Ulysses's utterance, "Take but degree away, untune that string, / And hark what discord follows. Each thing meets / In mere oppugnancy" (1.3.109–11), can be taken to summarize the last chapter's findings. The cosmos, robbed of the ordered relation of all things to the incarnate Lord becomes a vast battleground of contraries. It is in this steaming miasma of oppugnancy that the temporal unfolding of the cosmos occurs. The world we know is as Ulysses describes,

Then every thing include itself in power
Power into will, will into appetite,
And appetite, an universal wolf
(So doubly seconded with will and power),
Must make perforce an universal prey,
And last eat up himself.
(1.3.119–24)

A more Augustinian sentiment would be hard to find—the *libido dominandi* as "an universal wolf," whose last act is solipsistic self-consumption.

But Ulysses is only partly right. Shakespeare hints at this for us with the subtle and not so subtle ironies of the "Degree Speech." I have pointed to some subdued irony already, but one more hint that we cannot take Ulysses with perfect seriousness comes on the lips of Agamemnon. Before Ulysses launches into the speech, he offers Agamemnon and Nestor what can only be called a "tortive and errant" (1.3.9) introduction to his thought. The fawning Ulysses commends Agamemnon, "great commander," "nerve and bone of Greece," "Heart of our numbers," "soul and only sprite," "most mighty for thy place and sway," and "the hand of Greece" (1.3.54–64) all in the space of ten lines. But just before the "Degree Speech" begins, we catch a glimpse of Agamemnon's impatience with what borders on courtly buffoonery. He gives Ulysses permission to speak, but with this proviso,

> *Speak, prince of Ithaca, and be't of less expect*
> *That matter needless, of importless burthen,*
> *Divide thy lips, than we are confident,*
> *When rank Thersites opes his mastic jaws,*
> *We shall hear music, wit, and oracle.*
> *(1.3.70–74)*

One way to take these lines is as a vote of confidence in Ulysses's counsel: "Only needful and important matters come from the mouth of Ulysses." But the mention of Thersites challenges that reading. If instead you take Agamemnon's "be't" in the subjunctive rather than the indicative mood, the comparison to the play's fool is more apt. Read this way, Agamemnon is saying: "I had better not hear needless and unimportant matters coming from your mouth, Ulysses." Or, even more aggressively, the imperative, "Get on with it." There are good reasons internal and external to the speech—apart even from the general tone of the play—to make the reader question how far she ought to follow Ulysses on degree and disorder.

The inclination to accept Ulysses's explanation for the world's ills, locating them in disorder *simpliciter*, fails on two accounts. First, while it has great explanatory power for dealing with particular manifestations of evil, we are still no closer to being able to account for evil's origins in the rational creature's disordered will. The original untuning of the cosmic instrument remains entirely opaque. Second, distinct yet related, this view of the untuned cosmos does not provide expansive enough a view for the Christian thinker. That is, Ulysses is uninterested in or unaware of the way particular disorders might contribute to, or be necessary for, the accomplishment of a greater, more encompassing order. I will take these two failures one at a time. I will deal with the second one by turning now to the creation myth of Tolkien's

The Silmarillion. The first will have to wait until we can look more closely at the character of Troilus.

Tolkien, Nostalgia, and the New Creation

Ulysses suffers from a failure of imagination. You see this failure when he says, "O, when degree is shak'd / Which is the ladder of all high designs, / The enterprise is sick" (1.3.101–3). This failure is one to which we are all disposed. Whenever we see particular failures, sins, or evils as clear evidence of the world's disorder, whenever we are confident the whole "enterprise is sick" as a result, we succumb to Ulysses's temptation. Hamlet offers a different response by catching a glimpse of the broader field on which human lives and designs are played out. Think, for instance, of his comments to Horatio in act 5 of *Hamlet*,

> *Our indiscretion sometimes serves us well*
> *When our deep plots do pall, and that should learn us*
> *There's a divinity that shapes our ends,*
> *Rough-hew them how we will—*
> (Hamlet, *5.2.8–11)*

That indiscretion sometimes serves us well is not a view countenanced by Ulysses. Disorder is something to be corrected, by subterfuge if necessary. More often than not, our responses to the unruly cosmos incline toward Ulysses rather than Hamlet. And it is worth observing that it takes nearly the whole action of *Hamlet* to bring the young prince to see things aright. To be able to say, "There is a special providence in the fall of a sparrow" (*Hamlet*, 5.2.219–20), he has to overcome the twin temptations of fatalistic despair and its opposite number, Ulysses's nostalgic utopianism.

The creation myth that prefaces J. R. R. Tolkien's *The Silmarillion* is an astute piece of theology and angelology. It offers a response more akin to Hamlet's view of providence than to Ulysses's nostalgic paean for degree. In doing so, it provides a third way of responding to disorder. Tolkien calls his myth the *Ainulindalë* or "The Music of the Ainur."[5] In a letter to Milton Waldman, as part of an effort to convince his publisher that both *The*

5. J. R. R. Tolkien, *The Silmarillion*, 2nd ed. (Boston: Houghton Mifflin Company, 1999), 15.

Silmarillion and *The Lord of the Rings* should appear in print, Tolkien says this about the *Ainulindalë*:

> The cycles begin with a cosmogonical myth: the *Music of the Ainur*. God and the Valar (or powers: Englished as gods) are revealed. These latter are as we should say angelic powers, whose function is to exercise delegated authority in their spheres (of rule and government, *not* creation, making or re-making). They are "divine", that is, were originally "outside" and existed "before" the making of the world. Their power and wisdom is derived from their Knowledge of the cosmogonical drama, which they perceived first as a drama (that is as in a fashion we perceive a story composed by some-one else), and later as a "reality".[6]

The Ainur of Tolkien's cosmogonical myth bear a strong resemblance to Augustine's description of the angels as the created forms of uncreated Wisdom called into existence on the first day when God says, "Let there be light."[7] In the *Ainulindalë*, God is "Eru, the One, who in Arda is called Ilúvatar."[8] The Ainur "were the offspring of his thought, and they were with him before aught else was made."[9] Like Augustine's angels, the Ainur are intellectual creatures, made first by Eru. The Ainur do not create but "exercise delegated authority," much as the angelic powers were said in the last chapter to be ministers of God's cosmos, governing it as secondary causes.

In the *Ainulindalë*, the Ainur exercise this ministerial function through song. Eru teaches the Ainur to sing. Each individual Ainur sings a piece of music corresponding to part of the mind of Eru. As they sing, they begin to understand one another's music. Eventually, they learn to harmonize. At that point, Eru instructs them in a musical theme. After giving them the theme, he tasks them with making "a Great Music" together, each performing the

---

6. J. R. R. Tolkien, *The Letters of J. R. R. Tolkien* (Boston: Houghton Mifflin Company, 1981), 146.

7. Augustine, *Gn. Litt.*, 2.8.16–19.

8. Tolkien, *The Silmarillion*, 15.

9. Tolkien, *The Silmarillion*, 15.

portion allotted using the powers gifted by Eru.[10] As they played their music, "the places of the dwelling of Ilúvatar were filled to overflowing, and the music and the echo of the music went out into the Void, and it was not void."[11] Creation, in Tolkien's myth is ordered by harmonious music, played according to the wisdom and power of Eru. Eru's spiritual creatures, the Ainur, use their powers—those powers being themselves created and derivative—to shape and form a cosmos according to the will of Eru.

The harmonious music of the Ainur, woven together by the will of Eru, is perfectly ordered. There are no mistakes of degree until we read that, "as the theme progressed, it came into the heart of Melkor to interweave matters of his own imagining that were not in accord with the theme of Ilúvatar; for he sought therein to increase the power and glory of the part assigned to himself."[12] So begins an attempted usurpation of Eru's prerogatives. In doing so, Melkor introduces disorder, not because he is small or weak—Tolkien explains that he's the most powerful and knowledgeable of the Ainur[13]—but because he is not Eru. Like Ulysses's description of Achilles playacting as Agamemnon, his disregard for degree results in a mimicry that becomes mockery. "Such to-be-pitied and o'er-wrested seeming / He acts thy greatness in; and when he speaks, / 'Tis like a chime a-mending, with terms unsquar'd" (1.3.157–59). Melkor's seeming, when he desires "to bring into Being things of his own," has the effect of weaving "discord" into the song of the Ainur.[14] Like the chime in need of repair, that rings "with terms unsquar'd" Melkor's voice disturbs the music. The other Ainur attempt to change keys, to salvage the music by following Melkor's lead. The perturbations spread farther and wider until, "the melodies which had been heard before foundered in a sea of turbulent sound."[15]

The crucial difference of response to disorder is seen in Eru's response contrasted with Ulysses's. The possible responses are delimited in advance by the role each plays in his respective narrative. Ulysses is a creature and so has

10. Tolkien, *The Silmarillion*, 15.

11. Tolkien, *The Silmarillion*, 15.

12. Tolkien, *The Silmarillion*, 16.

13. Tolkien, *The Silmarillion*, 16.

14. Tolkien, *The Silmarillion*, 16.

15. Tolkien, *The Silmarillion*, 16.

a small set of possible responses to the upsetting of degree. His attempt to correct the disorder with deceit is not the only creaturely response available, but it is one that makes Ulysses relatable. This sort of solution is attractive to creatures. We imagine the disorders we perceive in the world to be things that can be corrected straightforwardly, by returning things to a state of affairs in an idealized past. Earlier, I called Ulysses's response a nostalgic one. Nostalgia is the fundamental logic at work in his desire to put things back the way they were.

The responses available to Eru are different. As the creator of Tolkien's narrative, Eru's options for reestablishing order are not limited to what has gone before. When Eru perceives Melkor's discordant music, he rises and lifts his left hand, "and a new theme began amid the storm, like and yet unlike to the former theme, and it gathered power and had new beauty."[16] To which new theme, Melkor responds with further strife, with such violent music that Tolkien goes so far as to say, "Melkor had the mastery."[17] But once more Eru rises up, this time raising his right hand, introducing a further theme. With its introduction there now seem to be two separate pieces of music. One is sweet and beautiful. The other lacks artistry, trying instead to drown out the subtle, soft music.[18] Finally, with both pieces of music vying against one another, Eru rises one last time. He raises both his hands, "and in one chord, deeper than the Abyss, higher than the Firmament, piercing as the light of the eye of Ilúvatar, the Music ceased."[19]

This is Tolkien's antinostalgic response to discord. Instead of attempting a backward-looking restoration, the creator God of Middle Earth looks quite like the God of Scripture who says, "Remember not the former things, nor consider the things of old. Behold, I am doing a new thing; now it springs forth, do you not perceive it?" (Isa 43:18–19, cf. Rev 21:5). To understand Eru's response to Melkor, and so also God's response to the rebellion of Lucifer and his angels, it is necessary to clarify what we mean by "response." Properly speaking, God does not respond to his creatures' actions, if response is taken to indicate a temporally sequenced reaction. You can see that this is usually

16. Tolkien, *The Silmarillion*, 16.

17. Tolkien, *The Silmarillion*, 16.

18. Tolkien, *The Silmarillion*, 16–17.

19. Tolkien, *The Silmarillion*, 17.

what we mean when we say so-and-so responded to someone else. Consider a televised debate, where one participant is given thirty seconds to respond to a point made by his opponent. Think, too, of the responsorial psalm sung during Mass, which follows in answer to the first reading. The point–counterpoint of the music of Eru and Melkor should not be understood in this way. How could it be if God (and in this case, Eru) knows all things because they are created and sustained by his creative act? This necessarily includes all Melkor's creaturely possibilities. If that is the case, then it is not clear what would count as a "response" from Eru or God in the ordinary sense of the word. For the things that are to be is for God to will them to be as they are.

Comparing Ulysses's response to Eru's is bound to fail. Eru is not responding to Melkor in the ordinary sense. He is instead wielding him, even and especially in his freely willed disobedience, to bring about the ordered whole of his creation. He says as much to the Ainur after the final, trembling chord comes to a halt. Tolkien writes,

> Then Ilúvatar spoke, and he said: "Mighty are the Ainur, and mightiest among them is Melkor; but that he may know, and all the Ainur, that I am Ilúvatar, those things that ye have sung, I will show them forth, that ye may see what ye have done. And thou, Melkor, shalt see that no theme may be played that hath not its uttermost source in me, nor can any alter the music in my despite. For he that attempteth this shall prove but mine instrument in the devising of things more wonderful, which he himself hath not imagined."[20]

This is a deep point of Christian grammar, carefully portrayed by Tolkien. In brief we might characterize it this way: God permits evils that greater goods might come about. Even a cursory look at Scripture shows this to be the usual way God acts providentially to bring about goods. Joseph is sold into slavery by his brothers only to save those same brothers and so the line of Abraham from famine (Gen 37–50). Holofernes lays siege to Bethulia and Uzziah makes oaths that put God to the test, causing Judith to singlehandedly defeat the attacking army (Jdt 1–16). The man born blind is without sight, not because of his or his parents' sins, "but that the

20. Tolkien, *The Silmarillion*, 17.

works of God might be made manifest through him" (John 9:3). This logic is embedded in the liturgy of the Church as well, when she proclaims the ancient hymn, the *Exsultet*, at the Easter Vigil. There we hear, "O certe necessárium Adæ peccátum, / quod Christi morte delétum est! / O felix culpa, / quae talem ac tantum méruit habére Redemptórem!"[21] The English missal for use in the United States renders this, "O truly necessary sin of Adam, / destroyed completely by the Death of Christ! / O happy fault / that earned so glorious a Redeemer!"[22] What the Church here unabashedly acclaims follows the same pattern as Eru's declamation to Melkor. Adam's sin is, in some way, *certe necessarium* and *felix*, so that—*mirabile dictu*—Jesus Christ, the incarnate Lord, might bring about humanity's salvation from sin and death.

In Tolkien and the *Missale Romanum* we discover the role evil is made to play in the ordering and reordering of the cosmos. This problem of the goods to be had, *that can only be had*, by way of evils (the *felices* only possible as the result of *culpae*), is a vexing one. In the last chapter I spent quite some time giving reasons why the problem of evil is not the kind of problem we tend to think it is. There is nothing logically inconsistent about God who is all good permitting evils. But there I also said the fracturing of the cosmos since its inception by the angelic fall, and the resultant damage done to all creaturely relations, is the origin of death. Death is a great disordering, the result of an untuning of the cosmos which ends in discord. The last chapter showed that we have an intuitive grasp of this when we reflect upon the scope and so the horror of death and disintegration. But this item of the Christian grammar of creation and evil depicted by Tolkien and affirmed in the *Exsultet*, means that it is not all there is to say about it. We instead find that we must say that the evils afflicting the cosmos, with their source in the voluntary evil of angelic and human creatures, are permitted even if not positively willed by God.

To say more on this, let us turn to Augustine and Gregory the Great. The theme of the cosmos rightly ordered by God not despite evils but through

---

21. *Missale Romanum Cum Lectionibus*, vol. 2 (Vatican City: Libreria Editrice Vaticana, 1977), 332.

22. *The Roman Missal* (Collegeville, MN: Liturgical Press, 2011), 351.

them, frequently recurs in Augustine's work.[23] A careful statement of his position appears in book XI of *De civitate Dei.*

> But just as God is the perfectly good creator of good natures, so also is he the perfectly just orderer of evil wills. So, while evil wills use good natures badly, he uses even evil wills well. . . . That is, the temptations, by which the devil wanted to do harm, are good for his saints. And since God, when he made him, was not ignorant of the use of his future malignity, he also foresaw those good things he himself was to bring about from the devil's evils.[24]

The thought expressed here is formally close to the one found in Tolkien, but it points up something only hinted at in the *Silmarillion*. That is, the devil proves to be God's instrument because God foreknows both the evil of the devil and the goods he will bring out of it. Augustine goes further than this. While it is true that if none had sinned there would only be good natures, the fact of sin does not detract from God's ordering all things rightly. "Because," Augustine says, "just like a painting with dark color in its proper place, so too the whole universe of things—if someone were able to see it—is beautiful even with sinners, even though considered in themselves their ugliness is hideous."[25] The beauty of the whole includes the negative space caused by sin and evil.

The position I am drawing out is clearer if we turn once again to the relation of time and eternity this discussion presupposes. In chapter 2, I showed what I take to be entailments of Augustine's position in *De trinitate*

23. Cf. *inter alia*, Augustine, *ord.*, 1.1.2; *lib. arb.*, 3.9.25–28; *civ.*, 11.17–18, 22–23, 33, and 12.4; *Gn. litt.*, 8.9.18, 23.44; 11.3.5, 9.12, 12.16.

24. Augustine, *civ.*, 11.17, *CSEL* 40.1:536–37: "Sed Deus sicut naturarum bonarum optimus creator est, ita malarum voluntatum iustissimus ordinator, ut, cum illae male utuntur naturis bonis, ipse bene utatur etiam voluntatibus malis . . . id est, ut prosint tentationes eius sanctis, quibus eas obesse desiderat. Et quoniam Deus, cum eum conderet, futurae malignitatis eius non erat utique ignarus et praevidebat quae bona de malo eius esset ipse facturus."

25. Augustine, *civ.*, 11.23, *CSEL* 40.1:545: "quoniam sicut pictura cum colore nigro loco sua posito, ita universitas rerum, si quis possit intueri, etiam cum peccatoribus pulchra est, quamvis per se ipsos consideratos sua deformitas turpet."

on knowledge of future things. There I provided a speculative answer to the ticklish problem of God's eternal knowledge. God's knowledge of past, present, and future things *is* their reality. Gregory the Great, perhaps also drawing on Boethius, sees something similar. In book XX of the *Moralia in Job*, Gregory has this to say about God's foreknowledge:

> And because he sees the things which to us are in the future, but which to him are always present, he is called "foreknowing." Even though he does not in any way foresee the future, which he sees happening at once. For certainly all the things that are, are not seen in his eternity because they are, rather they are because they are seen. When, therefore, his eternity is brought down to our mutable words, out of those words a kind of stairway is made that he who can may climb up to the immutability of God so that he may see one jealous without jealousy, irate without ire, sorry without sorrow and grief, full of pity without a pitiable heart, foreknowing without foresight. For in him neither past nor future can be found, but all mutable things endure immutably. And things which, in themselves, cannot be at once, at once all stand together for him, and nothing that passes by passes away, because in his eternity in a certain incomprehensible manner, the whole roll of ages remains while passing, while running stands still.[26]

As Gregory says, words like "foreknowing" cannot be properly predicated of God. This does not mean the words are useless for talking about God's eternity. Quite the contrary, our attempts to express the unchangeable in changeable (tensed) words give us a foothold, a step by which we can

---

26. Gregory the Great, *mor.*, 20.32.63, *CCL* 143A:1049–51: "Et quia ea quae nobis futura sunt videt, quae tamen ipsi semper praesto sunt, praescius dicitur, quamvis nequaquam futurum praevideat quod praesens videt. Nam et quaeque sunt, non in aeternitate eius ideo videntur quia sunt, sed ideo sunt, quia videntur. Dum ergo ad verba mutabilitatis nostrae descenditur, ex eis quibusdam gradibus factis ascendat qui potest ad incommutabilitatem Dei, ut videat sine zelo zelantem, sine ira irascentem, sine dolore et paenitentia paenitentem, sine misero corde misericordem, sine praevisionibus praescientem. In illo enim nec praeterita, nec futura reperiri queunt, sed cuncta mutabilia immutabiliter durant; et quae in seipsis simul existere non possunt, illi simul omnia assistunt nihilque in illo praeterit quod transit, quia in aeternitate eius modo quodam incomprehensibili, cuncta volumina saeculorum transeuntia manent, currentia stant."

begin to mount up to eternity. There, and only there, do these apparent contraries hang together. Most importantly, in Gregory's account we find all times present to God. In all their variability, they stand firm in his eternity.

What we are trying to get at with talk of God's foreknowledge is the entirely unique way God relates to things existing in our temporal future. Gregory unpacks this to say God's foreknowledge is of things that have not yet occurred in the march of time, but which already are in God. They already are because "creation" does not mark the beginning of things in time. "Creation" names the relation any creature you like and the whole set of creatures considered as a cosmos bear to their creator.[27] Creatures are made out of nothing and without movement from one state to another—as there are no states prior to creation.[28] In keeping with my speculations about the reality of past, present, and future times hanging together in the "whole roll of ages," as Gregory says, it makes sense to say the simultaneous creation of all things without change[29] includes all spatiotemporal, intellectual, and intentional relations considered as a whole. To say God makes this world is to say he makes it *this* ordered whole. And this ordered whole, the one God wills, is the one in which great evils occur.

But what does it mean to talk about evils this way, as unable to frustrate God's intention? The evils are unable to do so because God allows them to occur—though he does not intend the evils themselves—in order to bring about greater goods. God does not intend the evils themselves because an evil

27. This distinction between "creation" as beginning in time and "creation" as relation to the Creator forms the whole subtext for Augustine's treatment of Genesis 1:1–2:5 in *De Genesi ad litteram*. On this point, see especially *Gn. litt.*, 5.6.19, *PL* 34:327: "Haec enim jam per moras temporum fiunt, quae tunc non erant, cum fecit omnia simul, unde etiam tempora *inciperent*" ("For these things now happen through intervals of time, of which there were none when he made all things at once, from which moment even times began"). Thomas gives it a scholastic specificity in article 45 of the *Prima Pars* of the *Summa Theologiae*. On creation as relation, Thomas says in *ST*, 1.45.3 *resp*: "creatio in creatura non sit nisi relatio quaedam ad creatorem, ut ad principium sui esse" ("creation in a creature is nothing but a certain relation to the creator, as to the principle of its act of being").

28. *ST*, 1.45.2 *ad* 2: "creatio non est mutatio nisi secundum modum intelligendi tantum. Nam de ratione mutationis est, quod aliquid idem se habeat aliter nunc et prius" ("Creation is only a change according to a mode of understanding. For it belongs to the idea of change that the same something is different now than it was before").

29. *ST*, 1.45.2 *ad* 3: "cum creatio sit sine motu, simul aliquid creatur et creatum est" ("since creation is without motion, a thing is created and being created simultaneously").

is a privation. It makes little sense to say God wills to bring about a privation because a privation is not something but a lack of something. In order for a privation to be, God need do nothing at all. This belongs to the grammar of God's permissive will. God allows a privation to occur by doing nothing to prevent it. In this way, God's permissive will is distinct from God's positive will, which—according the doctrine of simplicity—is identical with himself. God's positive will for creatures is a matter of self-gift, whereas his permissive will is a matter of creaturely possibilities that are a function of being created from nothing, possibilities God does not impede, and so result in privation.

That God permits evils to bring about greater goods is a statement of faith and explicitly not one of sight. This way of presenting things—consonant though it is with the deep structure of Christian thought—is not an act of describing the world we see. It is easy to read Augustine, and probably my own account, as overly sanguine. Talk of sin and evil as the dark spots of a chiaroscuro, lending beauty to the whole, might even seem morally deranged. This would be true if what he or I meant were that it is somehow obvious that this is the case, or if the order of the whole somehow excused or justified the evils. That is not what I take Augustine to be doing, though he sometimes swerves further in this direction than seems advisable. Instead, what he and I are expressing is a commitment to the goodness of God, appearances notwithstanding. What we find in his account of the beautifully ordered whole is what he takes to be demanded in the light of faith. He says so explicitly in book XII of *De civitate Dei*. We are often incapable of seeing how the evils of the world contribute to its beauty, how our *culpae* are the source of our *felices*. But it is when we are least certain, least able to perceive it, that we are "most rightly directed to believe in the providence of the Creator."[30] To do otherwise is to find fault in God and his creation.

Augustine is aware of the brokenness of the world. He also believes God created all things very good (Gen 1:31). When God looks upon "everything that he had made" (Gen 1:31) and sees its goodness, what other perspective should we take these words to be expressing but the one from God's eternal vantage? For Augustine, this "very good" comes as a description of things under the aspect of the *conditio*. Its subject is "the whole roll of ages" as yet to

30. Augustine, *civ.*, 12.4, *CSEL* 40.1:571: "Unde nobis, in quibus eam contemplari minus idonei sumus, rectissime credenda praecipitur providentia Conditoris, ne tanti artificis opus in aliquo reprehendere vanitate humanae temeritas audeamus."

be unfurled in the order of time. Read this way, Augustine's almost cavalier discussions of rape in book I of *De civitate Dei*, my reframing of the problem of evil as no problem at all, and Hamlet's confident "the readiness is all . . . let be" (*Hamlet*, 5.2.222, 224) before rushing to meet his death all have something in common. They share the same expansive horizon, a recognition that on some level protology *is* eschatology. This is the third kind of response, which avoids appeals to nostalgia and despair. It takes the world to be God's good creation, even in its evident brokenness.

But even if this third kind of response to disorder is available to and even necessary for Christians, it cannot be allowed to occlude the damage done to creation. We must be able to say in the same breath, good yet broken, beautiful yet terrible, perfect yet costly. Tolkien's vision does not flinch. He is prepared to say both things at once. In doing so, his story models a kind of creaturely response to the fact of evil that trusts no particular evil could finally disorder the world God creates. Nor, however, does it imagine the final, perfected beauty of the cosmos as unmarred. The created order damaged and healed mimics the risen Christ whose wounds remain even when glorified. Or, like the martyrs whose resurrected bodies, Augustine speculates, retain the marks of the stripes they receive for Christ.[31] The final perfection of God's creation is scarified and somehow more beautiful for it.[32]

Tolkien expresses both sides of this by pointing to the beauty of Eru Ilúvatar's third musical theme. The beauty of this theme comes, he says, from "an immeasurable sorrow."[33] Melkor's music attempts to stand apart, "but it seemed that its most triumphant notes were taken by the other and woven into its own solemn pattern."[34] The deep and beautiful music of Eru does not

31. Augustine, *civ.*, 22.19.

32. My "somehow" here has in the background a line from one of Flannery O'Connor's letters to "A" written on July 20, 1955. There she says, "I think that the Church is the only thing that is going to make the terrible world we are coming to endurable; the only thing that makes the Church endurable is that it is *somehow* the body of Christ and that on this we are fed." Flannery O'Connor, *The Habit of Being: The Letters of Flannery O'Connor* (New York: Farrar, Straus & Giroux, 1979), 90. Emphasis mine. O'Connor's "somehow" is meant to signal the presence of a mystery, the fact that it has been revealed and offered to us as an article of faith, and the persistent difficulty of accepting it as such.

33. Tolkien, *The Silmarillion*, 16–17.

34. Tolkien, *The Silmarillion*, 17.

refuse or destroy by drowning out what stands opposed to it. The creator God in Tolkien's myth allows the music to continue and weaves an audible lament into his all-encompassing theme. Michael Elam picks up on the importance of sorrow in Tolkien's work in an article on the *Ainulindalë*. Drawing on Thomas Aquinas and Augustine, he shows how the beauty of the third theme comes from the sorrow itself. "Sorrow for evil is good," he explains, because it is the only appropriate response to a lack of a good that ought to be present.[35] As Elam says, "In the context of the *Ainulindalë*'s conflict, therefore, it may be the case that beauty rises according to sorrow's function: i.e., that sorrow properly recognizes the contrast between what-is-and-shouldn't-be (the actual) with what-ought-to-be-but-isn't (the ideal)."[36]

Paul Griffiths describes the function of lament similarly, but he points out something else important in this discussion that is only nascent in Tolkien's narrative and Elam's treatment of it. Sorrow and lament are appropriate responses to particular evils. By this I mean lament shows "that we recognize the marks of damage in the devastation for what they are."[37] When we lament those marks, we recognize particular instances of damage. Proper sorrow requires perceiving a specific lack and lamenting it as a lack. For this reason, Griffiths identifies lament as kind of understanding, "an understanding that this, whatever is being lamented now, is not the way things should be."[38] The "whatever" of that last sentence is important, because it shows lament's specificity. You might feel sad about nothing in particular, sadness being an emotion. It makes no sense to say you are lamenting nothing in particular. Cries of lament have to do with things gone wrong, and things do not go wrong in general, but in identifiable ways. When something is evil, it is so because it lacks a particular good. Lamentation is a form of judgment about these lacks.[39]

The reason to distinguish sorrow or lament for particulars from the way things are *in toto* is that it is here that we see how the Christian grammar

35. Michael Elam, "The *Ainulindalë* and J. R. R. Tolkien's Beautiful Sorrow in Christian Tradition," *VII: An Anglo-American Literary Review* 28, no. 1 (2011): 68.

36. Elam, "The *Ainulindalë* and J. R. R. Tolkien's Beautiful Sorrow in Christian Tradition," 62.

37. Griffiths, *Decreation*, 327.

38. Griffiths, *Decreation*, 327.

39. Griffiths, *Decreation*, 332.

functions with respect to the permission of evils. It makes sense to say, and the tradition has affirmed magisterially, that God permits evil and that his permission of it is good insofar as it brings about greater good or prevents greater evil.[40] We have a way to say, "O, felix culpa." What we do not have—and ought not to desire—is a way of affirming the particular evils permitted as good. In other words, what is *felix* is not the *culpa* itself, but what is wrought with it. Having a place in the overall ordering of the cosmos does not make those evils good or excusable or somehow not as bad as they appear. Instead, the proper response to permitted evils, as we find in Tolkien, Elam, and Griffiths, is sorrow. Specific evils are always privations of particular goods. Even if God wields these evils to bring about a greater good than would otherwise have been possible, the evils that allow it to be so remain in themselves lamentable.

Romano Guardini sees the same inexorable logic at work in what we say about the crucified Lord. He asks about Jesus's mission, "Does God know that it will result in the death of the Messiah? Certainly, from eternity. And yet it should not happen. Does he will the death of Jesus? Certainly, from eternity. If the people close themselves off, his love has to go that way. But they should not close themselves off."[41] And in commenting on Jesus's own prophetic knowledge of this death's necessity—necessary in the way things which are willed from all eternity and yet also occasions for lament are necessary—in Luke 13, Guardini explains, "what God wills and what ought not to be are intertwined."[42] In the same passage he also says, "in the event that at last accomplishes the will of God, goods and evils are woven together."[43] This interweaving of good and evil in the accomplishment of God's will, coupled with the requirement for lamentation of those evils knotted into the tapestry,

40. Cf. *ST* 1.19.9 *ad* 3 and Leo XIII, *Libertas praestantissimum*, *DS* §3251.

41. Romano Guardini, *Der Herr: Betrachtungen über die Person und das Leben Jesu Christi* (Würzburg: Werkbund-Verlag, 1949), 266: "Weiß Gott, daß es zum Tode des Messias kommen wird? Gewiß, von Ewigkeit. Und dennoch soll es nicht geschehen. . . . Will er den Tod Jesu? Gewiß, von Ewigkeit. Wenn die Menschen sich verschließen, muß seine Liebe diesen Weg gehen. Aber sie sollen sich nicht verschließen."

42. Guardini, *Der Herr*, 262: "Wie das, was Gott will, und das, was nicht sein dürfte, ineinadergeht."

43. Guardini, *Der Herr*, 262: "wie in dem Geschehen, das zuletzt doch den Willen Gottes vollbringt, Gutes und Böses sich verweben."

is an encounter with mystery. We feel our understanding begin to fragment in the attempt to hold the pieces together.[44]

The fragmentation we encounter in the face of these twin obligations—to see the whole as good and give thanks for it and to recognize the evils as products of rebellion against God—marks the tragedy at the heart of the Christian life. The Christian form of life is tragic because we have to say, "O certe necessárium Adæ peccátum." What kind of necessity is this? Necessary because God wills the goods he brings about with it, necessary in order for those goods to be. Not absolute necessity, if by that we mean things cannot have been otherwise. It is because they could be otherwise but are not that they are possible objects of lament. They are necessary supposing the fact of this world, supposing God intends this world and not another. God intends it always as the world created and redeemed by him. The lamb is slain "from the foundation of the world" ("qui occissus est ab origine mundi") (Rev 13:8, Vulg.). The world is, in this sense, created so that it might be redeemed by Jesus Christ. The sin of Adam and the sin of Lucifer are not less blameworthy because of this kind of necessity. They are not because this necessity obtains only with respect to the "whole roll of ages," the ordered whole God brings about in his act of creation. It is within this cosmos that created freedom is exercised.

In another letter, to Michael Straight, Tolkien claims that God's (or Eru's) actions in the order of time, "produce realities which could not be deduced even from a complete knowledge of the previous past, but which being real become part of the effective past for all subsequent time (a possible definition of a 'miracle')."[45] In the case of the *certe necessarium Adæ peccatum*, its necessity derives from the salvific action of God's incarnation, life, death, and resurrection in Jesus Christ. Adam's sin is necessary *because* "it was destroyed by the death of Christ" ("Christi morte deletum est"), *because* it "merited such and so great a redeemer" ("talem ac tantum meruit habere Redepmtorem").[46] God's

44. Guardini, *Der Herr*, 266: "Wir merken, hier kommen wir mit unserem Menschenverstande nicht durch. Gottes ewiges Wissen und unsere Freiheit; das, was nicht geschehen soll, aber geschehen wird; die Gestalt, die das Erlösungswerk eigentlich haben sollte, und jene, die es tatsächlich haben wird—alles das liegt in einem für uns unscheidbaren Geheimnis ineinander."

45. Tolkien, *The Letters of J. R. R. Tolkien*, 235.

46. *Missale Romanum Cum Lectionibus*, 2, 352.

action in Christ makes it part of "the effective past." This is the same trajectory of thought Paul offers in Romans 11. There, he says, "God has consigned all men to disobedience, that he may have mercy upon all" (Rom 11:32). It is no wonder this verse is followed quickly by, "O the depth of the riches and wisdom and knowledge of God! How unsearchable are his judgments and how inscrutable his ways!" (Rom 11:33). Paul's recognition that it is God who has consigned all to disobedience and the *Exsultet*'s insistence on the necessity of Adam's sin follow a similar pattern. Both turn our usual ways of thinking about sequentially ordered causes and effects on their heads. God intends from all eternity to destroy death, to redeem, to have mercy. These have necessary antecedents. To destroy death, there must be dying things; to redeem, there must be someone in need of redemption; to have mercy, there must be someone who deserves punishment. What we are taught to say by the liturgy and Scripture is that what God accomplishes in Jesus Christ somehow makes necessary the sin of his creatures. That is, if God is to make this world and save it gratuitously, to have mercy upon all, it is also true that there must be a fall.

But with this realization we should also cry out, "Deliver me from my necessities" ("de necessitatibus meis erue me") (Ps 24:17, Vulg.). According to the lines sketched above, the kind of necessity we are dealing with is not made less lamentable for being necessary. Neither do the goods they occasion mean lament is no longer called for. Acknowledging this is the course Augustine recommends in book XIX of *De civitate Dei*. There he looks at the impossible task of the judge, who must act according to his duty in support of human society and who at the same time recognizes the limits to his capacity to know. Even in the case where the judge's decisions do not proceed from an evil will, they are often accompanied by evils. His necessities in this case are twofold: the necessity of human ignorance coupled with the necessity of judging. "How much more circumspect, how much worthier a human who acknowledges misery in that necessity, who despises it in itself and, faithfully wise, cries to God, *Deliver me from my necessities!*"[47] The wise man knows his duty and knows what doing it entails.

The kind of necessity we wish to be delivered from because it need not have been and (we hope) will not be in the future, is at the very heart of tragedy

47. Augustine, *civ.*, 19.6, *CSEL* 40.2:383: "Quanto consideratius et homine dignius agnoscit in ista necessitate miseriam eamque odit in se et, si pie sapit, clamat ad Deum: De necessitatibus meis erue me!"

as described by Terry Eagleton and Stanley Cavell. Sorrow's knowledge, which occasions lament, depends on our being able to recognize things would have been better had they been otherwise.[48] Eagleton is right to say, "'as it happens' is an essential qualification" for tragedy, since "most tragic episodes which prove inevitable do so for contingent reasons."[49] This fits with the grammar of Christian talk about evil. It is the will of voluntary creatures that brings evil about. And this is so even if the primordial evil is situated in an ancient or even pretemporal past. Ancient evils develop the stink of inevitability, even as we remain capable of seeing how a particular evil need not have been perpetrated. It is also the case that we are now, as Augustine noted, slaves of our necessities. Cavell thinks tragedy exists because we are able to see this sorry state of affairs. As he puts it, "There is nothing and we know there is nothing we can do. Tragedy is meant to make sense of that condition."[50] But Cavell knows there is *something* we can do. We can write and perform tragedy, for one. Tragedy, we might say, is the literary genre most fit to elicit the cry of the psalmist, "Deliver me from my necessities!" It does so by laying those necessities bare. It offers them to view and asks us to see them as our own. It calls on us to acknowledge those necessities and weep. And if tragedy is meant to make sense of knowing there is nothing we can do, perhaps weeping is the way we bear it.

Bearing our necessities by acknowledging them as tragic, as something to be delivered from, is the proper Christian response to the disorder of the cosmos. The alternative, given perfect expression by Mammon in book II of Milton's *Paradise Lost*,[51] is to cease to see the evils that confront us and

---

48. As Eagleton puts it, "It is not quite true, then, as Karl Jaspers claims, that 'when man faces the tragic, he liberates himself from it'. It is rather that the whole liberation is part of the tragedy; but it would be better if the whole action had not been necessary in the first place." Terry Eagleton, *Sweet Violence: The Idea of the Tragic* (Malden: Blackwell Publishers, 2003), 61.

49. Eagleton, *Sweet Violence*, 127.

50. Stanley Cavell, "The Avoidance of Love: A Reading of *King Lear*," in *Must We Mean What We Say?* (Cambridge: Cambridge University Press, 2012), 304.

51. John Milton, "Paradise Lost," in *The Poems of John Milton*, ed. Helen Darbishire (London: Oxford University Press, 1958). All subsequent references to Milton's *Paradise Lost* will be given in-line using a roman numeral and arabic numeral indicating, respectively, book and line numbers.

demand something from us as evil at all. In counselling his fellow demons away from repeated war against God, he attempts to assuage their fears about the fallen state, saying,

> *Our torments also may in length of time*
> *Become our Elements, these piercing Fires*
> *As soft as now severe, our temper chang'd*
> *Into their temper; which must needs remove*
> *The sensible of pain.*
> *(II.274–78)*

To become used to our fallen state and so cease to be troubled by it is the devil's reasoning. The judge who did not lament the twin necessities of ignorance and duty would be a pitiable figure indeed. So too, Ulysses, who fails to see how he is implicated in the disorder when he embraces it as a tool for his stratagems—his torments become his elements. And when the disorder and death that permeate the cosmos fail to elicit our tears—Milton's "our temper" pointing out a certain hard-heartedness—we succumb to callousness that is a failure of faith and hope.

Before we move on to Troilus's response, I want to look at one more scene in the creation narrative of the *Silmarillion*. Tolkien's work offers a depiction of what it means to say greater goods come about as the result of evils. After the singing has ended, Eru shows the Ainur a vision of what they have wrought with their voices.[52] One of the Ainur, Ulmo—charged with stewardship of water—sees the effects of Melkor's discordant music on his own singing once both are caught up into Eru's architectonic theme. Ulmo wove the waters of the seas, rivers, and fountains. Melkor's music was bitter cold and blazing hot as he attacked the work of Ulmo and the other Ainur. His assaults on the waters issue in something neither Ulmo nor Melkor expected. The cold did not destroy Ulmo's work. Instead it produced snow and frost. The heat did not dry up the seas. It brought clouds and mist and the patter of rain upon the earth. Creation's beauty is not lessened but increased by Melkor's evils when put to work by Eru. Ulmo is moved to say, "Truly, Water is become now fairer than my heart imagined, neither had my secret thought conceived the snowflake,

52. Tolkien, *The Silmarillion*, 17.

nor in all my music was contained the falling of the rain."[53] Ulysses's nostalgic response to disorder cannot imagine this. The world coming apart at the seams brooks no hope for anything but an unapproachable past. Insofar as we are tempted to Ulysses's response, we have failed to understand how God responds to evil. Until we understand our responsibility to recognize and weep over the ills of the world and at the same time turn our faces in faith and hope to the one who can bend even radical evil toward the accomplishment of his ends, we have not grasped the tragedy of the Christian life evident in the orientation of our fallen wills toward God.

Troilus on Being the Truth

In my reading of Ulysses's "Degree Speech," I mentioned Agamemnon's words, asking his captains why they look so glum at the prospect of ongoing battle with the Trojans. Agamemnon's proposed purpose for the constant trials of war was, "To find persistive constancy in men" (1.3.21). "Constancy" bears particularly upon the two title characters of the play, Troilus and Cressida, who attempt a courtship in the midst of war. The question of whether "persistive constancy" is possible in the fractured world of the play is an important one for the pair of lovers. Tony Tanner, in his *Prefaces to Shakespeare*, answers in the negative, "It is not to be found in this play, in which there is more discontinuity and instability of character than anywhere else in Shakespeare."[54] This does not prevent Troilus from developing an obsession with constancy which threatens to overturn the whole enterprise of love. In Troilus's relentless pursuit of Cressida's constancy he proves himself inconstant. If this play is a tragedy this is why.

It is Troilus's continued demands for Cressida to "be true" (4.4.74) that bespeak what John Kerrigan calls Troilus's "fetishization of constancy."[55] It is not enough for Cressida to plight her troth; playing with the senses of "plight," Troilus doubts her capacity "to keep her constancy in plight" (3.2.161). He demands of her persistive, uninflected, absolute constancy. If Tanner is right,

53. Tolkien, *The Silmarillion*, 19.

54. Tony Tanner, *Prefaces to Shakespeare* (Cambridge, MA: The Belknap Press of Harvard University Press, 2010), 591–92.

55. John Kerrigan, *Shakespeare's Binding Language* (Oxford: Oxford University Press, 2016), 264.

no such thing is available in the world of this play. What I would like to ask is whether the constancy demanded by Troilus ever makes sense, whether it is ever a live option, not just in the play but in our world as well. If it is not, what does the desire for it mean, for Troilus and for us? This brings me to another sort of response to the disordered cosmos. In the seeming absence of order—having no eye for providence—Troilus tries to take it upon himself to *be* the order of the cosmos. Troilus recognizes his hubris as demonic when he worries over the possibility of Cressida's temptation, saying, "And sometimes we are devils to ourselves, / When we will tempt the frailty of our powers, / Presuming on their changeful potency" (4.4.95–97). But he is unable to see how these words apply to himself, only others. He demands an inhuman constancy from Cressida, removed from all consideration of circumstance. Fear that she will betray him prevents Troilus from receiving the sort of constancy creatures of "changeful potency" can offer. He is condemned by his own words, "Fears make devils of cherubins, they never see truly" (3.2.70). In the end it is he who is found wanting, not for demanding too little but too much from himself and others.

There are a few key moments in the play that illustrate Troilus's presumption. I will highlight these before showing how Troilus bears a resemblance to the Satan of John Milton's *Paradise Lost*. This opens up a broader discussion meant to address one of the failures that comes from an inclination to accept the Ulyssean view of the disordered cosmos. In all this, I intend to make good on my promise to give an account of evil's origin in Satan's disordered will. To do so, I will draw in some theological treatments of Satan's sin and offer a speculative account relating Troilus's desire to be the truth to the primordial angelic sin.

The first hint of Troilus's desire to transcend human limitation comes during the Trojan council. The occasion forms a matched pair with the Greek war council in which Ulysses delivers his "Degree Speech." Where the Greeks wonder why the war must continue with no hint of resolution, the Trojans debate the cost of the conflict and the worth of Helen. Hector argues at the outset that they ought to let Helen go, having received a promise from Nestor that this will end the hostilities. The cost of continued fighting, he says, is more than Helen is worth (2.2.1–25). To this suggestion, Troilus replies,

> *Fie, fie, my brother!*
> *Weigh you the worth and honor of a king*
> *So great as our dread father's in a scale*

> *Of common ounces? Will you with compters sum*
> *The past-proportion of his infinite,*
> *And buckle in a waist most fathomless*
> *With spans and inches so diminutive*
> *As fears and reasons? Fie, for godly shame!*
> (2.2.25–32)

Troilus's response to Hector's claim that the cost in blood is too great "To guard a thing not ours nor worth to us" (2.2.22) changes the register of the claim to value. We are not arguing over Helen's worth, but Priam's and so all Troy's. And that, Troilus declares, simply offers no scale for drawing Hector's conclusion. Priam is "infinite," "fathomless," and all forms of measure are against him "diminutive," especially cowardly "fears and reasons." But Troilus is making demands of his father's legacy and honor that cannot be met. Troilus desires to be without limit and demands his father be so, too. The casualty in this fight is the ability to offer reasons for your actions. He goes so far as to repudiate the attempt. "Reason and respect," Troilus says, "Make livers pale and lustihood deject" (2.2.49–50). His brother, Helenus, is a coward, Troilus argues, as much for attempting to reckon his father's limits as for fear of the enemy's sword.

Hector insists on his original assessment of Helen, that "she is not worth what she doth cost / The keeping" (2.2.51–52). Troilus replies with one of the play's crucial lines, "What's aught but as 'tis valued?" (2.2.52). Tanner comments, "Troilus is saying, or implying, that there are no intrinsic values, only attributed ones. Coming from a young man who regards himself as exemplifying, as incorporating, an absolute standard of fidelity, this is somewhat inconsistent—but inconsistency prevails in the play."[56] But this need not be seen as evidence of Troilus's inconsistency. Instead, in the face of what he sees as the disordering of valuation, Troilus retreats into an entirely subjective mode of judgment. You can see this change clearly by looking back to the play's first act. After an interchange with Pandarus about his unfulfilled desire for Cressida, Troilus hears an alarum. Here is his reply,

> *Peace, you ungracious clamors! peace, rude sounds!*
> *Fools on both sides, Helen must needs be fair,*

56. Tanner, *Prefaces to Shakespeare*, 595.

> *When with your blood you daily paint her thus.*
> *I cannot fight upon this argument;*
> *It is too starv'd a subject for my sword.*
> (1.1.89–93)

Troilus is unprepared to fight for Helen on the terms given him. She cannot be fair as she must be for so much blood to be spilt on her account. What change occurs between this scene and the Trojan council in the second act? Troilus is determined to find a subject less "starv'd" than Helen's fairness. Troilus is looking for something that can account for the whole world being turned upside down.

If we read Troilus's "What's aught but as 'tis valued?" as a genuine and not a rhetorical question, his words seem less inconsistent and more like a drive for consistency, or constancy. He is trying to make sense of the war up to this point. He rejects the "cramm'd reason" (2.2.49) of his brothers that would attempt to determine whether to continue the war based on the worth of Helen herself. If that is the reason, the war never made sense. At the same time, he rails against the council's inconsistency,

> *If you'll avouch 'twas wisdom Paris went—*
> *As you must needs, for you all cried "Go, go"—*
> *If you'll confess he brought home worthy prize—*
> *As you must needs, for you all clapp'd your hands,*
> *And cried "Inestimable!"—why do you now*
> *The issue of your proper wisdoms rate,*
> *And do a deed that never Fortune did,*
> *Beggar the estimation which you priz'd*
> *Richer than sea and land?*
> (2.2.84–92)

Priam's youngest son has come to a decision. To make sense of his father's and brothers' decision to support the "fair rape" (2.2.148) of Helen, he cannot believe they ever did so on account of her beauty. He "cannot fight upon this argument" and neither could they, if they are being honest. The fact of the war points to other criteria. To make sense of the lives lost in combat, it must be that value does dwell, contra Hector, "in particular will" (2.2.53). That particular will must make its object not Helen, but the honor of Priam and Troy herself. Even then, he must suppose that value infinite, fathomless, if he is supposed to kill and die for it. Helen is but "A spur to valiant and magnanimous deeds" (2.2.200), not the source of valuation of the action. Troilus shows himself opposed to the "cramm'd reason" of his brothers that would attempt to decide on the basis of Helen. By contrast, his reason is capacious, reclining on its own estimations of worth coupled with an inflexible commitment to the will's judgments once made. "There can be no evasion / To blench from this and to stand firm by honor" (2.2.67–68). Absolute constancy and infinite valuation are his answer to the uncertain, disordered world of *Troilus and Cressida*.

The effects of Troilus's turn to subjective value, coupled with the demand for unflinching commitment to the will's determination, is a powerful tool. It offers Troilus a way to make sense of the scale of bloodshed. It at once offers protection and a goad to heroic action when the objective reasons he can muster surely fail. Neither Priam's honor nor Helen's fairness are things of infinite value in themselves. But, as Troilus says, there is a limit to what reason can accomplish in cases like this. He is arguing against the straightforward moral calculus of his brother Hector, which would reduce Helen's situation to a syllogism: "Nature craves / all dues be rend'red to their owners" (2.2.173–74). The wife's due should be rendered to the husband, "What nearer debt in all humanity / Than wife is to the husband?" (2.2.175–76). Ergo, "If Helen then be wife to Sparta's king, / As it is known she is, these moral laws, / of nature and of nations speak aloud / To have here back return'd" (2.2.183–86). If this is true, it never made sense to take Helen in the first place. Troilus, in an attempt to make sense where none seems to lie, overshoots his target and settles on constancy of will. He overshoots his target because his way of dealing with the predicament lands him somewhere nonsensical, though not inconsistent. The demands of his solution end up being too high.

Troilus has settled on a form of valuation rooted in the "particular will" (2.2.53). Hector is right to accuse him of a shaky voluntarism. But looking beyond the Trojan council we can see the further implications of Troilus's new moral posture. In act III, scene 2, when Troilus and Cressida meet for the first time, the limitations of his stance become apparent. After Pandarus promises to bring Cressida to meet him, Troilus soliloquizes, giving us a look at his state of mind. "I am giddy; expectation whirls me round; / Th' imaginary relish is so sweet / That it enchants my sense" (3.2.18–20). What he might mean by having his sense enchanted is answered a few lines later, when he explains the fear, "That I shall lose distinction in my joys, / As doth a battle, when they charge on heaps / The enemy flying" (3.2.27–29). More than a reference to the fog of war, Troilus's mention of battle can be read as further commentary on his attempt to save the appearances of the Trojan War by attributing worth to subjective valuation. Troilus recognizes that the same method of reckoning value might soon overtake his relationship with Cressida.

The Troilus of the first act of the play, in the same soliloquy in which he explains he cannot wage war on the basis of Helen's fairness alone, also says this of Cressida,

> *Her bed is India, there she lies, a pearl;*
> *Between our Ilium and where she resides,*
> *Let it be call'd the wild and wand'ring flood*
> *Ourself the merchant, and this sailing Pandar*
> *Our doubtful hope, our convoy, and our bark.*
> *(1.1.100–104)*

Cressida is a pearl that stands apart from Troilus. Her uncle, Pandarus, is the go-between. Troilus sees the commercial quality of this transaction and bemoans it. Yet looking forward again to the Trojan council we find similar words on the lips of Troilus:

> *Is she worth keeping? Why, she is a pearl,*
> *Whose price hath launch'd above a thousand ships,*
> *And turn'd crown'd kings to merchants.*
> *(2.2.81–83)*

There is a lot going on here, with references to Marlowe's *Doctor Faustus* and the Gospel of Matthew elaborating the callback to Troilus's words in act I. If the reference to merchants and pearls from the first act did not spur the memory of Matthew 13, where the merchant finds "one pearl of great value" (Matt 13:46), these lines from act II leave the reader with no doubt. But is Troilus speaking of Helen or Cressida? The *mis*quotation of Marlowe, having "launch'd *above* a thousand ships" makes the referent doubtful.[57] But mention of the pearl in the lines from both act I and act II inclines me to imagine Troilus's mind wandering toward Cressida even as he argues in defense of Helen. Is she worth keeping? he wonders. In this conjunction of allusions we can see the same shift in valuation I described above in Troilus's attempts to make sense of the Trojan War. Cressida, as the pearl, is identified with the "kingdom of heaven" (Matt 13:45). She is imputed with an infinite value by Troilus. A valuation that still rises and falls on his "particular will."

In both cases—his love for Cressida and his dedication to ongoing war over Helen—Troilus has laid a trap for himself. In retreating from the moral calculus of his fellow Trojan nobles, he has landed where no distinctions are possible and proceeded to burn his boats. He fears, in act III, scene 2, "That I shall lose distinction in my joys" (3.2.27), but by that point distinction is already lost. The switch to purely subjective valuation coupled with absolute determination and, insulated by force of will from any external considerations, makes any such distinction impossible. This becomes increasingly evident in his interchanges with Cressida. Troilus sees the impossibility, and recognizes the horror of it, when he says, "This is the monstruosity in love, lady, that the will is infinite and the execution confin'd, that the desire is boundless and the act a slave to limit" (3.2.81–83). Troilus casts the terms of discussion as limitless. Cressida, perhaps a bit taken aback, replies with a bawdy joke (3.2.84–89). Uncowed or oblivious, Troilus answers her in earnest, ending with the assurance that "what truth can speak truest not truer than Troilus" (3.2.97–98). This is Troilus's repeated claim. All of Cressida's worries and uncertainties, which are genuine enough in the world of the play, are dismissed. She the daughter of a traitor in the midst of an endless war, he the son of the king, whom her father has betrayed. What stability can truly be had? She doubts even herself (cf. 3.2.147–51). But then comes Troilus's insistence, "I am as true as truth's simplicity" (3.2.169). Not only that, but "True swains in love shall in the world to come / Approve their truth by Troilus" (3.2.173–74). At this point, a brazen sequence follows. Troilus rehearses the

57. Faustus's lines from Marlowe's play run, "Was this the face that launch'd a thousand ships / And burnt the topless towers of Ilium?" Christopher Marlowe, *Doctor Faustus* (London: Routledge, 1965), 18.99–100.

ordered relations of creatures—and their witness to the nature of truth—in the natural world. Those swains who find their truth in comparison to Troilus's would discover,

> *When their rhymes,*
> *Full of protest, of oath and big compare,*
> *Wants similes, truth tir'd with iteration,*
> *As true as steel, as plantage to the moon,*
> *As sun to day, as turtle to her mate,*
> *As iron to adamant, as earth to th' centre,*
> *Yet after all comparisons of truth*
> *(As truth's authentic author to be cited)*
> *"As true as Troilus" shall crown up the verse,*
> *And sanctify the numbers.*
> (3.2.174–83)

This claim is astonishing in its forthrightness. Coupled with the two preceding references to Troilus's truthfulness, or rather, Troilus *as* truth, he is doing more than assuring Cressida of his honesty. Confronted by cosmic disorder, Troilus has taken it upon himself to *be* the truth.

In these verses Troilus makes explicit what up to now was only implicit in his attempts to make sense of the war and of his own limitless love for Cressida. He judges himself "truth's authentic author" whose infinite will is the yardstick against which all truth is not only measured, but even sanctified! Putting up so radical a claim, Troilus has issued a direct challenge to God, who is, in fact, invoked in the preceding scene by a servant in a comical exchange with Pandarus (3.1.5, 8). Shakespeare reminds us that though the play's setting lies in pagan antiquity, its context remains a squarely Christian one. Troilus's attempts to make sense of his world, a world wrecked by war, by the hunt for glory premised on a confrontation in which "All the argument is a whore and a cuckold" (2.3.72–73) results in total retreat into the self. His refusals are twofold. Troilus will not countenance the possibility that the war is what Thersites recognizes it to be. There must be more to all this bloodshed. In doing so, he also refuses his human limits. The only way to make sense of things, as far as Troilus is concerned, is to locate the source of value in his own will, ascribing to himself the role of God who is the truth (John 14:6). In this he shares Ulysses's inability to see an order that could encompass tragedy and redeem it. But even Ulysses's response did not swerve into this territory. He attempted to correct disorder but never to *be* the order of the world. Troilus is guilty not just of misprision but of pride. This difference makes Troilus's response diabolical.

How Lucifer Became Satan

John Milton's Satan in *Paradise Lost* resembles Shakespeare's Troilus. One of the most pronounced similarities is found in his response—when faced with the (apparent) disorder of the cosmos—to take the task of ordering upon himself. In Milton, it is during the angel Raphael's recounting Lucifer's rebellion to Adam that this similarity comes into focus. In book V of *Paradise Lost* Raphael is sent by God to warn Adam and Eve of their danger. By this point in the poem Satan has made his way from hell through Chaos, arrived at Earth, and penetrated its angelic defenses. He has done all this in the hope the fallen angels might more successfully "wage by force or guile eternal Warr" (I.121).[58] In the first book, the fallen Satan sees that God in his providence plans to bring about good from the evil of the angels' turn, explaining,

> *Our labour must be to pervert that end,*
> *And out of good still find means of evil;*
> *Which oft times may succeed, so as perhaps*
> *Shall grieve him, if I fail not, and disturb*
> *His inmost counsels from their destind aim.*
> *(I.164–68)*

Satan shows that he misapprehends the role God and God's providence play and how. Just as in Tolkien's *The Silmarillion*, great evils are only ever permitted by God to bring about greater goods. There is no getting behind God's will to "disturb / His inmost counsels from their destind aim." But this raises problems about the story of Lucifer recruiting angels to his cause in book V. While we may be able to see how a fallen angel could be mistaken about the nature and scope of God's providence, it makes less sense to say so before the fall. Attending to Raphael's account

58. From this point forward all references to Milton's *Paradise Lost* will be given in line.

of the angelic fall, and to the origin of Lucifer's rebellion, will help us to see how such a thing is even possible.

Raphael begins by explaining that what he has to tell Adam cannot be told straightforwardly, and so "what surmounts the reach / Of human sense, I shall delineat so, / By lik'ning spiritual to corporeal forms, / As may express them best" (V.571–74). This can be read as Milton's own apology for the treatment that follows. In the next few lines, Raphael (Milton?) wonders whether "Earth / Be but the shaddow of Heav'n, and things therein / Each to other like, more then on Earth is thought?" (V.574–76). With this caveat and its tentative recision in place, Raphael presses on with his tale. All the heavenly host is arrayed before God, when God the Father makes this proclamation:

> *Hear all ye Angels, Progenie of Light,*
> *Thrones, Dominations, Princedoms, Vertues, Powers,*
> *Hear my Decree, which unrevok't shall stand.*
> *This day I have begot whom I declare*
> *My onely Son, and on this holy Hill*
> *Him have anointed, whom ye now behold*
> *At my right hand; your Head I him appoint;*
> *And by my Self have sworn to him shall bow*
> *All knees in Heav'n, and shall confess him Lord*
> (V.600–608)

First, it is necessary to establish the subject of this decree. Is the Father's "onely Son" Jesus Christ, the Lord incarnate? There are good reasons to think so. An alternative approach might suppose that the Father here issues a decree about the Son in his divine nature only, the *Logos asarkos*. Much recommends this view. Raphael has just told Adam the events he is recounting took place when, "As yet this World was not, and *Chaos* wilde / Reignd where these Heav'ns now rowl, where Earth now rests / Upon her Center pois'd" (V.577–79). But this is straightforwardly true only if we are dealing with events occurring in the order of time. Remember, Raphael said he would have to make spiritual things intelligible in terms corporeal. He mentions the "Time" of heaven, but also says it is time "in Eternitie" (V.580), which argues for thinking of it as something less pellucid than the sequential order of time here below. This argues for Raphael trying to express something to Adam in terms he will understand.

I read this text to be referring to Jesus Christ as the "onely Son" who has ascended to his heavenly throne "in Eternitie." The first clue supporting this reading comes in the description of the Son having been anointed "on this holy Hill" (V.604–5). The reference to the Son being God's anointed, his Christ, the Messiah, seems a clear reference to the incarnate Son, Jesus. Jesus, not the fleshless Son in his divinity alone, is the Christ. The "holy Hill" could then be one of two places. It could be Golgotha, the place of Jesus's death on the cross. Golgotha is a good candidate because it is there that Jesus fulfills his mission as the anointed one. Another possibility, which I prefer, is to take the holy hill to be Mount Tabor. This is a better candidate because it is on Tabor that time and eternity touch for a brief moment in the transfiguration. Peter, John, and James who accompanied Jesus, "saw his glory" (Luke 9:32; cf. Matt 17:2, Mark 9:3) on that hill. It is there that Moses and Elijah converse with Jesus (Luke 9:30–31; cf. Matt 17:3, Mark 9:4). Finally, on Tabor there is a proclamation of the Father affirming, in Luke's gospel, that Jesus is his Son, the chosen one (Luke 9:35), and in Matthew and Mark, that Jesus is the Father's beloved Son (Matt 17:5, Mark 9:7). This forms a parallel to the Father's proclamation to the angels in heaven as described by Milton. The transfiguration is a moment in the narrative of Jesus's life that reveals his divinity to some of his followers. The way this is done, alongside two of the greatest, but long dead, prophets, points to this event occurring in a time outside of time. Likewise, the descent of a cloud, with echoes of the events upon Mount Sinai, points to a coincidence of the order of time and the order of eternity.

A second piece of evidence is found when the Father locates the Son "At my right hand" (V.606). This again is an explicit reference to Jesus. In the New Testament, the one seated at the Father's right hand is always the resurrected and ascended Jesus. The New Testament writings are citing Psalm 110, "The Lord says to my lord: 'Sit at my right hand, till I make your enemies your footstool" (Ps 110:1).[59] Apart from the five direct quotations of Psalm 110 in the New Testament, this locution identifying Jesus as the one "at the right hand of God" occurs at least fourteen times.[60] It is the enfleshed Lord whom Stephen

59. This verse appears as a quotation of the Psalm in the gospels of Matthew, Mark, and Luke, and again in Acts and Hebrews (Matt 22:44, Mark 12:36, Luke, 20:42, Acts 2:34, and Heb 1:13).

60. Matt 26:64, Mark 14:62, 16:19, Luke 22:69, Acts 2:33, 5:31, 7:55–56, Rom 8:34, Eph 1:20, Col 3:1, Heb 8:1, 10:12, 12:2, 1 Pet 3:22.

sees "standing at the right hand of God" (Acts 7:56) when the heavens open up before his martyrdom. And it is at God's right hand that Jesus Christ "sat down" after he "had offered for all time a single sacrifice for sins" (Heb 10:12). The reference to the Son being at the Father's right hand should immediately incline our thoughts toward the incarnation.

I will treat the third and fourth pieces of evidence together. Saying the Son has been appointed "Head" is again a reference to Jesus Christ, who, as Paul says, "is the head of the body, the church" (Col 1:18; cf. Eph 1:22, 5:23). Add to that Milton's reference to Philippians 2 with the Father's declaration that "to him shall bow / All knees in Heav'n, and shall confess him Lord" (V.607–8). In Paul's letter to the Philippians, it is to Jesus that knees "in heaven and on earth and under the earth" (Phil 2:10) bend, and it is Jesus Christ whom every tongue will confess is Lord (Phil 2:11). Milton wants to draw the reader's attention not just to the second person of the Trinity in his divinity, but to the second person of the Trinity who is the God-man, the Word-flesh. With this in mind, there are two things to do. First, I need to show how this emphasis on the incarnate Lord colors our reading of Lucifer's rebellion recounted in book V of *Paradise Lost*. And second, I need to situate these reflections on angelic rebellion against the person of Jesus Christ within the broader theological tradition. Although it is a minority view, Milton is inheriting a long line of reasoning by depicting Lucifer rejecting Jesus Christ.

Satan—we need to call him Satan now, Milton says (V.658)—hears the proclamation of God the Father to his great dismay. Like Thomas Aquinas, Milton thinks it likely that Lucifer was made at the pinnacle of the created order, "hee of the first, / If not the first Arch-Angel, great in Power, / In favour and præeminence" (V.659–61). The light-bearer turned deceiver envies the Son of God (V.662). It is an envy born of pride, says Milton (V.665). He "could not bear" the sight of the Son elevated as he was (V.664). Raphael says Satan "thought himself impaird" (V.665) by the Son's advancement. One of the payoffs of reading the subject of the Father's speech as Jesus and not the discarnate Word is the sense it makes of these verses. Lucifer, situated at the pinnacle of the created order, sees himself subordinated to another and is envious. This other would not be a candidate for this kind of envy if we were dealing with the second person of the Trinity considered in his divinity apart from his humanity. Lucifer knew God as only an angel can, immediately and intuitively. God's triunity is one of the things he would apprehend in this manner. That the second person of the Trinity should be considered before him in honor can hardly have been a matter displeasing to even the highest angel. There is no reason to think he would resent the Son's divinity any more than he would resent the Father's or the Holy Spirit's. Something about the Son causes Satan to think himself injured.

The text of *Paradise Lost* illuminates Satan's rebellion by pointing to the incarnation of the Son as its precipitating cause. Satan awakens his sleeping companion, "his next subordinate" (V.671) in heaven, the one named in hell as, "One next himself in power, and next in crime" (I.79), the demon Beëlzebub (I.81). To him Satan complains of the "new laws" (V.679) instituted during God the Father's proclamation. The most interesting lines come at the close of his discourse. Satan has his second go forth to assemble those under his command:

> *The Quarters of the North, there to prepare*
> *Fit entertainment to receive our King*
> *The great* Messiah, *and his new commands,*
> *Who speedily through all the Hierarchies*
> *Intends to pass triumphant, and give Laws.*
> *(V.689–93)*

This is an explicit reference to the Messiah, which explains Satan's complaint that he intends to pass "speedily through all Hierarchies." This could only be addressed to the Son possessed of both a divine and creaturely nature, Jesus Christ. Satan's difficulty is the elevation of the created nature of Jesus Christ above all other created natures. Humans, made of corporeal and incorporeal elements, flesh and spirit, stand below angels by nature. By grace, human nature is elevated "through all the Hierarchies" and enthroned with glory above even the highest angel.

The Letter to the Hebrews says of Jesus Christ: "When he had made purification for sins, he sat down at the right hand of the Majesty on high, having become as much superior to angels as the name he has obtained is more excellent than theirs" (Heb 1:3–4). This is what motivates Satan's envy in Milton's *Paradise Lost*. Seeing a created nature placed above his own to "give Laws" (V.693) seems unbearable to him. He "thought himself impaird" (V.665). His inability to endure this inclines him to sin.

Before exploring the nature of angelic sin, I want to point out how Milton's Satan resembles Shakespeare's Troilus in his response to the perceived disorder of the cosmos. The concept of "degree" features heavily in this section of *Paradise Lost*, as it did in *Troilus and Cressida*. Setting the stage for Satan's council in the North of heaven, Raphael says of him, "great indeed / His name, and high was his degree in Heav'n" (V.706–7). Satan then asks, addressing the host he has gathered to rebel against God,

> *Will ye submit your necks, and chuse to bend*
> *The supple knee? ye will not, if I trust*
> *To know ye right, or if ye know your selves*
> *Natives and Sons of Heav'n possest before*
> *By none, and if not equall all, yet free,*
> *Equally free; for Orders and Degrees*
> *Jarr not with liberty, but well consist.*
> *(V.787–93)*

Satan considers degree itself good, yet successfully convinces his companion angels that to presume to rule over those "who without law / Erre not" (V.798–99) is a grave violation of their freedom. Satan's deception is successful in the case of all but Abdiel, who affirms God created all things "in thir bright degrees" (V.838), through his Word. Satan embraces the idea of hierarchical ordering by degree. He sees, however, the elevation of a created nature above his own as a fundamental overturning of the order of things. Much like Troilus it is what he perceives as an overvaluation of a particular person—in Satan's case Jesus Christ and in Troilus's case Helen—that precipitates a crisis.

Abdiel, the lone faithful holdout of Satan's host, sees Satan's mistake with respect to degree and attempts to offer a correction. Far from "impaird" (V.665), Satan should understand that in making all things and marking them out by degree God,

> *Crownd them with Glory, and to their Glory nam'd*
> *Thrones, Dominations, Princedoms, Vertues, Powers,*
> *Essential Powers, nor by his Reign obscur'd,*
> *But more illustrious made, since hee the Head*
> *One of our number thus reduc't becomes,*
> *His Laws our Laws, all honour to him done*
> *Returns our own.*
> *(V.839–45)*

The rule of God does not infringe upon created freedom, it glorifies it. The honor redounds to God in a way that elevates the creature who submits to God's rule. Abdiel returns to the heart of the matter, the incarnation, when he refers to "hee the Head" who "One of our number thus reduc't becomes." It is the honor done to him, the Head who has become a creature, that is sure to magnify the glory of the angels. Abdiel inveighs against Satan's rejection of the incarnate Word.

Satan's rejection comes as the result of what seems to him a disturbance of the created order. But what he thinks of as a disordering of the hierarchy of creation is, if we follow Abdiel, a revelation of creation's proper order. It is "more illustrious made" (V.842) by the incarnation and ascension into heaven of the God-man. In this there is a dissimilarity between Troilus and Satan. The epistemic condition of the two characters follows a similar pattern. It seems wrong to each that one person be elevated above what is naturally called for. But in the order of being, the situation is not the same. Troilus is a sympathetic figure insofar as we can recognize the psychic wound done to him by the war when he says, "I cannot fight upon this argument" (1.1.92). He is facing a real difficulty. It is a reasonable thing to wonder whether Helen's life is worth the blood daily spilt on her behalf. Satan's situation is much less ambiguous. God the Father commands that Satan bend the knee to the incarnate Son. He will not. There is good reason to think Troilus perceives rightly the disordered state of affairs in Troy. Satan is wrong to see God's command as a disordering of the cosmos.

Satan's attempt to be God is on full display in his response to Abdiel's admonition. Instead of receiving Abdiel's correction, Satan replies as a skeptic. "Who saw / When this creation was? rememberst thou / Thy making, while the Maker gave thee being?" (V.856–58). He doubts God's trustworthiness and his own creaturely nature. He continues, more extravagantly,

> *We know no time when we were not as now;*
> *Know none before us, self-begot, self-rais'd*
> *By our own quick'ning power, when fatal course*
> *Had circl'd his full Orbe, the birth mature*
> *Of this our native Heav'n, Ethereal Sons.*
> *(V.859–63)*

Not knowing when or how he was created and no longer trusting God's proper ordering of the cosmos, he appropriates the role of creator to himself. Satan refuses to be the handiwork of another. Troilus claimed to be the truth. Satan claims to be the creator. And with this claim, he sends Abdiel to act as messenger "to th' anointed King" (V.870), Christ himself, to tell him,

> *Our puissance is our own, our own right hand*
> *Shall teach us highest deeds, by proof to try*
> *Who is our equal: then thou shalt behold*
> *Whether by supplication we intend*
> *Address, and to begirt th' Almighty Throne*
> *Beseeching or besieging.*
> *(V.864–69)*

Satan counts on his own strength to determine what is right, to "teach us highest deeds." It is clear that he will no longer evaluate his actions against any standard but his own might. In doing so he issues a threat. This "self-begot" angel will confront God himself with arms.

Situating Milton's Satan

Milton's Satan and Shakespeare's Troilus both attempt usurpations. Each takes a perceived disorder as license to refashion the cosmos in his own image, seeking to make himself the *regula* or *ratio* of the created order. In Milton's narrative this rebellion originates in a confrontation with the one who is the *ratio* of the cosmos. This is telling, and situates Milton's Satan in the broader theological tradition. To show where he fits, I will look to Jonathan Edwards, Matthias Scheeben, and Francisco Suárez. The Church's magisterium has not weighed in determinatively on the precipitating cause of the angelic fall, other than to say it is accomplished voluntarily by the angels. For this reason, it is a properly speculative matter. With the help of these thinkers, I will place Milton's account of the angels' fall within the theological tradition. In doing so, I will be looking for the roots of the doctrine and examining some of its entailments.

The idea that Satan's fall was precipitated by his knowledge of the incarnation is something argued for by Jonathan Edwards. There are a number of entries in his *Miscellanies* on the fall of the angels. In a section called "Devils," Edwards glosses the angelic fall this way:

> It seems to me probable that the temptation of the angels that occasioned their rebellion was that when God was about to create man, or had first created him, God declared his decree to the angels that one of that human nature should be his Son, his best beloved, his greatest favorite, and should be united to his eternal Son, and that he should be their head and king; that they should be given to him and should worship him and be his servants, attendants and ministers. And God, having thus declared his great love to the race of mankind, gave the angels the charge of them as ministering spirits to men. Satan, or Lucifer, or Beelzebub, being the archangel, one of the highest of the angels, could not bear it, thought it below him and a great debasing of him; so he conceived rebellion against the Almighty and drew away a vast company of the heavenly hosts with him.[61]

Like Thomas Aquinas and Milton, Edwards places Lucifer at the apex of the created order. In another place Edwards says, commenting on Isaiah 14:12, "This angel, before his fall, was the chief of all the angels, of greatest natural capacity, strength, and wisdom, and highest in honor and dignity, the brightest of all those stars of heaven, as is signified by what is said of him under that type of the devil, the king of Babylon."[62] Edwards also affirms the position taken in the last chapter, that the angels serve as ministers of the created order to bring about God's providential plan. In this vein, Edwards says Lucifer is given a certain dominion over the whole of

61. Jonathan Edwards, *The "Miscellanies": (Entry Nos. A–Z, Aa–Zz, 1–500)*, Works of Jonathan Edwards Online (New Haven, CT: Yale University, Jonathan Edwards Center, 2008), no. 320, pp. 401–2.

62. Jonathan Edwards, *The "Miscellanies": 833–1152*, Works of Jonathan Edwards Online (New Haven, CT: Yale University, Jonathan Edwards Center, 2008), no. 936, pp. 190–91.

creation.[63] His position resembles that of Gregory of Nyssa, who also took Satan to have had governance over the world prior to his fall.[64]

In his *Die Mysterien des Christenthums*, Matthias Scheeben calls this idea, that God revealed the incarnation of his Son to the angels, "a pretty commonly taught opinion."[65] He does not cite any sources, but does say that the opinion is something of an entailment of the teaching of "several Fathers" who "posit the sin of the angels in the envy of man."[66] It is possible that Scheeben had in mind Gregory of Nyssa's *Oratio catechetica*, where the devil's envy is a critical theme. To summarize Gregory's view, the angel given power over the earth grows envious upon witnessing the creation of humans and God's gift of his own image and likeness. The angel had been given the task of governing the world, and yet one beneath him was honored with a dignity surpassing even his own.[67] In Scheeben's argument, there is nothing in humanity itself, even the dignity of the image and likeness of God, that could incite the envy of the highest angel. The only thing that could produce such envy from Lucifer would be the knowledge "that a member of the human race was destined to the dignity of the Son of God and so to be head and king of the angel."[68] The revelation of God's hypostatic union with human nature is too much to bear for Lucifer and those who follow him. Scheeben recognizes the revelation as

63. Edwards, *The "Miscellanies": 833–1152*, no. 936, p. 191.

64. Gregory of Nyssa, *The Catechetical Oration of St. Gregory of Nyssa*, trans. J. H. Srawley (London: Society for Promoting Christian Knowledge, 1917), §6, pp. 40–41. *PG* 45, col. 28.

65. Matthias Joseph Scheeben, *Die Mysterien des Christenthums: Wesen, Bedeutung und Zusammenhang Derselben nach der in ihrem Übernatülichen Charakter Gegebenen Perspective* (Freiburg im Breisgau: Herder, 1865), §X.42, p. 254: "Nach einer ziemlich allgemein gelehrten Meinung hatten die Engel vor ihrem Falle die Offenbarung der zukünftigen Menschwerdung des Sohnes Gottes gehabt."

66. Scheeben, *Die Mysterien des Christenthums*, §X.42, p. 255: "Nur in diesem Sinne läßt es sich erklären, wenn einige Väter die Sünde des Engels in den Neid gegen den Menschen setzen."

67. Gregory of Nyssa, *The Catechetical Oration of St. Gregory of Nyssa*, §6, pp. 40–41. *PG* 45, col. 28.

68. Scheeben, *Die Mysterien*, §X.42, p. 255: "wenn nicht den, daß ein Glied seines Geschlechtes zur Würde des Sohnes Gottes, und damit zum haupte und könige der Engel ausersehen war."

"a great humiliation."[69] The angels must acknowledge the source of the grace they have received in a nature below their own. As Scheeben says, they must come to terms with God establishing his *Gnadenthron*, his mercy seat, in Jesus of Nazareth.[70]

But some of the angels are envious that God has condescended so far to establish his *Gnadenthron* in human nature, singling out Jesus Christ to be "the center of the universe."[71] For Scheeben, this solves the quandary of diabolical envy's source, and for him the solution is linked to the devil's pride.[72] Like Milton's Lucifer, Scheeben's glories in his own goodness and rebels against what he takes to be an inordinate elevation of another created nature above his own. Scheeben's treatment of it, however, does more than this. His account foregrounds the malevolence of the rebel angels. On this view, the rebellion is occasioned by the revelation of God's love for his creatures exemplified by the incarnation.[73] Sin as a response to the love of God "takes on . . . a new, more terrible, more horrific character of malice."[74] This primordial hatred of Jesus Christ also accounts for the devil's relentless pursuit of humanity and in particular his continued persecution of the Church. Satan's hatred of the Son of God extends also to those who belong to Jesus as members of his body.[75]

Gregory of Nyssa serves as a model for this way of thinking about the *invidia diaboli*, with Scheeben offering the revelation of the incarnation to the angels as a logical extension of this Patristic position.[76] Scheeben's

69. Scheeben, *Die Mysterien*, §X.42, p. 254: "eine große Demüthigung."

70. Scheeben, *Die Mysterien*, §X.42, p. 254.

71. Scheeben, *Die Mysterien*, §X.42, p. 254: "Ja sie sollten Gott dafür danken, das er gerade mit der Menschheit sich so innig vereinigt, in ihr die Sonne der Gnade niedergelegt, sie zum Mittelpunkte des Universums ausersehen hatte."

72. Scheeben, *Die Mysterien*, §X.42, p. 255.

73. Scheeben, *Die Mysterien*, §X.42, pp. 255–56.

74. Scheeben, *Die Mysterien*, §X.42, p. 256: "dann gewinnt auch ihre Sünde einen neuen, noch furchtbarern, grauenvollern Charakter der Bosheit."

75. Scheeben, *Die Mysterien*, §X.42, p. 256: "Er verfolgt den Menschen nicht bloß deßhalb, weil derselbe die Herrlichkeit zu erlangen bestimmt ist, welche er selbst verloren, sondern noch ungleich mehr, weil der Mensch ein Glied am Leibe des Sohnes Gottes ist."

76. This theme of the *invidia diaboli*, also occurs, as Francisco Suárez notes, in the works of Irenaeus of Lyons, Tertullian, Cyprian, and Basil the Great. Cf. Francisco Suárez, "Tractatus

and Milton's speculations lend a certain specificity to the devil's envy. If, as I have argued, death enters the world *ex quo creatus est* as the result of angelic sin, then giving an account of what occasions that envy is essential. It is essential because one way to understand the "devil's envy" in Wisdom 2:24 is to think of it as a description of an Edenic scene. The preceding verse, "God created man for incorruption, and made him in the image of his own eternity" (Wis 2:23) could refer to the creation of Adam and Eve. "Through the devil's envy death entered the world" (Wis 2:24), could be read as a gloss on Genesis 3, where death comes to Adam and Eve through the deception of the devil. The idea that it is God's revelation of the incarnation to the angels in the beginning that precipitates the angelic fall allows something more in line with the Augustinian reading of Genesis 1. In that account, all the days of the hexaëmeron are the result of the cyclical motion of the angelic intellect in the one day of God's creative act. If in the very same moment of their creation the end of humanity and of all creation is revealed to them in the person of Jesus Christ, then Wisdom 2:23–24 can support the reading offered by both Milton and Scheeben. As Scheeben notes, that the source of the devil's envy could lie in God's revelation of himself as the God-man to his heavenly host while purely speculative also "has a great intrinsic probability."[77]

Serge-Thomas Bonino's *Les anges et les démons* attributes a worked out version of this position to Francisco Suárez. Bonino refers to Suárez's *Tractatus de angelis* to provide an example of a thinker who attributes the origins of Satan's envy to the revelation of the hypostatic union. Suárez's position, Bonino says, "gives a christological connotation to the fall of Satan,"[78] though Bonino prickles a bit at the suggestion that the "angels *in via*" might have knowledge of the incarnation, tied as it is (in Thomas's system) to the sin of

---

de angelis," in *Commentarii Et Disputationes in Primam Partem D. Thomae* (Paris: Vivès, 1856), 7.13.16, p. 886.

77. Scheeben, *Die Mysterien*, §X.42, 258: "Indeß geben wir diese ganze Theorie über den Ursprung und die Geschichte der Sünde nur als das, was sie ist, als eine achtungswerthe theologische Meinung, die sich nicht stringent aus der Offenbarung be gründen läßt, aber eine große innere Wahrscheinlichkeit besitzt."

78. Bonino, *Les anges et les démons*, 207: "Certains pensent même qu'il a envié tout spécialement à l'homme la grâce insigne de l'union hypostatique, ce qui donne à la cute de Satan une connotation christologique."

Adam.[79] But Jonathan Edwards also drew upon Suárez for his thoughts on the angelic fall. And both Edwards and Suárez agree on the christological dimension of angelic sin. Edwards goes as far to call Suárez "the best of the Schoolmen"[80] in another of his entries about the fall of the angels. There he recapitulates the position of his earlier *Miscellanies*. This time he does so with direct reference to Suárez's position. Unlike Bonino, Edwards does not mention the *Tractatus de angelis* by name, but it is likely he is referring to the same text. It is probable Edwards read Milton,[81] who might be the source Edwards's demonology, but it is certain he heard the position from a scholastic theologian he held in high regard.

Suárez addresses the question at hand in book VII of his work on the angels in a chapter entitled, "Whether Lucifer's Sin Was About Inordinately Desiring the Excellence of the Hypostatic Union for His Nature."[82] Suárez first establishes the possibility of Lucifer sinning in this way. He argues that it is possible, but only if God were to reveal the hypostatic union to him.[83] Suárez then shows that desiring the hypostatic union for himself is not opposed to Lucifer's natural desires as an angel. In desiring the hypostatic union, he wants a "mode of existing" that is "better by a long shot [than his own] and brings with it many perfections."[84] There is nothing intrinsically sinful about desiring the hypostatic union. Intimate union with God is eminently desirable, "the

79. Bonino, *Les anges et les démons*, 207: "mais on peut hésiter, dans une perspective thomiste où l'Incarnation est liée au péché adamique, à reconnaître aux anges in via une connaissance du mystère de l'Incarnation rédemptrice."

80. Edwards, *"Miscellanies": 833–1152*, no. 1261, p. 198.

81. *Paradise Lost* appears twice in Jonathan Edwards, *The Works of Jonathan Edwards*, vol. 26: *Catalogues of Books* (New Haven, CT: Yale University Press, 2008), nos. 20, 225. As Peter Theusen says in his introduction to the *Catologues*, "Whether he [Edwards] owned Milton's epic himself is not certain, but by the end of Edwards' life, Milton had become part of what one scholar has called a 'canon of the religious sublime'" (p. 105, quoting David Shields).

82. Suárez, "Tractatus de angelis," 880. My citations of Suárez's text will be by book, chapter, and section number (e.g., 7.13.1, for the first section of this question about whether Lucifer's sin is the result of his desire for the hypostatic union).

83. Suárez, "Tractatus de angelis," 7.13.1, pp. 880–81: "quia nec peccari potest sine cognitione, nec cognitio talis mysterii imo fortasse nec illius apprehensio sine aliqua revalatione haberi potest."

84. Suárez, "Tractatus de angelis," 7.13.2, p. 881: "Nec refert, quod non maneret eadem persona, quia per hoc solum variaretur in me quidem modus existendi meae naturae, et loco

most lovable thing in itself."[85] So if he can desire it and the desire is not contrary to his nature and it is not sinful to want it for himself, what can Lucifer's sin be?

Lucifer's sin, according to Suárez, lies in desiring the right thing for the wrong reason. Suárez gives some examples of bad reasons for an angel to desire the hypostatic union for himself. Lucifer might, for instance, desire it in order to dominate others or out of contempt for creatures less perfect than himself or by desiring it against a contrary ordinance of God.[86] With each of these cases, Suárez shows how Lucifer could sin through inordinate desire. His desire is marked out as disordered in each case due to the sin of pride—*superbia*.[87] But, following Thomas Aquinas, Suárez does not want to attribute erroneous judgment to the angels.[88] And so, he says, "To sin with this kind of pride was not by some necessary error of judgment or speculatively false, but an imprudent practical judgment, or it was not sufficiently considered."[89] Instead, "it was enough and more than enough" that all of his considerations "cloud the eyes of his heart."[90] With the eyes of his heart clouded he "considers, with his whole intention, that dignity [of the hypostatic union] to be most fitting for himself and—by reason of his own natural existence—sort of owed, and the

---

illius daretur modus unionis cum divina persona, qui longe excellentior est, et secum quam plures perfectiones affert."

85. Suárez, "Tractatus de angelis," 7.13.3, p. 881: "Hinc vero dixerunt alii, licet potuerit Angelus illud bonum sibi appetere, non tamen in eo peccare, quia ille appetitus non esset malus, neque peccatum, quia est de bono honestissimo, et maxime amabile propter seipsum."

86. Suárez, "Tractatus de angelis," 7.13.4, pp. 881–82.

87. Suárez, "Tractatus de angelis," 7.13.4, p. 882: "quia talis appetitus unionis hypostaticae sub tali motivo gravissima superbia est."

88. Suárez, "Tractatus de angelis," 7.13.6, p. 882: "Sicut ergo tale judicium Angelus habere non potuit, ita neque peccatum, quod illud supponit"; cf. *ST* 1.63.1 *ad* 4: "Hoc autem modo in angelo peccatum esse non potuit, quia nec in angelis sunt passiones, quibus ratio aut intellectus ligetur . . . nec iterum primum peccatum habitus praecedere potuit ad peccatum inclinans."

89. Suárez, "Tractatus de angelis," 7.13.10, p. 884: "ad peccandum hoc genere superbiae non fuisse necessarium judicium aliquod erroneum, aut speculative falsum, sed judicium practicum imprudens, seu inconsideratum fuisse sufficiens."

90. Suárez, "Tractatus de angelis," 7.13.10, p. 884: "satis, superque fuit, ab his omnibus objectis, et considerationibus oculos cordis claudere."

other order prescribed by God as though it were of little account, and falls in contempt of his own nature."[91] This is not the result of a speculative error, but rather a "rash practical judgment" by which he saw the greatness of the union with a divine person and desired it for himself as if it were his final end.[92] Suárez tries to show that it is by desiring something good according to the wrong rule that Lucifer errs and becomes Satan. He goes further than Thomas, by arguing that the rule he rejects is the *ratio* of the whole created order, to whom he refused to be subjected.[93]

I think it is possible to press this line of thinking further than Suárez. I do not choose to follow Thomas or Suárez on the nature of diabolical sin. Both of them fall victim to the understandable desire to make too much sense of the fall of the angels. They do this by imagining the angelic intellect to be something quite similar to the human intellect. As Thomas tries to home in on the source of angelic sin in the *Summa Theologiae*, he suggests that an angel might freely choose "something which is good in itself, but not with the order of proper measure or rule."[94] Thomas is trying to give reasons for angelic sin and explain how it might come about in the first place. But the way he describes it—and Suárez follows him on this—tends to anthropomorphize the angels. Scheeben, who inherits Thomas's view of the angelic fall, does so explicitly. The only instance we have, Scheeben argues, for reasoning about how rational creatures fall comes from our knowledge of what it is like for humans to turn away from God.[95] Humans can turn away because they are created in a state

91. Suárez, "Tractatus de angelis," 7.13.10, p. 884: "et tota intentione considerare dignitatem illam sibi convenientissimam esse, et ratione suae naturalis existentiae, quasi debitam, et alium ordinem a Deo praescriptum, quasi in vilipendium, et contemptum suae naturae cedere."

92. Suárez, "Tractatus de angelis," 7.13.10, p. 884: "Quae omnia potuit Lucifer, vel explicite, vel saltem implicite judicare sine proprio speculativo errore, praecise spectando congruitatem illam, quae ex parte excellentioris naturae resultare potest, et quid sibi esset commodius, indeque pracipitando judicium practicum, et consequenter affectum in tali commodo suo, tanquam in ultimo fine constituendo."

93. Suárez, "Tractatus de angelis," 7.13.10, p. 884: "et nollet Christo voluntarie subdi: vel illum, ut caput, et dominum voluntarie recognoscere."

94. *ST* 1.63.1 *ad* 4: "Alio modo contingit peccare per liberum arbitrium, eligendo aliquid quod secundum se est bonum, sed non cum ordine debitae mensurae aut regulae."

95. Matthias Scheeben, *Handbuch der katolischen Dogmatik*, Buch 3, Band 2 (Freiburg im Breisgau: Herder Verlagshaudlung, 1878), §181, p. 484: "When so-and-so and so-and-so frequently speak of an original beatitude of the angels, then that is only intelligible in the

that does not yet correspond to their final end. The first humans were graced, but were not yet experiencing the beatific vision. On this model, humans are able to turn away from God in part because they lack this immediate apprehension of God. According to this view, the angels must be created in an analogous position, graced yet not seeing God face to face. As Scheeben puts it, "To merit the supernatural beatitude, however, the angels require no less of actual and habitual supernatural grace than humans."[96] If this obtains, angels are like humans who could choose according to the wrong rule or measure. They would lack, prior to their elevation to supernatural beatitude, a perfected awareness of that rule. They would only attain that perfected awareness once they had chosen to turn themselves to God and received the gift of being raised to this new and different state.

But why think this? There is another possible view on offer. In *De civitate Dei*, Augustine claims that the angels are created beholding God himself.[97] In *De Genesi ad litteram* he argues that the very nature of angels, as intellectual creatures, is to behold God.[98] Contemplating God is what angels do and are. The only thing angelic creatures lack at the moment of their

---

manner of the human paradise: namely 1) by the freedom from all evil, 2) by the full use of their higher natural virtues, and 3) by the self in a state of being on the way (*in statu viae*) to supernatural community with God resulting in beatitude ("Wenn VV. und TT. vielfach von einer ursprünglichen Seligkeit der Engel reden, dann ist das nur in analogem Sinne zu verstehen, wie beim paradisischen Menschen: nämlich 1) von der Freiheit von allem Uebel, 2) von dem Vollgenusse ihrer höheren natürlichen Vorzüge, und 3) von der selbst in statu viae aus der übernatürlichen Gemeinschaft mit Gott resultirenden Seligkeit").

96. Scheeben, *Handbuch der katolischen Dogmatik*, §181, p. 484: "Zum Verdienste der übernatürlichen Seligkeit aber bedurfen die Engel nicht weniger, als die Menschen, der aktuellen und habituellen übernatürlichen Gnade."

97. Augustine, *civ.*, 11.9, *CSEL* 40.1:525: "certainly they have been made participants of the eternal light, which is itself the unchangeable wisdom of God, through which all things are made, which we call the only begotten Son of God" ("profecto facti sunt participes lucis aeternae, quod est ipsa incommutabilis sapientia Dei, per quam facta sunt omnia, quem dicimus unigenitum Dei filium").

98. Augustine, *Gn. litt.*, 1.9.17, *PL* 34:252–53: "If, however, light—which was the first thing about which it was said that it should be made, and it was made—should be understood to hold the first place in creation, it is itself intellectual life. Which life, unless it were turned to the Creator to be illuminated would have been formlessly fluid. When, however, it was turned and illuminated what was said in the Word of God happened: 'Let there be light.'" ("Si autem lux, quae primum dicta est ut fiat, et facta est, etiam primatum creaturae tenere intelligenda est, ipsa est intellectualis vita; quae nisi ad Creatorem illuminanda converteretur,

creation, Augustine says, is knowledge of their perseverance in God.[99] Whether they will persist in cleaving to him for all eternity is opaque to them. Angels do not need to do anything but continue to cast their loving gaze upon God in order to be assured of their eternal communion with the divine. Distinct from the Thomistic position, Augustine does not think there is a decision for the angel to make for or against God which results in a corresponding elevation or fall. There is instead faithful adherence to the God who made them or a turning away from that God's countenance. This turn just is the angelic fall.[100] The holy angels are not elevated further, they are simply given the surety of their continued persistence in God's truth just as they are.[101]

The Augustinian reading challenges the intellectualist account of the good. We must say it is possible to misdirect our wills in such a way that we are not pursuing a good, but a lack. Put another way, we have to be able to succeed at failing.[102] Augustine presents this terrifying possibility in his most famous analysis of sin in book II of *Confessiones.* While trying to understand his motivations for stealing some pears as a young man, Augustine gropes along for something intelligible to hold on to in the sinful act. He begins with a confession to God, "Let my heart tell you here, what it was searching for there: that I was evil for nothing (*gratis*) and the cause of my malice was

---

fluitaret informiter. Cum autem conversa et illuminata est, factum est quod in Verbo Dei dictum est, 'Fiat lux'"). Cf. *inter alia*, *Gn. litt.*, 2.8.17, 4.24.41, 5.4.10.

99. Augustine, *civ.*, 11.13, *CSEL* 40.1:532: "Cuius illi alii quia certi non fuerunt (non enim erat eorum aeterna felicitas cuius certi essent, quae finem fuerat habitura), restat, ut aut inpares fuerint, aut, si pares fuerint, post istorum ruinam illis certa scientia suae sempiternae felicitatis accesserit."

100. Augustine, *civ.*, 12.9, *CSEL* 40.1:579: "eoque sunt isti ab illorum societate discreti, quod illi in eadem bona voluntate manserunt, isti ab ea deficiendo mutati sunt, mala scilicet voluntate hoc ipso quod a bona defecerunt."

101. Augustine, *civ.*, 11.13, *CSEL* 40.1:531: "procul dubio multo est durius nunc putare angelos sanctos aeternae suae beatitudinis incertos, et ipsos de semet ipsis ignorare, quod nos de illis per scripturas sanctas nosse potuimus."

102. Paul Griffiths, *Intellectual Appetite: A Theological Grammar* (Washington, DC: The Catholic University of America Press, 2009), 43: "The drama of the world of darkness and light is that the tragedy of human existence is neither getting nor not getting what you want, but rather the real possibility that you will guarantee yourself success at failure by seeking the darkness of absence that you can in fact obtain."

nothing (*nulla*) but malice."[103] He goes on to rule out the idea that it was his love of a lesser good motivating his action. It was not that he loved *something* other than God; he loved *nothing*. "I loved to come to nothing. I loved my fall, not what I fell for. I loved my fall itself."[104] Augustine is horrified by this discovery. You get the sense when reading these sections of the *Confessiones* that he would like to be able to make sense of it. He is looking for rational solutions, trying them on in turn. First, that his sin was the pursuit of lower-order goods—loving things, but not loving them rightly. He dismisses this option, comparing himself to Catiline, who could at least give a sense to his evils.[105] Then, he attempts to frame the action with reference to the gang with whom he committed the evils—"alone, I never would have done it."[106] But he dismisses this view as well, admitting the love of the gang to be nothing at all.[107]

This capacity to turn toward nothing is best understood as a negative possibility of creatures possessed of intellect and will. It does not belong to freedom itself. Freedom is being able to choose your final end. But when freedom breaks, when we sin and so fail to be free, we turn away from our final end. Being creatures made from nothing, this negative possibility includes the possibility of attempting to return to nothing. What Augustine realizes, to his great consternation, is that while it might *seem* like something to us to sin, on final analysis sin is not an orientation toward something but toward nothing. We are tempted to make sense of sin, but this is a species of self-deception. We offer explanations for our actions, but these are accounts of what it seems like to us to be sinning, not accounts of what sin is.

Attempting to specify the sin of the angels as pride falls into this trap. If what Augustine says in *Confessiones* II is right, it is a trap we can avoid on his own terms. But Augustine also elsewhere identifies the sin of the devil as one of disordered love in the form of pride. Satan prefers himself to God,

103. Augustine, *conf.*, 2.4.9, *CSEL* 33:36: "dicat tibi nunc ecce cor meum, quid ibi quaerebat, ut essem gratis malus et malitiae meae causa nulla esset nisi malitia."

104. Augustine, *conf.*, 2.4.9, *CSEL* 33:36: "amavi perire, amavi defectum meum, non illud, ad quod deficiebam, sed defectum meum ipsum amavi."

105. Augustine, *conf.*, 2.5.10–11.

106. Augustine, *conf.*, 2.8.16, *CSEL* 33:41: "solus omnino id non fecissem."

107. Augustine, *conf.*, 2.8.15, *CSEL* 33:41–42: "non ergo nihil aliud quam furtum amavi; inmo vero nihil aliud quia et illud nihil est."

Augustine argues.[108] The angels who fall love themselves more than they love God. But what do they love when they love themselves this way? If we follow Augustine's own rationale from book II of *Confessiones*, this love is at root the love of nothing at all. That is because to love yourself for what you are apart from God is to be in love with nothing. On its own, that is all any creature is. Angelic sin turns out to be stupefying because it is nonsensical. Pointing to pride is a way of trying to save the intentionality of the act. Without an object, it is not clear what could be moving the will. Augustine's attention to pride, and Thomas's and Suárez's specifications of angelic inattention are each attempts to make too much sense of sin.

In order to capture the absurd quality of sin, I suggest giving some attention to the older tradition to which I have already adverted in Gregory of Nyssa's writings, which calls the devil's characteristic defect envy rather than pride. Cyprian of Carthage, too, in his treatise *De zelo et livore*, identifies envy as the primordial sin of Satan. At the beginning of the world, the devil saw humans made in the image of God.[109] And "from envy he launched into a malevolent jealousy."[110] Gregory the Great inherits this line of thought as well, in his *Regulae pastoralis*. While advising pastors how to deal with the envious, he cites Wisdom 2:24, "Through the devil's envy death entered the world." As in Cyprian, the devil envies the making of humans.[111] Unlike Cyprian, Gregory does not attribute the devil's fall to envy itself. For Gregory, envy is a consequence rather than a cause of the fall. But from Gregory we learn something about the character of envy. The envious person does not desire anything for himself. Envy instead begrudges another his good things. "How very unhappy they are, who become worse by the improvement of their neighbors."[112] Gregory explicitly compares it to a plague (*peste*) and rot (*putrescere*).[113]

108. Augustine, *civ.*, 12.6, *CSEL* 40.1:573: "Noluerunt ergo ad illum custodire fortitudinem suam, et qui magis essent, si ei qui summe est adhaererent, se illi praeferendo id quod minus est praetulerunt."

109. Cyprian, *zel.*, 4, *CSEL* 3.1:421.

110. Cyprian, *zel.*, 4, *CSEL* 3.1:421: "in zelum malivolo livore prorupit."

111. Gregory the Great, *reg. past.*, 3.10, *PL* 77:63c–63d: "Quia enim ipse caelum perdidit, condito hoc homini invidit, et damnationem suam perditus adhuc alios perdendo cumulavit."

112. Gregory the Great, *reg. past.*, 3.10, *PL* 77:63b: "Quantae infelicitatis sunt, qui melioratione proximi deteriores fiunt."

113. Gregory the Great, *reg. past.*, 3.10, *PL* 77:64a–64b.

Envy is a sort of infection. When it takes root, it tends toward the undoing of the one who has it, not by being directed outwardly toward some good, but by being consumed internally by the desire that another experience a lack.

This makes envy an ideal way of specifying what angelic sin is. It does not require the added machinery of angelic misapprehension or inattention. John Cassian provides an excellent description of the envious person in his *Conlationes*: "For however much more another might have made progress in the obedience of humility or the virtue of patience or in the attainment of generosity, so much will he be incited by the greater torments of envy, because he desires nothing except the ruin or death of him whom he envies."[114] Envy grows in proportion to another's attainment of perfection, and its object is nothing. What the envious person wants is nothing for someone else. It is possible to attempt an appropriation of this sin to pride. You could say the reason an envious person wants this for someone else is a relative increase in his own state. But it is not necessary to make this leap, unless you are committed to the intelligibility of sinful action. And it is not clear we ought to be, or should want to, on Augustinian grounds. Cassian, in fact, thinks the fact that the envious person does not want anything for himself is why it is the most difficult vice to overcome.[115]

If this is the case, you can see how Suárez's solution to the cause of the devil's fall might fit. Lucifer, seeing the incarnation in the divine light in which he as an angel is created, perceives the elevation of human nature in the hypostatic union above his angelic nature. Following Cyprian's insight, we could posit that what Lucifer sees is the human being made in the image of God, achieved perfectly in the person of the incarnate Son. In seeing it, Lucifer's will is not inclined toward himself, toward a good. He desires ruin, nothing, the absence of this great good bestowed upon human nature. We might be tempted to say he wants the good for himself. That is where Suárez's thought inclines. But it is better to say that his will defects in his desire not for his own misperceived good but for nothing at all. It is a culpable failure of perseverance in the love in which he was created. The diabolical sin is not properly an act but a failure

114. John Cassian, *con.*, 18.16.10, *CSEL* 13:529–30: "quanto enim amplius alius aut humilitatis subiectione aut patientiae virtute aut munificentiae laude profecerit, tanto ille maioribus invidiae stimulis incitatur, quia non nisi ruinam aut mortem eius cui invidet concupiscit."

115. John Cassian, *con.*, 18.16.8, *CSEL* 13:528: "sciendum sane est invidiae morbum difficilius ad medellam quam cetera vitia pervinire. nam eum quem semel veneni sui peste corruperit paene dixerim carere remedio." Cf. also *con.*, 18.16.11, *CSEL* 13:530.

to act as he ought given the powers and capacities he possesses. It is the vision of Jesus Christ that precipitates this movement of the will, but the movement remains entirely deficient, obsessed with the destruction of another rather than any particular good to be obtained by him in his angelic nature.

While we can make sense of Troilus's sin by attributing it to pride, trying to do the same for the primordial sin of the angels requires some leaps that do more harm than good. By pointing to envy rather than pride, we are left with a sin that can be specified without rendering it intelligible. There is no reason for Lucifer to defect and become Satan, and that is precisely the point. Troilus has a history we need to make sense of, which becomes an occasion of his pride. Lucifer does not. Neither does he have the sorts of limitations Troilus has in his knowledge of the good—Lucifer is face to face with God. In Troilus's case, pride is a coping mechanism lending intelligibility to an action that lacks it. Applying the same mechanism to Lucifer leaves us with more questions than answers. How is Lucifer able to make this mistake? What does it mean for an angel to misapprehend the good ordering of creation? Does he perceive the good order when created, and then fail to? If so, why? Angelic envy, by contrast, leaves us at the heart of the mystery without solving it. It retains the origin of the fall in the will of Satan as a free creature, but it shows us more clearly what sin is: a turn toward nothing.

Like Scheeben, Suárez admits speculations about the fall of the angels because they have seen the incarnation are just that, speculative. He does not think there is enough in Scripture or in the writings of the Fathers to prove it as a necessary deduction of reason.[116] Still, he calls it a probable doctrine congruous with both Scripture and the Fathers, and so one that can be freely held.[117] Like Scheeben, Suárez thinks this position accounts for the patristic position on the *invidia diaboli* because it shows how the envy of the devil is intimately linked to his pride in desiring the hypostatic union for himself.[118] I am pushing the position further by asking whether the *invidia diaboli* must

116. Suárez, "Tractatus de angelis," 7.13.13, p. 885: "Fateor enim non esse certam, quia nec ex Scriptura vel Patribus sufficienter ostenditur, nec ratione convinci potest."

117. Suárez, "Tractatus de angelis," 7.13.13, p. 885: "nihilominus tamen inter eas [Scripture and the Fathers] huic tanquam probabiliori libenter adhaereo."

118. See especially Suárez's treatment of the occurrence of this patristic *topos* in the works of Bernard of Clairvaux; Suárez, "Tractatus de angelis," 7.13.17–22, pp. 886–88.

be subordinated pride. As Suárez asks, "If probable conjectures or deductions from Scripture and the Fathers are enough in other cases, why not on this point?"[119] Leaning on the insights of Augustine on sin itself coupled with Cyprian, Gregory, and Cassian on the nature of envy, I think there are good reasons to affirm this as a probable speculative position. Suárez's final answer on the question of the origin Lucifer's sin is christological, which returns us to Bonino's Thomistic worry. Against Thomas, Suárez argues that the coming of Christ was not merely a remedy for sin. Suárez says,

> the advent of Christ in the human nature assumed by the Word viewed absolutely and in itself was not in itself first to abolish the work of the devil, nor on the pretext of human or angelic sin, but on account of itself, and because of the excellence of the mystery, and for the manifestation of divine goodness, and for the sake of the sanctification of humans and of the angels accomplished through faith in him.[120]

The incarnation does not depend on human or angelic sin. In this world, it is the case that Christ comes to heal its brokenness. But the incarnation is not contingent upon the fact of the world's brokenness. Jesus Christ is the means of sanctification for humans and angels considered apart from the freely chosen evil actions of rational creatures. For this reason, Suárez goes on to say the revelation of Christ's incarnation "was most able to be the occasion of offense and pride and foolishness."[121] Christ's incarnation

119. Suárez, "Tractatus de angelis," 7.13.27, p. 889: "Assumptum ostendo, interrogando, quodnam objectum superbiae Luciferi sit nobis in Scriptura clare propositum, aut magis significatum, vel quod possit sola ratione convinci? nullum profecto. Si ergo in aliis rebus probabiles conjecturae, vel deductiones ex Scriptura et Patribus sufficiunt, cur non in hoc puncto?"

120. Suárez, "Tractatus de angelis," 7.13.27, p. 889: "Adventus autem Christi in humana natura assumpta a Verbo absolute, et secundum se spectatus on fuit per se primo ad dissolvenda opera diaboli, nec occasione peccati hominum, vel Angelorum, sed propter se, et propter excellentiam mysterii, et divinae bonitatis manifestationem, ac summam communicationem, et propter hominum, et Angelorum sanctificationem per fidem in ipsum factus est."

121. Suárez, "Tractatus de angelis," 7.13.27, p. 889: "et ita optime potuit esse occasio, et offensionis superbum, et insipientium Angelorum."

can be the occasion of angelic sin because the Son's taking human flesh is not *simply* the result of angelic sin or the consequent temptation and fall of humans. As I have argued so far, the incarnation of the Son is the condition for the possibility not only of the sanctification but also of the creation of all that is not God.

Passed over in Silence

The turn to literature in this chapter is meant to illustrate more concretely, though still perhaps only "By lik'ning spiritual to corporeal forms" (*Paradise Lost*, V.573), the mystery of sin and evil. What I have offered are things that can, and in some cases must, be said by Christians about the disfigurement of the cosmos by the blight of evil. Much remains that cannot and should not be said. By that I mean that nothing I have said here can make sense of the origins of the voluntary evil of rational creatures. Why the revelation of Jesus Christ to Lucifer should provoke his envious response, bringing about his self-destruction, remains incomprehensible. It remains incomprehensible even if we can specify what occasions it and how. This is a good thing. If we were able to make sense of sin, we would no longer be dealing with evil as an absence, a *privatio boni*. Explicable sin is an oxymoron. To think we can give reasons for it is to imagine sin as something rational. It is to imagine Augustine's incident with the pears in book II of the *Confessiones* ends with a solution rather than an aporia. Instead we ought to recognize every sin as a flight from God, who is intelligibility itself. To recognize our sin for what it is requires that we say with Augustine, "I became to myself a land of lack."[122]

Tolkien's treatment of the kind of care the creator is capable of exercising over his creation remains a cause for hope. The reason Christians remain hopeful is that our deficiencies are no limitation on God's action. Those deficiencies become the means by which God brings about greater goods. This point of Christian grammar is embedded deep in the Church's liturgical practice and her Scriptures. It may be that the only way to give any sort of reason for the angelic fall is to exhibit the goods brought about by it, the *felices* occasioned by the demons' *culpae*. If there are any reasons for the devil's fall, they are God's reasons for bringing these felicities about. Sin remains unintelligible

122. Augustine, *conf.*, 2.10.18, *CSEL* 33:43: "factus sum mihi regio egestatis."

in itself, but it makes certain intelligible goods possible. To specify how this is so is beyond me, and perhaps beyond what it is possible to say. What I will try do next is show what the devil's fall and the consequent disordering of the cosmos brings about in our world, whose beauty, as Tolkien suggests, comes in large part from its sorrows.

CHAPTER FIVE

"There Is a Crack in Everything"

"He will swallow up death for ever, and the Lord God will wipe away tears from all faces, and the reproach of his people he will take away from all the earth, for the Lord has spoken" (Isa 25:8). God is the one who will bring death to nothing. In the verse before this one, death is called "the covering that is cast over all peoples, the veil that is spread over all nations" (Isa 25:7). Death is something which weighs us down and obscures our vision. But this state of affairs is temporary. That is the force of God's promise to swallow it up forever. The Vulgate says death will be cast down—*praecipitabit* (Isa 25:8 Vulg.). Death's dominion must come to an end. The claim that death needs destroying is implicit in Isaiah. It pairs well with Paul's claim in the Letter to the Romans that "death no longer has dominion" over Jesus (Rom 6:9). That death did—or seemed to—have dominion over Jesus is assumed by Paul. That this is a future state, something achieved in Christ but not yet in us, can be seen in Paul's first letter to the Corinthians, where he says, "The last enemy to be destroyed is death" (1 Cor 15:26). The prophecy of Isaiah is accomplished and not yet fully realized in the life, death, resurrection, and ascension of Jesus.

In addition to being temporary, death is also temporal. Its dominion extends only as far as the distention, the painful stretching out, of fallen spacetime. This is not the only kind of spacetime there is. In addition to it, there is also the spacetime of heaven. To offer a formal definition, I mean by "heaven" wherever the ascended flesh of Jesus Christ and the assumed flesh of the Blessed Virgin are. Having bodies, they occupy space. In occupying space, they also occupy time. Space and time are intimate with one another in just this way. To be in one is to be in the other conjointly. And so it is fitting to say that death's dominion over spacetime obtains where the spacetime of heaven does not. The spacetime over which death wields power is fallen.

The title of this chapter is from the Leonard Cohen song "Anthem," from *The Future* (studio album) (Columbia Records, 1992).

Death's dominion in fallen spacetime is entirely negative in itself. Its rule is one of lack. This lack manifests itself in distention. What fallen spacetime lacks is the wholeness, the all-at-onceness, of heaven, a wholeness that makes it the image of God's eternity.

Nothing in fallen spacetime, including spacetime itself, escapes the effects of the angelic fall. The distortion set in motion by angelic rebellion ramifies outward such that no creatures but heavenly ones escape its grip. The holy angels are not and have not ever been distended in spacetime. Holy angels occupy spacetime at its center—the still eye around which the hurricane rages. Distinguished from their diabolical counterparts by their recognition and embrace of God incarnate, the holy angels cleave to Jesus Christ. Jesus Christ, who puts an end to death's dominion, "bore our death and slew it by the abundance of his life."[1] He did so by being the Word made flesh—the eternal made timely. God enters fallen spacetime as a creature, *the* creature. He is the *ratio* of the cosmos because he is both God and man. Not only are space and time "created through him and for him" (Col 1:16), they are also redeemed by him who reconciles all things to himself, "whether on earth or in heaven, making peace by the blood of his cross" (Col 1:20). Not only does the Son of God make time and space, he makes them right as well.

The holy angels are gathered to Jesus Christ and minister to him during his time on earth. The events of Christ's earthly life are marked by the presence of the angels. Angels are present at the annunciation, the nativity, the temptation in the desert, the agony in the garden, the resurrection, and the ascension. Unfallen angels are active in fallen spacetime, and yet we should not think they suffer the effects of temporal distention. Even while acting in the fallen order, they remain fixed in heaven. Evidence for this view comes from the Gospel of Matthew, "See that you do not despise one of these little ones; for I tell you that in heaven their angels always behold the face of my Father who is in heaven" (Matt 18:10). The angels given the task of guardianship accomplish it without ceasing to also gaze upon the face of God.

In *De Genesi ad litteram*, Augustine takes the "Let there be light" of Genesis 1:3 to be an account of the creation of angels. He calls the angels the created form of God's uncreated light. I want to extend this language with an analogy to help account for angelic action inside and outside of fallen

1. Augustine, *conf.*, 4.12.19, *CSEL* 33:79: "tulit mortem nostram et occidit eam de abundantia vitae suae."

spacetime. Compare the intellectual light of the angels in heavenly spacetime to a beam of white light in the visible spectrum. Crisp and simple, it illuminates what it touches. In heaven, what it illuminates will include other angels, the souls of the saints, and the bodies and souls of Jesus Christ and Mary. But a beam of visible white light, while simple in appearance, is also a complex of electromagnetic radiation, oscillating at different frequencies along the visible spectrum. When that beam of white light passes through a prism, it refracts. The various frequencies of visible light, of which the beam of white light is composed, bend at different angles. They exit the prism along distinct trajectories, and if you set up a screen on the far side of the prism to catch the light it lands as a rainbow.

Angels in heaven are like beams of unrefracted white light. Entering fallen spacetime is like passing through a prism. The single beam of created intellectual light is refracted. The unitary action of the angel in heaven, the unceasing praise and worship of God in the "Holy, holy, holy, is the Lord God Almighty, who was and is and is to come!" (Rev 4:8), reveals its component frequencies. The "colors" of the angelic light spectrum land at different locations in fallen spacetime. The angel Gabriel's actions when he helps Daniel to interpret his visions (Dan 8–9) and when he announces the birth of Jesus Christ to Mary (Luke 1:26–38) are discrete events within fallen spacetime. They are also ingredients in the composite "white light" that is the angel's unending hymn of praise before the face of God. As Gabriel says to Zechariah, when Zechariah questions him about the birth of his son, John the Baptist, "I am Gabriel, who stand in the presence of God; and I was sent to speak to you and bring you this good news" (Luke 1:19). He is standing in the presence of God, and he is speaking to Zechariah. The angel touches down in the devasted temporal order without being dragged into it. In so doing, the angel also snatches those moments up into the heavenly liturgical act.

This idea comports well with the Church's liturgical practice. Each time the Mass is celebrated, the Church invokes the angels, uniting the prayer of the earthly liturgy to that of the heavenly one. This happens first in the preface to the eucharistic prayer. So, for example, in Preface I for Sundays in Ordinary Time, the priest says, "And so, with Angels and Archangels, with Thrones and Dominions, and with all the host and Powers of heaven, we sing the hymn of your glory, as without end we acclaim."[2] This is followed by

2. *The Roman Missal*, 572.

the people's singing of the "Holy, Holy, Holy" in unison with the angels in heaven. But while you might think the liturgical action of the Church simply points upward, straining to sing with the angels on high, it is also true that the angels themselves play an active role in the eucharistic sacrifice. In the Roman Canon, Eucharistic Prayer I, the priest asks God for the aid of an angel. He says, "In humble prayer we ask you, almighty God: command that these gifts be borne by the hands of your holy Angel to your altar on high in the sight of your divine majesty, so that all of us, who through this participation at the altar receive the most holy Body and Blood of your Son, may be filled with every grace and heavenly blessing."[3] The angels are active in offering the sacrifice of the Mass. At God's command, the angels allow the sacrifice offered on the altar on earth to be offered at the heavenly altar. It is this angelic action that allows the worshipping Church to receive "every grace and heavenly blessing."

Angels touch down with their various colors, refracted out of that one intellectual light in heaven, during each instance of the Mass. Angelic action dapples fallen spacetime with light from heaven. The refracted angelic light catches those moments of liturgical sacrifice and draws them into the heavenly worship of unfallen spacetime. This view offers a speculative account of what the dominical word of Matthew 18:10 might mean. On this model, any angelic action in the fallen world belongs to the singular act of that angel's continual worship of God in heaven. An angel can act in fallen spacetime without becoming mired in it. This view also gets us some of the way toward understanding what the fall means for angelic creatures who cease to gaze upon the face of God.

In chapter 3, I suggested reading Revelation 12 as a two-level drama. The events in Revelation 12:1–12 are best understood as cosmic in scope. They are a narrative of the battle demons have waged against God seen under the aspect of the *conditio*—the order of eternity. Michael and his angels throw down the dragon and his angels. They conquer Satan not by their own power, nor by some abstract might of God, but "by the blood of the Lamb and by the word of their testimony" (Rev 12:11). The devil has been defeated, the victory is won, and the victory is Christ's and the martyrs' who bore witness to the Lamb, "even unto death" (Rev 12:11). The angelic war is made effective, the devil is "thrown down to earth" (Rev 12:9), by Christ's sacrifice on Calvary. To consider this under the aspect of the *administratio*, we must ask what it means

3. *The Roman Missal*, 641.

to say that the fallen angels are cast down from heaven to earth. An answer has already suggested itself in my remarks on the holy angels. The most immediate effect upon the fallen angels who are cast down from heaven is that they no longer behold God's countenance. Unlike the holy angels, whose perpetual adoration of the face of God in heaven allows them to act in fallen spacetime without being distended in it, the demons' punishment includes being turned out of their heavenly participation in God's eternity and painfully stretched out in the order of time.

The fall of the angels from heaven is not only into the successiveness of fallen spacetime, it is also the cause of its distention. Time is one of God's creatures. "For you have made time itself," Augustine says to God in book XI of his *Confessiones*.[4] It is one of God's good creatures. The fall of the devil and his angels corrupts time's goodness. As Paul Griffiths has put it, the time that belongs to the devastation, "metronomic time," is nothing other than time damaged.[5] It is "an artifact of the fall."[6] The ticking of metronomic time "is what time is like when it has been devastated. The principal mark of that devastation for us—the sign that shows us most clearly that metronomic time is devastated—is that time is a metronomic countdown to death."[7] This identification of the ticking of time and the reign of death is an Augustinian claim. In book XIII of *De civitate Dei*, where Augustine deals most explicitly with the fact of death, he says something coordinate with Griffiths's remark on death's countdown. "And daily," Augustine says, "what remains becomes less and less, so the whole time of this life is nothing other than a march toward death in which no one is permitted either to stand still for a little while or to go a bit slower."[8] The fall of the angels is an atemporal event that damages all creation apart from the holy angels, including the fabric of spacetime.[9] The

4. Augustine, *conf.*, 11.13.14, *CSEL* 33:291: "id ipsum tempus tu feceras."

5. Griffiths, *Decreation*, 89–93.

6. Griffiths, *Decreation*, 91.

7. Griffiths, *Decreation*, 91.

8. Augustine, *civ.*, 13.10, *CSEL* 40.1:626: "et cottidie fit minus minusque quod restat, ut omnino nihil sit aliud tempus vitae huius, quam cursus ad mortem, in quo nemo vel paululum stare vel aliquanto tardius ire permittitur."

9. In this I follow Griffiths in his reflections on the fall of the angels and the damage this does to the temporal order. Cf. Griffiths, *Decreation*, 131–35, esp. 133.

angels being thrust out of heaven is coincident with the painful stretching out of the fallen temporal order.

The light of the demons, the created form of uncreated light, is not extinguished. It is distended in the order of fallen spacetime. To stick with the analogy of light, we might say demonic light is diffracted rather than refracted. Passing out of heaven and into the medium of fallen spacetime, the demons' light is occluded, though not entirely. Were their light to be entirely obscured, they would cease to be. Instead, the light of the fallen angels is forced to pass through tiny openings in a barrier. Because light behaves like a wave, passing through these narrow openings means their angelic light no longer illuminates clearly. The light waves exiting the far side of the barrier end up fragmented. When a beam of light passes through two or more slits in a barrier, diffraction occurs. It happens because the ripples of light, like intersecting ripples on the surface of a pond, bump into one another and cause interference. When the peak of one light wave intersects the trough of another of the same intensity they cancel one another out. The light caught by a surface on the far side of the barrier will not appear as the differentiated spectrum colors as in refraction through a prism. What you find instead are bits of light interspersed with darkness.

The bits of darkness caused by diffraction are not caused by the slits in the barrier they pass through. Two slits in the barrier do not issue in two points of light on the far surface. The far surface receives many points of light and darkness in a wave interference pattern. The absences are caused by the light itself, interfering with its own activity. The light shines, the waves roll, and when peak and trough meet, light cancels light. This is a fitting analogy for the fallen angels. Passing out of the participated eternity of heaven and into fallen spacetime, they are the cause of their own darkness. Their powerful and beautiful light is marred when it comes into conflict with itself. Their light ceases to be what it is created to be. The light of the fallen angels spreads out in fallen timespace—the ripples extend to its edges—but it is a broken, ineffectual light. The light of the fallen angels does not help us to see clearly. The light interspersed with darkness illuminates just enough to deceive, "for even Satan disguises himself as an angel of light," says Paul (2 Cor 11:14).

The punishment of the devil and his angels is self-imposed and self-inflicted. The essential piece of this argument is that this is an event occurring *ex quo creatus est*—since the devil was created. Time begins ticking in its metronomic, death-dealing fashion from the moment of the fall, which happens outside of the clock-ticked temporal order. With this claim, I am arguing against a time of idyllic perfection in the created order. God creates all things from nothing and makes them good, but that is a claim made under the aspect of eternity. In the temporal order, where things have a beginning and an end, creation is stretched out and unfolds in a cosmos that is good and fallen at all times. The great disjunction that causes spacetime to fall happens outside fallen spacetime and so permeates it. The always already fallen world means the good things God creates will have certain possibilities and eventualities foreclosed to them. Entropy and decay are woven into and corrupt the fabric of the cosmos from the beginning of fallen time.

Next, I am going to offer a speculative account of this good and fallen world—the only world we know—from the beginning of time. I want to show what it might look like for fallen spacetime, seeded with the *rationes seminales* to develop. In the last chapter's discussion of Tolkien's creation myth, God's providential care for, and instrumental wielding of, his damaged creatures formed a central part of the reflection. In this chapter, I will look at how Augustine's talk of death as an *instrumentum* implemented by God during the crucifixion of Jesus can clarify death's role in the whole history of the cosmos. This will also include a treatment of a move in contemporary theology to naturalize death, along with an argument for why this is a mistake. Finally, I will offer an interpretation of Genesis 2–3, which builds on the foregoing conversation, to explain the role of human creatures in a cosmos already shot through with nonhuman creaturely death. This brief foray into theological anthropology will conclude with a treatment of the human Fall and Original Sin, and its role in Christian theological thinking about human death in the light of the Cross of Jesus Christ.

Cosmology

I do not have much invested in a particular origin story of the mechanics or physics at the beginning of spacetime. It is not my specialty, and it makes little difference to me whether things began with an infinitely dense primordial pinpoint or an oscillation occurring at the level of quantum phenomena—or both. That work is best left to astrophysicists and cosmologists. The consensus view seems to have coalesced around the theory proposed by the Catholic priest George Lemaitre, whose observations of the red-shift in the electromagnetic radiation emanating from the observable universe led to the theory of an expanding universe. On this view, the Big Bang is an event traceable through measurable doppler effects and the rate of expansion of the observable universe to a time roughly thirteen-and-a-half billion years ago. This time horizon accounts for the unthinkably vast recesses of interstellar space, the distances of which boggle the mind and make the space between the planets of our solar system seem cozy by comparison.

While I am not interested in adjudicating any particular theory that purports to make sense of the vastness of the cosmos in the terms of physics, I do think something like the narrative offered by Charles Taylor in *A Secular Age* about the effects of the human encounter with the seemingly infinite expanse of spacetime is useful. His account includes the tagline naming the shift in the way modern people experience the world as one from "cosmos to universe."[10] This shift is important because the problem of death becomes more pressing once you recognize the sheer quantity of it contained in the ever-expanding universe. The world feels less tidy and comprehensible as a result. For those committed to the position that all death, without remainder, is a product of sin, the burden of that sin begins to look immeasurably weighty. Time and space are now much deeper. As Taylor puts it, "we have moved from a world which is encompassed within certain bounds and static to one which is vast, feels infinite, and is in the midst of an evolution spread over aeons."[11] With those bounds removed, or put at such a distance that they cease to be meaningfully present, Christian thinking about death could not avoid being affected.

Taylor identifies the publication of Charles Darwin's *On the Origin of Species* in 1859 as the last major event in a long series of scientific discoveries, beginning in the seventeenth century, that solidified an evolutionary universe as a background assumption for modern people.[12] Darwin and his approach to evolutionary theory are important because they highlight some key developments that make necessary a study like the one I am writing now. I will focus on two. The first is the role death plays in Darwin's treatment of evolution

10. Charles Taylor, *A Secular Age* (Cambridge, MA: The Belknap Press of Harvard University Press, 2007), 323.

11. Taylor, *A Secular Age*, 323.

12. Taylor, *A Secular Age*, 327.

in terms of natural selection. If it is the case that death and dying have been around for at least three-and-a-half billion years, and that it is a *structural* feature of the coming-to-be of all the kinds of living things there are, then we need an intelligible account of how this fits into God's providential care for the cosmos. The second development I will treat is a flaw specific to Darwin's approach. While all things seem to indicate Darwin was a good scientist, it is also reasonably clear he was a lousy metaphysician. As some of the earliest Catholic responses show, Darwin's unfortunate and unreflective thoughts about the nature of God and how God works in the cosmos tended to infiltrate his scientific conclusions.

Before discussing the problems associated with death as a structural feature of the created order, it will be useful to look at one of these Catholic responses to Darwin. The reception was almost immediate. The first edition of Charles Darwin's *On the Origin of Species by Means of Natural Selection* hit the shelves in November 1859.[13] *The Rambler*, an English Catholic periodical, published a review of the work by Richard Simpson the following March. It begins inauspiciously enough:

> The infidelity we have to combat is no longer the grinning sarcasm of Voltaire, or the blasphemous buffoonery of a half-sceptical libertine; but it is the calm philosophic discussion of men with their minds stocked with facts and instances, who, if they are without metaphysics enough to see the fallacies of their induction, yet earnestly believe the cogency of their proof.[14]

Given the tension that often obtains between Christians and apologists for evolutionary theory, a contemporary American reader is primed for a familiar conflict. The Christian and the scientist have entered the lists once again. But the bout of jousting we are primed to expect given the present state of the discourse does not come to pass. Simpson takes Darwin to task, but not for lack of faith or submission to the authority of Scripture and Tradition.

---

13. Charles Darwin, *On the Origin of Species by Means of Natural Selection, or the Preservation of Favoured Races in the Struggle for Life* (London: John Murray, 1859).

14. Richard Simpson, "Darwin on the Origin of Species," *The Rambler* 2, no. 6 (1860): 361.

What Simpson points out is Darwin's extraordinary credulity with respect to his own theory of evolution. He pairs this with a very satisfying critique of Darwin's metaphysical presuppositions and simplistic notions of how God acts in order to create the cosmos and all life within it. This is coupled with a readiness to receive, gratefully even, the genuine empirical, scientific work Darwin presents in *On the Origin of Species*. In a pointed critique of the "theory of simplicity," which argues against intellectual subtlety in defense of doctrine, Simpson concludes,

> Those believers, on the contrary, who have confidence that all truth will be ultimately found to harmonise, will enter into the controversy without fear either of the subtleties with which they will be forced to repel his subtle attacks, or of admitting whatever truths in the physical order he seems to have established on a fair foundation.[15]

Darwin's theory has the advantage of simplicity, the elegance of parsimony, and the Christian should not fear Darwin's findings. The harmony between the truths established in the physical order might require subtle argumentation to show how they hang together. The confidence of the Christian is that all truth has a single source. Findings in the book of creation and the book of Scripture will hang together. God creates the cosmos and reveals himself through it, and this same God reveals himself in Scripture. God is himself the truth of both.

As Simpson shows, Darwin's work can be divided into two distinct elements. These elements are confusingly arrayed because intertwined throughout. The first is "his accumulation and arrangement of scientific facts," which is "most striking."[16] The second is "the mythological conclusion" he claims to have derived from that same accumulation of scientific facts, but which Simpson argues is "fabulous."[17] It is so because Darwin has built up a metaphysical conclusion based upon his physical observations about the biological differentiation of species. Simpson calls this conclusion "subversive

15. Simpson, "Darwin on the Origin of Species," 363.

16. Simpson, "Darwin on the Origin of Species," 365.

17. Simpson, "Darwin on the Origin of Species," 365.

of psychology, metaphysics, and theology, all these sciences must cover their mouths, and await with resignation the decision of physical science, their new 'mother and mistress.'"[18] But it is Darwin's willingness to ascribe so much explanatory power to his theory of natural selection that allows him to punt, in the conclusion of his work, on the decisive question of the origins of life itself.[19] As Simpson points out, the mythos of Darwin's theory seems to have enamored him of its infinite applicability, to include the origins of life, without feeling the need to explain how that would be the case.[20] Or, as Simpson says further on, "He allows full play to his own imagination, while he requires his opponents to adhere strictly to proved facts."[21]

I will return to the metaphysical problems with Darwin's approach in a moment. First, I want to emphasize Simpson's readiness to accept Darwin's empirical claims. After highlighting how Darwin's theory of evolution by natural selection can be divided into two parts, mythological and scientific, Simpson insists that a Christian who holds to the doctrine of creation is free to receive the scientific facts if they rest upon good authority.[22] This is reminiscent of Augustine's insistence that those things provable by "most certain reason" should be accepted by Christians and factored into the interpretation of Scripture.[23] On Simpson's account, Christians are relieved from thinking of God as continually fiddling with his creation as though it were necessary to help things along here, or polish something up there. Simpson invokes the authority of the Church Fathers, "On one point they were agreed, and that is, that the law of creation is no exceptional rule that acts by fits and starts, by catastrophes and miraculous interpositions; but an equitable ever-present force, embracing all nature as the ocean embraces the land, and active throughout

18. Simpson, "Darwin on the Origin of Species," 365.

19. Darwin, *On the Origin of Species*, 483.

20. Simpson, "Darwin on the Origin of Species," 366.

21. Simpson, "Darwin on the Origin of Species," 369.

22. Simpson, "Darwin on the Origin of Species," 373.

23. Augustine, *Gn. litt.*, 1.19.39, *PL* 34:261: "Plerumque enim accidit ut aliquid de terra, de coelo, de caeteris mundi hujus elementis, de motu et conversione vel etiam magnitudine et intervallis siderum, de certis defectibus solis ac lunae, de circuitibus annorum et temporum, de naturis animalium, fruticum, lapidum, atque hujusmodi caeteris, etiam non christianus ita noverit, ut certissima ratione vel experientia teneat."

the whole duration of the world."[24] The point is that God's governance of all things does not come in fits and starts. The *administratio* is nothing more or less than the working out in time of God's eternal will for creation considered under aspect of the *conditio*.

On this basis Simpson makes his strong claim concerning the scientific results of Darwin's work: "It is clear, then, that the doctrine of creation does not prevent us from recognizing as truths, not only the universal reign of law, but also the most strange origin for different races. If the ancient saints did not adopt the conclusions of modern science; it is not because they condemned them, but because they knew nothing about them."[25] In this, Simpson shows how a Christian can appreciate Darwin's scientific work and attempt to fit it into his understanding of the cosmos. This move does not require taking on board the metaphysical baggage Darwin unnecessarily imports. And if the metaphysical presumptions of Darwin are implicit in *On the Origin of Species*, they become explicit in some of his later work. His 1868 *The Variation of Animals and Plants under Domestication* provides a very clear example in the concluding remarks.[26] Pushing back against those who declare "natural selection explains nothing," he offers an image of teaching "a savage utterly ignorant in the art of building" why stones with certain shapes are used in particular structures—arches, roofs, and so on.[27] Would he have explained nothing to this man if the "precise cause of the shape of each fragment could not be given"?[28] The point here is true, as one need not give a complete account of the entirety of the events on the timeline in order to have provided an explanation of how to construct a building. A description of how the bits of rock go together and why just is what it means to explain how to build a structure.

Darwin lays a trap for himself by giving an account of the kind of explanation he is offering. With his analogy, he is claiming that the theory of evolution by natural selection is a limited description of what best explains the available data—the features found in extant species (the buildings in his analogy).

24. Simpson, "Darwin on the Origin of Species," 374.

25. Simpson, "Darwin on the Origin of Species," 374.

26. Charles Darwin, *The Variations of Animals and Plants under Domestication*, vol. 2 (London: John Murray, 1868).

27. Darwin, *The Variations of Animals and Plants under Domestication*, vol. 2, 430.

28. Darwin, *The Variations of Animals and Plants under Domestication*, vol. 2, 431.

As soon as this description is offered, Darwin transposes his reasoning into another key. Returning to the image of the stones used for building, he explains how the shape of any given rock fragment used for building is accidental. This does not mean that the shape of each rock is uncaused, just that we need not assume any particular shape of rock is there for the purpose of being used in his building.[29] This is where he begins to make a mistake. When Darwin switches the register of his discourse, he moves from talk of secondary causes—rockslides and cliff faces—to talk of God as primary cause—without seeing the need to modify his manner of speech. He knows he is wading into unfamiliar waters when he says, "And here we are led to face a great difficulty, in alluding to which I am aware I am travelling beyond my proper province."[30] Darwin marks the departure and its dangers, but he presses on.

Before continuing with his analogy, Darwin adverts to the omniscience of a creator who knows all the consequences of the laws he establishes.[31] Everything that comes about, God knows. Darwin calls this foreknowing, but as I have argued it is helpful to specify "foreknowing" as shorthand for God's knowledge of all the things in his eternal present. Darwin presses this picture of foreknowledge when he asks, incredulously, "But can it be reasonably maintained that the Creator intentionally ordered, if we use the words in any ordinary sense, that certain fragments of rock should assume certain shapes so that the builder might erect his edifice?"[32] It is not exactly God's knowledge that Darwin is questioning, but rather his knowledge as enacted in the providential ordering of all things. One response to his question might be to point out that what he means by the "ordinary sense" of "intentionally ordered" is what is at issue here. Darwin has moved from talk about the secondary causes of the shape of stones to talk about God as their primary cause. He wants to retain a kind of talk about ordering and causing that does not fit this new context. There is no specification of what the "ordinary sense" of ordering might be. We might infer, from his analogy, that it looks like the kind of thing the builder is doing when he selects stones to construct an edifice. This is a perfectly reasonable way to talk about ordering. The art of building

29. Darwin, *The Variations of Animals and Plants under Domestication*, vol. 2, 431.

30. Darwin, *The Variations of Animals and Plants under Domestication*, vol. 2, 431.

31. Darwin, *The Variations of Animals and Plants under Domestication*, vol. 2, 431.

32. Darwin, *The Variations of Animals and Plants under Domestication*, vol. 2, 431.

is just this kind of thing, the imposition of an order upon building materials that was not there before. But this is always a derivative and dependent sort of order. It requires that there be something capable of being ordered. Because humans cannot create *ex nihilo,* this means dependence upon God for not only the existence of the materials, but also of ourselves and our powers of ordering. Darwin's analogy breaks down rapidly under this pressure. The kind of ordering God does is radically different from the kind a human builder does. To demand that our descriptions of it fit with an "ordinary sense" of ordering is to miss this point entirely.

From his analogy of the builder and the rocks, he returns to the matter at hand: the variations in domesticated animals and plants. Taking himself to have proved his point in the case of the shapes of the rocks, he asks why we would suggest that the variations in organisms are ordained by the creator. This is a question that demands an answer. It demands one because the Christian theological tradition claims God knows and ordains all things having created them from nothing. It is necessary to understand what that claim entails. As Darwin says, we would have to establish God's claim over not just the beneficial variations in any given species, but also those that do them injury.[33] Before sorting out the relation of both beneficial and harmful variations to God's providence, I want to take a look at what Darwin's elision of primary and secondary causes does to his discourse.

This elision is the source of the mythological element, identified by Simpson, of Darwin's writing. As Darwin puts it,

> If we assume each particular variation was from the beginning preordained, the plasticity of organisation, which leads to many injurious deviations of structure, as well as that redundant power of reproduction which inevitably leads to the struggle for existence, and, as a consequence, to the natural selection or survival of the fittest, must appear to us superfluous laws of nature.[34]

This way of putting it—preordination rendering the mechanism of selection superfluous—confirms the inference I made above. Darwin

33. Darwin, *The Variations of Animals and Plants under Domestication*, vol. 2, 431.

34. Darwin, *The Variations of Animals and Plants under Domestication*, vol. 2, 432.

does not distinguish between primary and secondary causes and for this reason sees preordaining and selection standing in opposition to one another. There is no reason to draw this conclusion. In fact, there is good reason to think that anyone describing creation this way is not speaking about the Christian God. Darwin's creator is no creator at all. He is a builder operating on the same level of causality as the human builder constructing a building's edifice. Darwin's analogy swallows his conclusion whole.

Darwin's contemporary, St. George Mivart,[35] saw the same problem. His is another of the early Catholic responses to Darwin's theory of evolution by natural selection, *On the Genesis of Species*.[36] It has an entire chapter dedicated to theology and evolution. There he cites this same passage from Darwin's *Variations* and identifies the same weakness, a "low anthropomorphism."[37] From there he issues a flamboyant rebuttal to Darwin's *dubium*:

> Why, surely every theist must maintain that in the first foundation of the universe—the primary and absolute creation—God saw and knew every purpose to which every atom and particle of matter should ever subserve in all suns and systems, and throughout all coming aeons of time. It is almost incredible, yet nevertheless it seems necessary to think that the difficulty thus proposed rests on a sort of notion that amidst the boundless profusion of nature there is too much for God to superintend; that the number of objects is too great for an infinite and *omnipresent* being to attend singly to each and all in their due proportions and needs![38]

Mivart has rightly diagnosed the major theological difficulty in Darwin's work. It has a number of consequences. First, to adopt this picture of a creator means you are no longer speaking of the God Christians worship. Second, it leads people to say things about death that are not compatible with a Christian view of the cosmos. This second problem maps onto

35. For the record, he's not a saint, just British.

36. St. George Mivart, *On the Genesis of Species* (London: Macmillan & Co., 1871).

37. Mivart, *On the Genesis of Species*, 258.

38. Mivart, *On the Genesis of Species*, 258–59. Emphasis original.

considerations of nonhuman creaturely pain, suffering, and death. But it comes into even sharper focus when considering the death of humans.

And it is along these lines that I want to turn my attention to some contemporary theologians who have been captivated by Darwin's mythological picture of the cosmos. The first instance I will point out comes from Celia Deane-Drummond's work. Deane-Drummond is an interesting figure in this conversation because she is both a trained evolutionary biologist and a theologian. Sadly, she is also prone to Darwin's "low anthropomorphism." In *Christ and Evolution: Wonder and Wisdom*, Deane-Drummond falls victim to the mythological element of Darwin's evolutionary theory. Mirroring Darwin's own skepticism about God's omniscience and omnipotence, she says,

> as someone trained in biological science, I find the possibility that God might influence mutation in a particular direction for usefulness perhaps many thousands of years hence somewhat strange. . . . It would seem to anticipate, if it is to work, that God knows the whole history of the intervening period, which goes against how I would interpret the action of God in creation and history.[39]

Of course it is strange to try to think of God's panoptic view of all creation, but, as Mivart explained, this is just what Christians have taken to be characteristically true of God. Imagining that God does not know "the whole history of the intervening period" is simply to say he is not God. God's knowledge of that history and all the particulars that occur within it just is their existence. Attempts to speak of God's "action" in "creation and history" that lose sight of God's causative knowing and willing of all the things that are in all the times that are serve to show how far a given attempt has gone astray from Christian discourse about God.

Deane-Drummond's theological positions are even more problematic when she extends her evolutionary theology into the question of sin, suffering, and tragedy. In her essay for a volume called *Evolution and the Fall*,[40] Deane-Drummond makes a consequential error. She mistakes theological

39. Celia Deane-Drummond, *Christ and Evolution: Wonder and Wisdom* (Minneapolis: Fortress Press, 2009), 27.

40. William Cavanaugh and James K. A. Smith, *Evolution and the Fall* (Grand Rapids, MI: William B. Eerdmans, 2017).

positions on original sin for theologoumena.[41] It seems she thinks there is nothing Christians are obliged to think about original sin that might norm or govern what it would be possible to say respecting the scientific evidence for death and evolution. She is not entirely wrong. Christians can hold a number of possible views about what original sin brings about. But whatever position one holds is answerable to the Church's magisterial instruction on the subject, if there is any (there is). Against Deane-Drummond's view that there is nothing "required or necessary for Christian faith" about any specific teaching on original sin,[42] let us turn to the sources and see if that claim is supportable.

There are some non-negotiable elements to the doctrine of original sin, and they are incompatible with the opinion offered by Deane-Drummond. Look, for instance at the Synod of Carthage in 418. The first canon of the synod anathematizes the idea that humans were created so that whether or not they sinned, they would die a bodily death.[43] The synod explicitly condemns the idea that human bodily death comes about "by the necessity of nature" (*necessitate naturae*).[44] This synod also condemns two positions concerning the inheritance of original sin. Those who say either that infants ought not to be baptized or that they should be baptized but that original sin does not come from Adam are both anathematized.[45] The Second Synod of Orange also has something to say about original sin. There we are taught that it is not only the body that suffers a change for the worse but that the soul is also diminished

41. Celia Deane-Drummond, "In Adam All Die? Questions at the Boundary of Niche Construction, Community Evolution, and Original Sin," in *Evolution and the Fall*, ed. William Cavanaugh and James K. A. Smith (Grand Rapids, MI: William B. Eerdmans, 2017), 45.

42. Deane-Drummond, "In Adam All Die?, 45.

43. Synod of Carthage, *DS* §222: "ut quicumque dixerit, Adam primum hominm mortalem factum ita, ut, sive peccaret sive non peccaret, moreretur in corpore, hoc est de corpore exiret non peccati merito, sed necessitate naturae, anathema sit."

44. Synod of Carthage, *DS* §222.

45. Synod of Carthage, *DS* §222: "Item placuit, ut quicumque parvulos recentes ab uteris matrum baptizandos negat aut dicit in remissionem quidem peccatorum eos baptizari, sed nihil ex Adam trahere originalis peccati, quod lavacro regenerationis expietur, unde fit consequens, ut in eis forma baptismatis 'in remissionem peccatorum' non vera, sed falso intellegatur, anathema sit."

by Adam's sin.[46] The teachings of both Carthage and Orange are taken up and taught definitively by the Church at the Council of Trent, in session five's "Decree on Original Sin." Death is not only a consequence of sin, it is also a kind of captivity, in which the devil holds us.[47] Physical death and the damage done to the human soul in sin are held together. Both the death of the body and the death of the soul (i.e., spiritual separation from God), must be held to be diffused into the whole human family from Adam's sin, under threat of anathema.[48]

By contrast, here is how Deane-Drummond puts things:

> My own view is that original sin can be reinterpreted to mean that a person is born in each generation into an imperfect community of others, including other creaturely kinds. That community shapes the particular tapestry of sin as expressed in the life of an individual sinner, where sin represents a cutting off from relations with God and with each other, leading to concrete wrongful acts to which each person can be held to account. It is not so much that guilt is inherited through original sin, but that original sin creates the distorted social context in which it is impossible not to be a sinner.[49]

It is possible to affirm much of what she says here as true. Our sins are shaped by the sins of our community. These particular sins and the toll

---

46. Second Synod of Orange, *DS* §371: "Si quis per offensam praecaricationis Adae non totum, id est secundum corpus et animam, 'in deterius' dicit hominem 'commutatum', sed animae libertate illaesa durante, corpus tantummodo corruptioni credit obnoxium, Pelagii errore deceptus adversatur Scrupturae."

47. Council of Trent, "Decree on Original Sin," *DS* §1511: "amisisse incurrisseque per offensam praevaricationis huismodi iram et indignationem Dei atque ideo mortem, quam antea illi comminatus fuerat Deus, et cum morte captivitatem sub eius potestate, 'qui mortis' deinde 'habuit imperium, hoc est diaboli' [Heb 2:14]."

48. Council of Trent, "Decree on Original Sin," *DS* §1512: "'Si quis Adae praevaricationem sibi soli et non eius prpagni asserit nocuisse' . . . aut inquinatum illum per inoboedientiae peccatum 'mortem' et poenas 'corporis tantum in omne genus humanum transfudisse, non autem et peccatum, quod mors est animae': anathema sit."

49. Deane-Drummond, "In Adam All Die?," 45.

they take on our lives and the lives of others do affect our relations with God. But saying this much is not enough. There is nothing here you could not discover about human persons from a sociology or political science textbook. The radical claim the Church makes is that sin and death hold us captive and that to be freed from them you must be baptized, "so that what they contracted by generation, might be cleansed in them by regeneration."[50] Not only that, the Church also claims that original sin has damaged our human nature. This damage is a sort of congenital defect belonging to all humans. It is a disease which needs to be cured, an evil from which we must be saved.

Deane-Drummond suggests that "we might balk at the early church's supposition that the fall is also a fall in physical capacities as well as moral capacities."[51] There is something right about the doctrine of original sin, she thinks, just not this. What is needed, in her estimation, is a reconfiguration of the theology of original sin that takes into account what we know from evolutionary science. Here, she and I agree. We have to say something to account for our changed perspective on the natural world. At the same time, any such reinterpretation cannot abandon the magisterium by scoffing at the primitive early Church. As Deane-Drummond sees it, the "classic accounts" of original sin contain a major flaw.[52] They assume "that suffering and the tragic follow from the fall into sin, rather than precede it. Evolutionary theory demands, then, an adjustment in such a perspective, so that sin takes place in a tragic context and the unity hoped for is an eschatological expectation of the end, rather than a return to a paradisiacal state."[53] Like Darwin, Deane-Drummond's moral impulses are attuned to creaturely suffering and death. She is right to see the problem, but she blinks too soon. Instead of asking whether the Christian tradition might have resources internal to itself to answer the question of moral tragedy—here I mean the moral tragedy of the millions of years of creaturely

50. Council of Trent, "Decree on Original Sin," *DS* §1514: "ut in eis regeneratione mundetur, quod generatione contraxerunt."

51. Deane-Drummond, "In Adam All Die?," 45.

52. Deane-Drummond, "In Adam All Die?," 46.

53. Deane-Drummond, "In Adam All Die?," 46.

suffering and death evolutionary science presents us with—she assumes we must pitch overboard the teaching of the Church.

This kind of thinking about original sin and death is not exclusive to Deane-Drummond. Another example in contemporary theology comes from David Kelsey. In *Eccentric Existence: A Theological Anthropology*, Kelsey attempts a theology of creation and the human person that can account for contemporary scientific knowledge about human origins. He does so by drawing on the accounts of creation in Scripture's wisdom tradition. Kelsey presents arguments for human creaturely existence that is fragile and finite from the very beginning. Humans and all other creatures have a proper integrity, but our finitude and our death go hand in hand. As Kelsey puts it, "Such creaturely finitude makes their [human creatures'] deaths essential possibilities. Relating to us creatively, God creates dying life."[54] The language gets stronger as he goes. Kelsey pushes back against the idea that original sin leads to human biological death. Drawing on the creation accounts in the biblical wisdom literature he argues for "an understanding of human creaturely finitude according to which mortality and dying are inherent features of what it is to be a personal body. Hence it cannot be said that somehow adventitious distortion of personal identities [i.e., sin] causes personal bodies to die."[55] We should be skeptical about this approach. In an attempt to make sense of what we know of the cosmos by way of the natural sciences, the author ends up abandoning a central axiom of the Christian faith, that we are in need of salvation from death and death's mistress, sin.

It might be possible to object that this reinterpretation of original sin, which emphasizes its spiritual, moral, and communal rather than the physical, biological, and inherited aspects, is a natural development in Christian thought about the nature of human beings. Now that we have come to understand more fully what humans are and where we have come from in evolutionary terms, it is necessary to reconfigure our doctrines accordingly. This seems to align with Augustine's argument about the relation between biblical interpretation and scientific knowledge in the first book of *De Genesi ad litteram*. Here I say both yes and no. We do need a way of speaking about God and creation that can account for what the natural sciences have taught

---

54. David H. Kelsey, *Eccentric Existence: A Theological Anthropology*, vol. 1 (Louisville, KY: Westminster John Knox Press, 2009), 284.

55. Kelsey, *Eccentric Existence*, vol. 1, 437.

us. But we must recognize the priority of the rule of faith in our speculative suggestions. Casting to one side the teaching of an ecumenical council on the origins of human death in sin, especially when it is claiming to offer a definitive interpretation of the scriptural witness of St. Paul at Romans 5:12,[56] should not be our first option. Sin and physical death go hand in hand.

And the Council of Trent is simply codifying as doctrine what can be found throughout the Old and New Testament. Sin and death must be held together or else the gospel turns out to make very little sense. Remove death from the network of evils consequent upon sin and you will have a very hard time saying why creation needs salvation from it. If death is a natural reality, intrinsic to what it is to be a finite creature, and in particular of what it is to be a human, how can it also be "the last enemy to be destroyed" (1 Cor 15:26)? Is there a way to speak intelligibly of sin as "the sting of death" (1 Cor 15:56) or of death as "the wages of sin" (Rom 6:23) without connecting physical, bodily death with the voluntary evil of rational creatures? It is not clear we can give reasons why God should become a human, suffer, and die in order to save us from death, if it is also the case that he created us to die. In Deane-Drummond's view, tragedy precedes sin—death is just part of what it means to be a creature. For Kelsey, finitude and death go hand in hand. But the Word becomes flesh so that "he might taste death for every one" (Heb 2:9). In Jesus Christ, God tastes death to "deliver all those who through fear of death were subject to lifelong bondage" (Heb 2:15). But why fear what belongs to us properly? How can our natures as created by God constitute bondage?

The short answer is that these positions cannot be reconciled with the Christian witness to a crucified God who goes to his death willingly to save us from death. It is more than a little ironic that Darwin's *Variations* ends with a comparison of the problem he presents, of natural selection and its compatibility with divine foreknowledge, with another perennial problem, free will and predestination.[57] I have already established that Darwin is dealing with a confused picture of God and God's causal agency, and so I do not think he has anything useful to say about this theological conundrum. But free will and predestination—the compatibility of God's saving action and human free choice—is at the heart of the Pelagian controversy. Pelagius, who taught that

56. Cf. *DS* §§1512, 1514.

57. Darwin, *The Variations of Animals and Plants under Domestication*, vol. 2, 432.

the faculties of human creatures had not suffered diminution from the fall of Adam and Eve, imagined it was possible to keep God's commandments apart from the help of grace. The passages I cited from the Synods of Carthage and Orange and the Council of Trent all address the question of original sin from this angle. The Church's definitions of original sin and its interpretation of the relevant passages from Scripture are meant to put to bed a particular heresy.

The Pelagian controversy is about the effects of the human fall. In Augustine's opposition to Pelagianism we find a stout defense against the tendency to naturalize death. Augustine opens his *De peccatorum meritis et remissione et de baptismo parvulorum* on this note. "They say, 'Adam was so created that even without sin it would be his due to die, not as punishment for guilt, but by the necessity of nature.'"[58] Those who follow the teaching of Pelagius claim human death is a natural phenomenon, not the punishment due to original sin. The death promised to Adam and Eve for disobedience in the garden, say the Pelagians, is a soulish death, not something affecting the human body.[59] Augustine does not claim human creatures are made with something other than a mortal body. In *De civitate Dei*, for instance, drawing on the teaching of Paul in First Corinthians 15:42–50, Augustine says the first man was made "from the earth, earthly, into a living soul not into an enlivening spirit, which was laid up for him after being earned by obedience."[60] Not yet clothed with immortality, Adam has an animal body—alive by way of an *anima*, a soul. But were he to persist in obedience—to return to *De peccatorum meritis*—he would have been "changed into a spiritual body and into that incorruption, which is promised to the faithful and the saints, without having to pass through the punishment of death."[61] The Pelagian position is consistent, though, with their more fundamental position on the nature of original sin.

---

58. Augustine, *pecc. mer.*, 1.2.2, *CSEL* 60:1: "Qui dicunt 'Adam sic creatum, ut etiam sine peccati merito moreretur non poena culpae, sed necessitate naturae.'"

59. Augustine, *pecc. mer.*, 1.2.2, *CSEL* 60:1–2: "profecto illud, quod in lege dictum est: qua die ederitis, mori moriemini, non ad mortem corporis, sed ad mortem animae, quae in peccato fit, referre conantur."

60. Augustine, *civ.*, 13.23, *CSEL* 40.1:648 "Primus autem homo de terra terrenus in animam viventem factus est, non in spiritum vivificantem, quod ei oboedientiae meritum servabatur."

61. Augustine, *pecc. mer.*, 1.2.2, *CSEL* 60:2: "si non peccasset, in corpus fuerat spiritale mutandus et in illam incorruptionem, quae fidelibus et sanctis promittitur, sine mortis supplicio transiturus."

The Pelagians argue that biological death is not an effect of original sin. It cannot be because sin is not transmitted by propagation, but rather by imitation.[62] Augustine refutes this claim with the help of Paul's Letter to the Romans. The textual conflicts around Romans on sin and death are interesting in their own right. David Hart, for example, has levied a straightforward critique of the "mistranslation" of Romans 5:12, which he finds responsible—in part, at least—for the trajectory of Western theological reflection on the topic of original sin.[63] Augustine's reading of Romans is intriguing because while he does deploy the text of Romans 5:12 in his argument against the Pelagians, he does not first tack to the controversial "in quo omnes peccaverunt." Instead he points back to Wisdom 2:24, "through the devil's envy death entered the world." Imitation is how the first sin occurs. The devil tempts, and humans fall by following him away from God. If imitation is how sin is propagated, Augustine thinks it would better to name Satan instead of Adam in Romans 5.[64] This is a subtler move than what he will do with "in quo omnes peccaverunt" in the next section.[65] It is worth attending to because the claim that Augustine, or the Western tradition following him, has built its theology of original sin on a shaky foundation is less convincing once you see the range of arguments Augustine deploys to support it—this being just one of them. Romans 5:12 is one piece (a big piece to be sure) in a much larger puzzle of doctrine and practice.

The upshot of Augustine's reading of Wisdom 2:24 and Romans 5:12 together is that Adam is identified as the *princeps*, the originator, of sin.

62. Augustine, *pecc. mer.*, 1.9.9, *CSEL* 60:10: "ipsum peccatum non propagatione in alios homines ex primo homine, sed imitatione transisse."

63. David Bentley Hart, *The New Testament: A Translation* (New Haven, CT: Yale University Press, 2017), 296–97, note p. An interesting situation presents itself here, however, as the Council of Trent offers a decisive interpretation of Romans 5:12 in its "Decree on Original Sin." Whatever the Greek manuscripts say, the Roman Catholic Church has codified not only the text of the Vulgate, "Per unum hominem peccatum intravit in mundum, et per peccatum mors, et ita in omnes homines mors pertransiit, in quo omnes peccaverunt" (Rom 5:12), but also its meaning (especially what it means to say "in whom all have sinned") as part of the doctrinal deposit of the Church. Whatever your position on the Greek is, Catholics cannot resolve the difficulty simply by returning to the text of Paul's letter.

64. Augustine, *pecc. mer.*, 1.9.9, *CSEL* 60:10: "Sed si peccatum apostolus illud commemorare voluisset, quod in hunc mundum non propagatione, sed imitatione intraverit, eius principem non Adam, sed diabolum diceret."

65. Cf. Augustine, *pecc. mer.*, 1.9.10.

Augustine draws a distinction between the way sin comes through Adam's imitation of the devil and the way it comes to us. Were Paul speaking of sin that comes through imitation, were we in no way subject to inherited guilt, he would have had us all marked out as imitators of the devil. As it happens, Paul has connected death to Adam's sin, and so it must come to us in a way distinct from imitation. We do imitate Adam each time we sin, Augustine says.[66] But Adam also passes along his sin to all humans who come after him. Here Augustine deploys Romans 5:12 to drive home the distinction he has made between imitation and propagation. Adam "in himself corrupted by the hidden corruption of his carnal concupiscence all who were to come from his lineage"[67]—and this is why the devil is not named as the originator of sin by Paul.

The Pelagian rejects death as punishment for sin because he also rejects original sin as something that is contracted and propagated through inheritance. This parallels the move in contemporary theology that seeks to naturalize human death. Both Kelsey and Deane-Drummond want to reinterpret the doctrine of original sin, decoupling it from death. Being born into a context that is ineluctably tragic and so also drinking in the sins of the human family, as Deane-Drummond's reinterpretation offered, sounds like the position Augustine is critiquing in *De peccatorum meritis*. I think this stems from a worry shared by both Darwin and Deane-Drummond that if God is omniscient and omnipotent, knowing and willing all the things that are, something of the drama of life is lost. They are both in search of a world that could surprise God himself. And that is exactly the sort of worry Pelagius has when he encounters Augustine's theology of grace. The story of Pelagius hearing Augustine's words from book X of the *Confessiones*, "grant what you command, and command what you will,"[68] centers on a worry that God might know and will too much, leaving no room for creatures to be themselves. If the ability to do good is something God must grant, Pelagius worries the moral

66. Augustine, *pecc. mer.*, 1.9.10, *CSEL* 60:11: "Imitantur quidem Adam, quotquot per inoboedientiam transgrediuntur mandatum dei."

67. Augustine, *pecc. mer.*, 1.9.10, *CSEL* 60:11: "occulta etiam tabe carnalis concupiscentiae suae tabificavit in se omnes de sua stirpe venturos."

68. Augustine, *conf.*, 10.29.40, *CSEL* 33:256: "da quod iubes et iube quod vis."

seriousness of the Christian life is in jeopardy. Darwin's inclination to tie natural selection and species variation to the vexed question of free will and predestination represents the same set of concerns at the level of biological processes rather than the life of faith. The structure is similar in each case. In response, I return to the thoughts of Herbert McCabe, which I cited earlier. McCabe says, "every action in the world is an action of God; not because it is not an action of a creature but because it is by God's action that the creature is *itself* and has its *own* activity."[69] The desire to be yourself, to have your own activity that is not also an action of God is to desire to be nothing at all. There is something demonic lurking in the Pelagian demand for moral autonomy as there is in Darwin's for physical autonomy. In each case, a person wants himself or the world to be what it is apart from God. But, apart from God and what he brings about, there is just nothing.

Now I want to return to the moral problem identified in both Darwin's and Deane-Drummond's work. I want to turn back to it because the desire to naturalize death and to exclude the natural processes by which things come to be, propagate themselves, and die, from God's providence arises from a specific set of worries. As I have made clear, I am inclined to view all death, not just human death, as evidence that things are not as they should be. To say the death of the zebra in the jaws of a lion is simply the way things are and that it can be explained away by recourse to natural evil misses something of the evolutionary biologist's horror at finding the pluriformity of life on earth has its origins in a colossal meat grinder. This is clearly on Darwin's mind when he notices that if all the variations of plant and animal life are superintended by God, this includes those that are "not beneficial" and "far more injurious to the creatures themselves."[70] So, too, in Deane-Drummond's desire to preserve the tragic, we see an awareness of the moral difficulty posed by the sheer scope of nonhuman creaturely death.

This moral judgment about creation is expressed in a number of genres. Alongside Darwin's worries we can place his more polemical heir, Richard Dawkins, who takes the evidence of the vast scales of evolutionary death, dismemberment, and general suffering to argue decisively against the idea

69. McCabe, "Creation," 7.

70. Darwin, *The Variations of Animals and Plants under Domestication*, vol. 2, 431.

of beneficent (or at least an omnipotent) creator. In a section of his book *The Greatest Show on Earth*[71] called "Evolutionary Theodicy?" Dawkins gives the example of Ichneumon wasps. The females of the species paralyze their victims before laying their eggs within the living, but immobile, bodies of their prey. The larvae of the wasp then hatch within the still-living victim and devour it from the inside out.[72] According to Dawkins, Ichneumon wasps were a common cause of worry among Victorian biologists, including Darwin himself.[73] It is easy to see why. How could such a thing as the Ichneumon wasp come about? Why would God devise such a cruel mechanism for the propagation of the species? In this section Dawkins cites another of his works with a description that ought to dissuade us from hasty or glib dismissals of the very real concern expressed. He says,

> The total amount of suffering per year in the natural world is beyond all decent contemplation. During the minute that it takes me to compose this sentence, thousands of animals are being eaten alive, others are running for their lives, whimpering with fear, others are being slowly devoured from within by rasping parasites, thousands of all kinds are dying of starvation, thirst and disease. It must be so. If there is ever a time of plenty, this very fact will automatically lead to an increase in population until the natural state of starvation and misery is restored.[74]

All of this is right and terrifying. It ought to give Christians pause and cause us to ask whether we have answers to objections of this kind.

It is not only Dawkins or Darwin who are shaken in this way. Tennyson, too, sees the difficulty, in a poem called *In Memoriam A. H. H.* The work begins "Strong Son of God, immortal Love, / Whom we, that have not seen thy face, / By faith, and faith alone, embrace, / Believing where we cannot

---

71. Richard Dawkins, *The Greatest Show on Earth: The Evidence for Evolution* (New York: Free Press, 2009).

72. Dawkins, *The Greatest Show on Earth*, 395.

73. Dawkins, *The Greatest Show on Earth*, 395.

74. Dawkins, *The Greatest Show on Earth*, 391.

prove."[75] Faith, and faith alone, is what is required by the fifty-fourth canto. Looking upon the ills of death, Tennyson says, perhaps trying to convince himself, "Oh yet we trust that somehow good / Will be the final goal of ill."[76] Faith in the goodness, and perhaps also of the strength of the "Strong Son of God" is necessary when staring nature in the face. By the end of this same canto, he will find there are no words to express what it is he sees, "And with no language but a cry."[77] But he does continue to speak or limp along, now asking, "Are God and Nature then at strife, / That Nature lends such evil dreams?"[78] Tennyson wonders how he can hold together the strength and "immortal Love" of God with the brutality of Nature. He offers a solution which fits the suggestion from the last canto that good is the goal of ill. "So careful of the type she seems, / So careless of the single life."[79] Maybe species are the goal, the final goal, the good that comes from ill. He finds that this does not quite satisfy, though, so now we hear, "I falter where I firmly trod" and "I stretch lame hands of faith, and grope."[80] Tennyson feels his own weakness in the face of death, registering the feebleness of his own attempt at resolution.

He ends the fifty-fifth canto with, "And faintly trust the larger hope."[81] His attempts to offer something more than wordless cry do not satisfy him. And it gets worse. The larger hope, that of the preservation of the species at the expense of the individual, is also shattered by the voice of Nature herself, in the next canto. I will quote this one at length, as it includes the best-known line from the poem, and sums up the poet's difficulty in the face of the world depicted for him by evolutionary biology.

> *"So careful of the type?" but no.*
> *From scarped cliff and quarried stone*

---

75. Alfred Tennyson, "In Memoriam A. H. H. Obit MDCCCXXXIII," in *Tennyson: Poems and Plays* (London: Oxford University Press, 1965), 230.

76. Tennyson, "In Memoriam A. H. H., canto LIV, p. 243.

77. Tennyson, "In Memoriam A. H. H., canto LIV, p. 243.

78. Tennyson, "In Memoriam A. H. H., canto LV, p. 243.

79. Tennyson, "In Memoriam A. H. H., canto LV, p. 243.

80. Tennyson, "In Memoriam A. H. H., canto LV, p. 243.

81. Tennyson, "In Memoriam A. H. H., canto LV, p. 243.

She cries, "A thousand types are gone:
I care for nothing, all shall go.

"Thou makest thine appeal to me:
I bring to life, I bring to death:
The spirit does but mean the breath:
I know no more." And he, shall he,

Man, her last work, who seem'd so fair,
Such splendid purpose in his eyes,
Who roll'd the psalm to wintry skies,
Who built him fanes of fruitless prayer,

Who trusted God was love indeed
And love Creation's final law—
Tho' Nature, red in tooth and claw
With ravine, shriek'd against his creed—

Who loved, who suffer'd countless ills,
Who battled for the True, the Just,
Be blown about the desert dust,
Or seal'd within the iron hills?[82]

Not even the species or "type" can save him, for types themselves perish at Nature's hands. Wielding life and death, Nature confronts Man. Man, who trusted in the immortal Love of God, now sees Nature for what she is, gorged on the flesh of not just individuals but whole species.

One more striking instance of this moral impulse comes in Graham Greene's *The Power and the Glory*, where the lieutenant in pursuit of the whisky priest feels, viscerally, the cruelty of the world. Greene writes,

> The lieutenant sat down upon his bed and began to take off his boots. It was the hour of prayer. Black beetles exploded against the wall like crackers. More than a dozen crawled over the tiles with injured

82. Tennyson, "In Memoriam A. H. H., canto LVI, p. 243.

> wings. It infuriated him to think that there were still people in the state who believed in a loving and merciful God. There are mystics who are said to have experienced God directly. He was a mystic, too, and what he had experienced was a vacancy—a complete certainty in the existence of a dying, cooling world, of human beings who had evolved from animals for no purpose at all. He knew.[83]

The absurdity of a beetle maiming itself by repeatedly bashing into the wall until it loses the ability to fly provokes the lieutenant's rage. His mystical vision presses in on him as a felt lack. The lieutenant experiences God's absence in the suicidal beetles as palpably as the Christian mystic does God's love. His contemplation of nature leaves him unable to imagine a loving and merciful creator.

It would be a mistake to insist on God's love and mercy by dismissing the moral concerns of Darwin, Deane-Drummond, Dawkins, Tennyson, and Greene's lieutenant. Mivart does make this mistake in his critique of Darwin. He tackles Darwin's questions about variations that prove detrimental to a creature's survival. These maladaptations might be the source of pain or suffering for the animal, but Mivart's gruesome response is to explain the pain away by insisting the specter of animal suffering is something of a canard. Suffering, he claims, can be directly correlated to the mental acuity of the sufferer.

> The Author has been assured that lower races of men appear less keenly sensitive to physical pain than do more cultivated and refined human beings. Thus only in man can there really be any intense degree of suffering, because only in him is there that intellectual recollection of past moments and that anticipation of future ones, which constitute in great part the bitterness of suffering. The momentary pang, the present pain, which beasts endure, though real enough, is yet, doubtless, not to be compared as to its intensity with the suffering which is produced in man through his high prerogative of self-consciousness.[84]

83. Graham Greene, *The Power and the Glory* (New York: Penguin Books, 1983), 24.

84. Mivart, *The Genesis of Species*, 260–61.

Not only does Mivart think anecdotal pseudoscience sufficient evidence for hierarchically ordering the pain of nonhuman animals, he applies the same standard to talk of human pain and suffering. His characterization of the phenomenology of pain is extremely problematic, though this is not the place to show why. It is enough to offer his as an example of a certain kind of response—and a particularly distasteful one—to the concerns of those struck by the insights of evolutionary biology, and who are not able to easily reconcile what they have learned about the world with what they have heard about God.

Given Mivart's response, it is no wonder that he is able to cheerily respond to Darwin, "The natural universe has resulted in the development of an unmistakable harmony and beauty, and in a decided preponderance of good and happiness over their opposites."[85] The point of Mivart's manly, rational dismissal of Darwin's sentimentalism toward plants and animals is to paper over the concern altogether and simply insist on the world's goodness and beauty. Never mind how one would measure goodness and happiness so as to be able to announce so blithely their preponderance. Never mind, that is, the sound of the lieutenant's exploding beetles.

On this point, I find myself siding with those who see the horror of the natural history of carnage. It is something that needs to be made sense of, not something to be brushed aside. It does not seem at all obvious to me that there is a preponderance of goodness and happiness. I am more inclined to hear the whole creation groaning (Rom 8:22). At the same time, I want to affirm the cosmos created by God is good and very good. The task now is to see whether the work I have done to interpret Augustine's theology of creation provides something robust enough to bear the sometimes tragic weight of evolutionary biologists' discoveries. There is a way through the confrontation of Greene's lieutenant with the vacancy he experiences when confronted with the realities of death and suffering. But to take this path you cannot deny these evident evils. Averting your eyes will not make them disappear, and the attempts to lessen their significance are grotesque. What I am proposing is that we head straight for the death and suffering. We have to see it as the working out in the order of time of the real consequences of the angelic fall. The rest of this chapter will be a speculative attempt to see how that plays out and what the theological payoff of this view might be.

---

85. Mivart, *The Genesis of Species*, 261.

The *Rationes Seminales* in the Order of Time

To recapitulate, the devil is fallen *ex quo creatus est*—from the moment of his creation. That was the conclusion of chapter 3. This should not be misunderstood as a claim that the devil was created evil. The devil was created good and yet falls in the blink of an eye. Because of this fall the world is always already broken, shot through with the devil's sin. There is never a time when the good and very good creation of God is not also damaged. This is because the creation of the angels occurs before all times and so affects all times. I have also made the provisional claim that because the angels administer all things, and do so through the *rationes seminales*, there is good reason to suppose the damage the demons do by falling is not limited to themselves. The damage inflicted by the fall of the angels ramifies outward in a cascade of effects, leaving no part of the cosmos untouched by the effects of sin.

I am offering an interpretation of Paul's assertion, "the wages of sin is death" (Rom 6:23), that applies it to the entirety of the cosmos. The principal effect of the fall of the angels, with respect to all other creatures, is to incline them to die. "Through the devil's envy death entered the world" (Wis 2:24), and when the good and very good creation of God—made all at once in the *conditio*—marches along in the order of time, it does so with a limp. In other words, the *rationes seminales* God created in the *conditio* unfurl in the *administratio* in a cosmos with a tendency toward dissipation and dissolution. This is the "bondage to decay" Paul identifies holding creation captive in Romans 8:21. It is a tendency toward death that affects all creatures, living or otherwise. Entropic decay, the movement of the physical universe toward a thermodynamic equilibrium state, is a structural feature of the cosmos. It begins, so far as we can tell, at the very beginning. It will end, so it seems, with a cold, dark, and lifeless material world. Augustine's claim that "the whole time of this life is nothing other than a march toward death"[86] applies equally well to the whole physical world as it does to any individual human life.

Assuming that the march begins just shy of fourteen billion years ago with a big bang, the decay begins right away. Things start to cool down, but they also start to take shape. Eventually galaxies and stars form—all the heavenly bodies dance to gravity's tune. But how do they form? There is one level at which to ask this question where I am unqualified to answer. Astrophysicists, I assume,

86. Augustine, *civ.*, 13.10, *CSEL* 40.1:626: "ut omnino nihil sit aliud tempus vitae huius, quam cursus ad mortem."

can give perfectly cogent explanations of the how of stellar and galactic genesis. This is not my primary concern. That it happens, and happens predictably, is something I am willing to trust them on. But this is not the only sort of "how" at stake here. How do the seed-like rules at the heart of creation, which relate all things to Christ, give this cosmos its particular shape after the fall of the angels? They do so while always being marked, marred, by the sin of the angels. Augustine's thinking about the *rationes seminales* in *De genesi ad litteram* is congruent with this thought. There Augustine looks into a couple of possible ways of interpreting the *rationes*. Is each thing created in its seed-like state with the tendency to develop in the course of time, through normal periods of growth? Or, does God prescribe that things will emerge already developed, fully formed, without passing through any intermediary stages?[87]

"But why should we not believe they had both possibilities?" Augustine asks.[88] We might instead assume God creates the *rationes* with aptitudes (*habiles*) toward either mode of development.[89] If God acts to bring an event about miraculously, we need not suppose he acts against his own original creation of all things in the *conditio*. Instead, we can assume a latent possibility toward either timebound or miraculous unfurling. Perhaps even better, Augustine thinks, we may be inclined to reflect upon the miracle that there is anything at all. Augustine gives the example of Jesus's miracle of turning water to wine. It is not, he points out, as though water is not apt to become wine. This happens all the time, but doing so normally involves temporal processes: being drunk in by the roots of a vine, budding into grapes, being pressed into juice, and fermenting into an alcoholic beverage.[90] But, Augustine asks, "Did

87. Augustine, *Gn. litt.*, 6.14.25, *PL* 34:349: "Quaeri autem merito potest, causales illae rationes, quas mundo indidit, cum primum simul omnia creavit, quomodo sint institutae: utrum ut, quemadmodum videmus cuncta nascentia vel fruticum vel animalium in suis conformationibus atque incrementis, sua pro diversitate generum diversa spatia peragerent temporum? an ut, quemadmodum creditur factus Adam sine ullo progressu incrementorum virili aetate, continuo conformarentur?"

88. Augustine, *Gn. litt.*, 6.14.25, *PL* 34:349: "Sed cur non utrumque illas credimus habuisse."

89. Augustine, *Gn. litt.*, 6.14.25, *PL* 34:349: "Restat ergo ut ad utrumque modum habiles creatae sint."

90. Augustine, *Gn. litt.*, 6.13.24, *PL* 34:349: "Quis enim nescit aquam concretam terrae, cum ad radices vitis venerit, duci in saginam ligni illius, atque in eo sumere qualitatem, qua in uvam procedat paulatim erumpentem; atque in ea grandescente vinum fiat, maturumque dulcescat, quod adhuc fervescat expressum, et quadam vetustate firmatum ad usum bibendi utilius jucundiusque perveniat?"

the maker of time need the help of time?"[91] The upshot of Augustine's thinking here is that God can bring things about in a way that seems unusual to us when he acts upon the latent possibilities contained in the *rationes seminales*. It is this sort of action that we call miraculous.

This notion of an aptitude for becoming deserves further attention, and it can be applied more broadly than the cases of God's miraculous action or development over time. Augustine's thoughts on the *rationes seminales* and their indeterminacy give us a way of talking about what happens when certain possibilities for the created order are foreclosed from the very beginning with the fall of the angels. The angelic fall prematurely closes off some of these possibilities, resulting in a cosmos enslaved to death and decay. The aptitudes toward which the *rationes seminales* are disposed unfurl within that structure. At the same time, the introduction of angelic sin is not a surprise to God, so what is actualized through those aptitudes is pleasing to God.[92] God acts in and through the brokenness of the cosmos to bring about what is good, but the goods that God brings about develop under the conditions of slavery to sin. It is not clear to us, on the far side of this catastrophe, what a world without angelic sin would have looked like or precisely what aptitudes are left unactualized. What is clear is that this world is the one with which we have to do. And this world is a world in which sin and sin's damage play a role. To play with Tolkien's symphonic picture of creation from *The Silmarillion*, sin's damage sets the musical score of the cosmos in a minor key. To complete that picture, we need a way of describing how God draws the damage wrought by sin into a melody more glorious than would have been apart from the wounds it inflicts.

To understand this I turn to book XIII of *De civitate Dei*, where Augustine describes what the grace of Jesus Christ accomplishes with respect to death. There he explains, "So, through the ineffable mercy of God the very punishment of sins becomes the armor of virtue, and even the death sentence of the sinner becomes the merit of the just."[93] Augustine is exploring the strange

91. Augustine, *Gn. litt.*, 6.13.24, *PL* 34:349: "Numquid adjutorio temporis eguit conditor temporis?"

92. Augustine, *Gn. litt.*, 6.14.25, *PL* 34:349: "Sed cur non utrumque illas credimus habuisse, ut hoc ex eis futurum esset, quod factori placuisset."

93. Augustine, *civ.*, 13.4, *CSEL* 40.1:620: "Sic per ineffabilem Dei misericordiam et ipsa poena vitiorum transit in arma virtutis, et fit iusti meritum etiam supplicium peccatoris."

state of affairs that obtains because of the grace of Christ. Death takes on a new character because the second person of the Trinity has gone down into death. Martyrs who go to their death now do honor to God by undergoing the very thing that once was a shameful punishment for sin. God is able, in other words, to put death to good use. Augustine is careful not to obscure the evil of death: "It's not that death, which once was bad, became something good."[94] Instead, he explains, "God showed so much grace to faith that death, which is known to be opposed to life, has become the instrument (*instrumentum*) by which one may pass over to life."[95] God wields death like a tool and uses his own death to put death to death. He does not make death good, but he turns it toward a good end.

This is the logic of the incarnation. The Son descends to take on our infirmity. He makes our weakness the means by which we can attain eternal life. Death plays a crucial role. Christ's death stands at the center of the liturgical life of the Church, and through death the resurrection. Given the revelation on the Cross of God's willingness to use death as a tool in this way, we can find a certain fittingness (a *convenientia*) to death being wielded as an instrument by God in the always already fallen creation. God created the *rationes seminales* with aptitudes. The aptitudes actualized in a cosmos whose rule is death and decay are those that put death to work. God uses death, thereby catching death's evil up into his own purposes. When he does so, God creates the whole panoply of living things. These living things only are what they are because they have come to be in a dying world. But this is a dying world whose true rule, whose *regula* and *ratio*, is life. As Augustine explains in book IX of *De Genesi ad litteram*, the seminal rules written into the cosmos at their inception determine the capabilities of those same creatures.[96] Everything God works in his providential governance of the cosmos—to include what we

---

94. Augustine, *civ.*, 13.4, *CSEL* 40.1:620: "non quia mors bonum aliquod facta est, quae antea malum fuit."

95. Augustine, *civ.*, 13.4, *CSEL* 40.1:620: "tantam Deus fidei praestitit gratiam, ut mors, quam vitae constat esse contrarium, instrumentum fieret, per quod transiretur ad vitam."

96. Augustine, *Gn. litt.*, 9.17.32, *PL* 34:406: "Omnis iste naturae usitatissimus cursus habet quasdam naturales leges suas, secundum quas et spiritus vitae, qui creatura est, habet quosdam appetitus suos determinatos quodammodo, quos etiam mala voluntas non possit excedere. Et elementa mundi hujus corporei habent definitam vim qualitatemque suam, quid unumquodque valeat vel non valeat, quid de quo fieri possit vel non possit."

would ordinarily call miracles—is a possibility already there in the *rationes seminales*.[97]

This matches up well with what we see at work in the natural processes of the world as we encounter it. Through the decay and death of stars, heavier elements come to be. Planets form and cool, making possible the kinds of living thing we find on earth, plants and animals, bacteria and fungi. And given this model, there is no reason to posit a special intervention of God with the advent of the most primitive forms of life on our planet three-and-a-half billion years ago. This is because in Augustine's account of creation everything has already been made, sown into the world as seeds. The coming to be of creatures in time is the outworking of God's hidden act of creation. Those first living creatures, primitive plants and animals, are no less a product of God's intentional creation of the cosmos if God did not prod at a puddle of primordial goo to give it life. God brought into being the very laws by which they would be governed, the context in which they would exist, the time in which they would live and die. It is a strange demand to insist that God must do this by what is sometimes called "special creation." To insist on this would be to assume that God could only govern his cosmos immediately and not through secondary, created causes.

But the damage of the cosmos evident in the death and decay of all things does not stop with the advent of life. Life resists entropic decay, but it remains the case that living things undergo this evil at the hands of time and of one another. Predation, the sustenance of life through the death and consumption of other creatures, is a mark of the fallen cosmos. So is the necessity of competition for finite resources like sunlight, water, or soil. This is the case in single-celled creatures and complex organisms alike. The struggle for survival, which staves off decay and death by boxing out other creatures or actively killing them, is evidence of the damage wrought by the fall of the angels. But God uses this feature of fallen life to bring about marvelous things. The bright colors and eye spots of the Io moth, the delicate, flowing elegance of the leafy seadragon, the powerful jaws of the American alligator, the sleek, streamlined body of the bottlenose dolphin, are all the product of God putting death

97. Augustine, *Gn. litt.*, 9.17.32, *PL* 34:406: "Super hunc autem motum cursumque rerum naturalem, potestas Creatoris habet apud se posse de his omnibus facere aliud, quam eorum quasi seminales rationes habent, non tamen id quod non in eis posuit ut de his fieri vel ab ipso possit."

to good use. The variations of species, the evolutionary successes that allow creatures to avoid death in another's jaws or by starvation are also the source of the multiplicity of life. Remembering the necessary caveats about natural and voluntary evils, it is possible to affirm that the competition among created goods is a feature of the world as it stands, without needing to say these evils are not a cause for alarm, disgust, or horror.

Greene's lieutenant and his exploding beetles, Tennyson's "Nature, red in tooth and claw," Deane-Drummond's awareness of the tragic context of biological speciation, and Darwin's concern for maladapted plants and animals all recognize something true. This world is a broken one. It is the occasion of unimaginable suffering. Not just individuals but entire species blink in and out of existence, often dying horribly. There is no need to deny the moral outrage of the biologist trying to reckon with what she knows to be the very processes by which life has staked its claim. As I have shown, these attempts often end up not only wrong but nearly as horrifying as the realities they are trying to ameliorate. But we can direct the outrage. We can do so by pointing out that it is the sin of rational creatures that creates the conditions in which *rationes seminales* unfold in time. As I want to show now, this means our outrage must be self-directed. Because while the angelic fall *ante omnia tempora* gives us a way of talking about the deaths of nonhuman creatures before—in the order of time—the sin of humans, this does not let humanity off the hook.

The Creation and Fall of Humans

If it is through the processes of death and decay that nonhuman creatures are given their particular shape—if, that is, the unfurling of the *rationes seminales* in the order of time means their unfurling in a world already marked by sin and death—then we should also suppose that this same process is the one by which human creatures come to be. This connection between human and nonhuman creatures is one we can see in Scripture and in the Fathers. Augustine, in *De civitate Dei*, affirms humans are created with animal bodies.[98] And in *De Genesi ad litteram* he explains that the human body when first created could be said to be both mortal and immortal: "That is, mortal, because it

98. Augustine, *civ.*, 13.23, *CSEL* 40.1:648: "non spiritale, sed animale fuisse non dubium est."

was able to die; immortal, because it was able not to die."[99] On this account, it is possible to say that God uses death as his instrument to shape the animal body of the human being.

This position is compatible with the text of Genesis 2 and with the position offered by Augustine in *De Genesi ad litteram*. When treating this text, Augustine appears to have at least two and possibly three variants of the scriptural account in front of him in Latin. None of the texts match the Vulgate's text describing the making of humans, which begins, "The LORD God formed man from the slime of the earth" ("formavit igitur Dominus Deus hominem de limo terrae") (Gen 2:7, Vulg.). Augustine's two texts contain components of this. One of them reads, "God formed the man, dust of the earth" ("formavit Deus hominem pulverem terrae"). Another looks like, "And God shaped the man, dust from the earth" ("Et finxit Deus hominem pulverem de terra").[100] And a third, "And God shaped the man from the slime of the earth" ("Et finxit Deus hominem de limo terrae").[101] I am mainly interested in this last one. First, because it tracks closest to the Vulgate,[102] and next, because it presents a provocative possibility. I have translated "de limo terrae" as "from the slime of the earth," but the Latin *limus* is a rich word, with a semantic range including plain old mud as well as something closer to "intestinal filth." Being formed not just from mud or dust, but from the cycle of ingestion, digestion, and excretion helps connect the evolutionary perspective with the theological one in Genesis 2.

Georges Bataille recognized the intimacy of decay and life. One line from his *L'histoire de l'érotisme* stands out as particularly astute. There he says, "death is that putrescence, that stench . . . which is at the same time the source and the repulsive condition of life."[103] Interpreting "de limo terrae"

---

99. Augustine, *Gn. litt.*, 6.25.36, *PL* 34:354: "id est mortale, quia poterat mori; immortale, quia poterat non mori."

100. Augustine, *Gn. litt.*, 7.1.1, *PL* 34:339.

101. Augustine, *Gn. litt.*, 3.22.34, *PL* 34:293.

102. Though not the Nova Vulgata, which reads "formavit Dominus Deus hominem pulverem de humo" (Gen 2:7).

103. Georges Bataille, "L'histoire De L'érotisme," in *Œuvres Complètes* (Paris: Gallimard, 1976), 69: "la mort est cette corruption, cette puanteur . . . qui est en même temps la source et la condition repoussante de la vie."

as intestinal filth or digested matter opens up the possible meanings of Genesis 2:7. Death, decay, and rot become the means by which God brings about even human life in its bodily, animal dimension. Augustine does not interpret Genesis 2 this way, but his teaching on the aptitudes of the *rationes seminales* makes it a live possibility. This reading of the text is in keeping with Augustine's mode of exegesis in *De Genesi ad litteram* because it remains focused on the *ad litteram* meaning of the text. By attending to the word *limus*, we find a depth of meaning that has room for the timebound processes of predation and digestion and the accumulation of critical masses of organic material that create the conditions necessary for human life. On this reading, the text of Genesis inclines us toward Augustine's affirmation that humans have animal bodies. We are, as he says with First Corinthians 15 in mind, "from the earth, earthly."[104]

Like all plants and animals humans remain implicated in death. It is both the condition for the coming to be of our material bodies and also the means by which we sustain them. But this is not all human beings are. Genesis 2:7 does not end with the shaping of the human out of the dust or mud or slime. The verse continues, "he breathed into his face the breath of life and the human was made a living soul" ("inspiravit in faciem eius spiraculum vitae et factus est homo in animam viventem") (Gen 2:7 Vulg.).[105] One way to read this verse is as a description of the bringing to life of inanimate matter generally. To live is to be animated, to be given an *anima*, a soul. But this act of animation occurs in a description of the making of the human in particular. God breathing into Adam's face, the action that makes the human a living soul, is omitted in Genesis 2's account of the creation of "every beast of the field and bird of the air" (Gen 2:19). God forms other creatures "out of the ground" (Gen 2:19)—"de humo" (Gen 2:19 Vulg.), and in this way they resemble the human, or humans resemble them. Both are made of earth—the digested organic matter that makes the continuation of life possible. The human form of life requires something extra, something that marks it out from plants and animals.

---

104. Augustine, *civ.*, 13.23, *CSEL* 40.1:648: "de terra terrenus."

105. Augustine's text also has a few different possibilities here, to include, *Gn. litt.*, 7.1.1, *PL* 34:339: "et insufflavit in faciem ejus flatum vitae; et factus est homo in animam viventem"; and *Gn. litt.*, 6.11.19, *PL* 34:347: "et inspiravit sive insufflavit in ejus faciem spiritum vitae, et factus est homo in animam vivam."

Augustine was notoriously unwilling to offer a definitive teaching on the origin of the human soul. In book VII of *De Genesi ad litteram*, however, he does go as far as to say what he thinks can be said with certainty about the soul breathed into Adam. What he thinks can be said definitively is that the soul is made by God from nothing. In this way it is from God but it is not the same substance as God. At the same time, the human soul is incorporeal. It does not come about in the same manner as animal bodies or nonrational souls. The human soul is immortal and also mutable. It is capable of living forever and also of changing for better or for worse. But it can also be called mortal, insofar as true immortality belongs to God alone.[106] Augustine's non-negotiables about the human soul comport well with the case I am laying out. God shapes the animal body of the human, using the processes of birth, death, and decay, just as he does for all other plants and animals. Death is a feature of the fallen cosmos, but one which God puts to work. Having shaped the human body using these processes, God does something new, giving humans a soul distinct from the souls of plants and animals. There is a beautiful moment in Gregory of Nyssa's *De hominis opificio*, where he reflects on how this situates humans between heaven and earth. Being a commingling of things divine[107] and earthly, humans are disposed by nature toward the enjoyment of God and also toward things of the earth.[108] Cyprian points out this twofold makeup of

---

106. Augustine, *Gn. litt.*, 7.28.43, *PL* 34:372: "Nunc tamen de anima, quam Deus inspiravit homini sufflando in ejus faciem, nihil confirmo, nisi quia ex Deo sic est, ut non sit substantia Dei; et sit incorporea, id est, non sit corpus, sed spiritus; non de substantia Dei genitus, nec de substantia Dei procedens, sed factus a Deo; nec ita factus ut in ejus naturam natura ulla corporis vel irrationalis animae verteretur; ac per hoc, de nihilo: et quod sit immortalis secundum quemdam vitae modum, quem nullo modo potest amittere; secundum quamdam vero mutabilitatem, qua potest vel deterior vel melior fieri, non immerito etiam mortalis possit intelligi; quoniam veram immortalitatem solus ille habet, de quo proprie dictum est, Qui solus habet immortalitatem."

107. Gregory should not be read to be saying something opposed to Augustine's claim that the human soul is not of the same substance of God. In the same sentence he says humans enjoy God "through the more divine nature" ("per naturam diviniorem"). Gregory of Nyssa, *De hom. op.*, 2.2, *PG* 44:133–34. By "divine" Gregory is referring to that which is not material or earthly. He does not mean humans are by nature divine.

108. Gregory of Nyssa, *De hom. op.*, 2.2, *PG* 44:133–34: "Propterea duabus ut rebus hominis opificium constaret, fecit commistis nimirum divinis ac terrenis, ut ipsi tam Dei quam terrestrium rerum fruitionem naturae suae consentaneam ac propriam statueret: Deoque per naturam diviniorem, bonis autem terrenis per sensum, qui eiusdem esset generis, frueretur."

the human creature in his treatise *De Dominica oratione*. There he says, "For we have a body from earth and a spirit from heaven, we are ourselves earth and heaven, and we pray that the will of God may be done in both, that is in both body and spirit."[109] Humans are made to stand at the midpoint of the whole created order, an admixture of what is heavenly and earthly, material and immaterial, physical and spiritual.

I am not going to venture into the question of monogenesis or the existence of an aboriginal community of hominins. Whether Adam and Eve are the first human pair or whether the biological requirements of genetic diversity necessitate a population minimum significantly higher than two is not something I intend to resolve here. Incidentally, the reading of Genesis 2 I am giving is compatible with both.[110] Instead I am going to focus on what the situation of humans at the midpoint of creation indicates, given the picture of the cosmos painted so far. Thinking of humans as the midpoint of the created order tells us something about the role of humans given to them by God. God calls humans out of the cycle of death, destruction, and decay. He does so by giving them a new possibility distinct from the other creatures of the corporeal world. God makes humans capable of knowing and of loving him. Humans have the spiritual capacity to cleave to God in a manner similar to that of the angels. They are able, as Augustine says, not to die.

But humans are corporeal creatures, too. Adam is given the garden of Eden to till and keep (Gen 2:15). He is also given charge of the animals, naming them (Gen 2:19), a mark of the dominion he has over them (Gen 1:28). Human dominion parallels the case of the angelic administration of the cosmos. God governs his creation not only immediately but also through secondary causes. Humans have an administrative role, a mandate to care for and rule the material cosmos in accordance with its rule, who is Christ. This cosmos is already off kilter and always has been due to the sin of the angels. Because of this, the position humans occupy when they are first created is a

109. Cyprian, *dom. orat.*, 16, *CSEL* 3.1:278: "Nam cum corpus e terra et spiritum possideamus e caelo, ipsi terra et caelum sumus et in utroque id est et corpore et spiritu ut Dei voluntas fiat oramus."

110. Separating the shaping of our animal bodies *de limo terrae* from the creation out of nothing of the human soul would allow us to admit there was an original community of hominins and that God made Adam and Eve human by plucking them out of that community and giving them rational souls.

mediatorial one. Humans are given care of a creation that is groaning from the first. God is bringing about the reconciliation of the fallen cosmos through human beings. Humans have a soul that makes them like the angels, and like the angels they are given charge of a piece of God's creation in order to bring it back into alignment with its *ratio*.

That is the intention, but humans fail at this task just as some of the angels failed at theirs. Like the fall of the angels, the fall of humans means a turning away from God. Humans fail in their duty to serve in a mediatorial role between the fallen material cosmos and things divine by failing to be what they are. Unlike the angels, the human fall is precipitated by temptation. Satan in the garden, pursuing humanity out of malice and envy, beguiles Eve (Gen 3:13) and Adam follows her into sin (Gen 3:6). The die is cast, and the possibilities of obedience are foreclosed, recapitulating the fall of the angels. Certain potencies lying dormant in the *rationes seminales* are cut off. The wound at the heart of the cosmos opens wider. The cracks in the architecture of the universe penetrate deeper. Humans, who might have served to reconcile the fallen cosmos by keeping God's commandment, are given over to the possibilities of their animal bodies. They fall back into the cycle of violence, death, and decay out of which they had been called.

Here we must compare Wisdom 2:24 and Romans 5:12. There are a few possibilities for reading them alongside one another. The first sees "through the devil's envy death entered the world" (Wis 2:24) as a description of how "sin came into the world through one man and death through sin" (Rom 5:12). Given that my position takes the devil's envy and death's entrance into the world to be an event that occurs before fallen time starts ticking away, this reading will not suffice. Another possibility limits the scope of what is described in Romans 5:12. The "world" into which sin and death enter could refer only to the human world. Before human sin, the necessity of human death was not there; with human sin, death follows of necessity. To retain the cosmic scope of both verses requires another way of reconciling them which intimately links the human and angelic fall and which points forward to the saving work of Jesus Christ.

The devil's envy is born when he sees the person of Jesus Christ in God's eternal present. What he sees is himself supplanted as the highest creature by the God-man Jesus Christ. Human nature is united to divinity in the second person of the Trinity. Satan's desire for this to be otherwise, for humans to lack this dignity, is what turns him away from God. This envy is his fall, which tears the fabric of the cosmos from the beginning. But Satan's fall from heaven into the order of fallen time is what makes possible his temptation of humans. Humans are prompted to fall by the devil. Temptation is what distinguishes the human fall from the angelic fall. But the human fall, too, has consequences. It is the "truly necessary sin of Adam," the "happy fault / that earned so glorious a Redeemer!"[111] In other words, what Satan sees in God's eternal present—the incarnation of the Son—which causes him to fall, is something Satan himself brings about through his temptation of humans. Human sin, succumbing to the temptation of Satan in the garden, is what makes necessary the reconciling work of God in the person of Jesus Christ. This is not a claim about whether or not God would have become incarnate apart from human sin. The incarnate Lord is the heart of this cosmos in the person of Jesus Christ. The incarnation is God's act of creation and of recreation. The incarnation, which follows upon human sin as God's saving act, is the very thing Satan sees when gazing upon the light of God at the moment of his creation. What Satan despised in the order of eternity is the very thing he brings about in the order of time. This is the self-mutilating quality of sin on full display. The diffracted angelic light which results in its admixture with darkness sows the seeds of its own destruction in the very act of sinning. Satan's recognition of this fact is a fitting account of his judgment as it is hard to imagine a greater torment than the recognition that your actions have brought about the very thing you hate.

Human sin is also thereby implicated in the original fall of the cosmos that occurs in the devil and his angels. The human fall necessitates the salvation of humans through the God-man. This salvific act, the union of divine and human nature, elicits Satan's envy. This makes it possible to say both "through the devil's envy death entered the world" (Wis 2:24) and "sin came into the world through one man and death through sin" (Rom 5:12). The cosmic scope of human disobedience is revealed. The human failure to carry out the mediatorial task has consequences that permeate the whole of time-space. The rent yawns wide enough for the natural history of carnage to take its toll within it. But death and destruction are not the end of the story. The mediatorial role of the human being is not abandoned by God. God sends "the last Adam" (1 Cor 15:45), Jesus Christ, the true mediator, who accomplishes

111. *The Roman Missal*, 351.

the mediation of fallen humanity back to God. Because Jesus is divine, he can mediate humanity back to God. Because Jesus is human, he can also act as mediator for the rest of the fallen cosmos. The God-man stands at the heart of creation, a creation that is fallen, broken, and dying because of the voluntary evil of his rational creatures. As God and man he comes to save it, "in Christ God was reconciling the world to himself" (2 Cor 5:19). Death does not have the last word.

Conclusion

TWO DIFFICULTIES PRESENT themselves in the account I have offered. The first arises if one wishes to insist that God's omnipotence is such that he could have accomplished all the goods of creation without allowing evil. He chose this way, the way of our world, for reasons opaque to us yet clear to him. But it would have been possible to achieve his purposes for us otherwise than through the permission of sin. Against this view I have claimed that the particular goods of this created order—some of them, anyway—are goods that can only be had because of certain evils. It makes no more sense to say God could have been merciful without the need for mercy than to say God could make a four-sided triangle. There are created conditions necessary for the achievement of created goods, and the insistence that God is the *bonum commune*, the good of all things in general, does not negate the fact that goods in particular, which created goods are, have certain logical dependencies.

At the same time, it is important to see that this does not make the evils permitted into goods. God's reasons for bringing about this particular creation, with particular goods occasioned by particular evils, remain mysterious to us. As Augustine does in his explanation of the reorientation of death from curse to *instrumentum*, I affirm that the evils brought about by the angelic and human falls are in fact evils. But the liturgy of the Church demands that we attempt to say how they can be construed as the results of the *felix culpa*—the happy fault. What is felicitous about them is that they bring about these goods, which could not be had another way.

A second problem presented by my argument arises from an insistence that sin, to be the action of a rational creature, must have an object. The fall of the angels, when construed as a turn away from God toward nothing, lacks intelligibility and so appears as indistinguishable from involuntary activities. In order to be an angelic act, one could argue, sin must be oriented toward some good—a lesser good than God, but a good nonetheless. Were it not to be so oriented, it would be no more culpable than a sneeze or a yawn. But if we take seriously Augustine's thought about what angels are, something like my account follows. It is possible to take another view on the nature of angels, but the Augustinian one has excellent scriptural and traditional bona fides. Augustine's thoughts incline toward sin as a kind of negation when he says sin has no efficient cause, but rather a deficient one.[1] Defect, failure, lack, these are the marks of the primordial sin of the angels. They mark angelic sin out even from the sin of Adam and Eve, which, while imitative of the first sin, has proximate causes that cannot have obtained for the angels: ignorance, distraction, and deception.

The worry that angelic sin might not be explicably narratable in terms of its intelligibility has only so much purchase. I am interested in its possibility, not its rationale. On this view, it is only necessary to affirm that angelic sin results from a culpable failure of will. Angelic sin is a failure to love God rightly and persistently given the full knowledge, capacity, and power necessary to do so. That rational creatures are culpable for such failures, for ceasing to act as they ought, seems clear enough. Augustine speaks of the angels as cleaving to God. One way to imagine this cleaving is by describing it as an embrace. If my only task were to remain locked in an embrace with my beloved, but I instead loosened my grip and finally let go, it would be a moral failure. This image of the embrace helps to illustrate something important. The action of the devil, in releasing his embrace, is a purely negative one. We do not need to be able to specify reasons for loosening his grip. It is enough to say he has failed to do so. I have offered some speculations of what might have precipitated that failure, but I hope I have prescinded from offering a rationale, since I do not think one is specifiable.

Apart from these potential objections, I take it that I have accomplished what I set out to do. My aim in asking after death was to see if the resources of the Christian tradition, especially Augustine's account of creation in *De Genesi ad litteram*, might be put to work to discover death's origin. This task is a particularly pressing one because Scripture's insistence that "God did not make death, and he does not delight in the death of the living" (Wis 1:13) stands in prima-facie contradiction with what natural scientists have been able to discover about the cosmos. Death is not just something we find in the

1. Augustine, *civ.*, 12.7, *CSEL* 40.1:577: "Nemo igitur quaerat efficientam causam malae voluntatis; non enim est efficiens sed deficiens, quia nec illa effectio sed defectio."

world, it is a structural element and the mechanism by which all the various kinds of life come to be what they are. Thomas Aquinas's gloss on this verse, that God did not intend death for its own sake,[2] turns out to be possibly true and possibly false. It is true in my account, insofar as God ends up wielding death as an instrument to accomplish his ends for creation. It is false if it is taken as support for a vision of the cosmos that sees death as necessary, strictly speaking, for the existence of any material cosmos.

What we are left with is a vision that is both bleaker and more hopeful than many of the ways of approaching the phenomenon of death in the created order. It is bleaker because we are forced to say that the good cosmos created by God is deeply damaged, and has been since it was created. God made all things good, but due to the fall of rational creatures there is never a time when the ravages of sin and decay and death have not been felt. There is no idyllic past to which we can return. This is true not just for human creatures, prevented by the flaming sword of the cherubim from returning to Eden (Gen 3:24), it is also true for all creatures taken together as a whole. Reconciliation, the healing of the cosmos's original wounds, is the work of the Christ, who will heal the brokenhearted and bind up their wounds (Ps 147:3). He stands at the heart of the created order, the *ratio* of all things. The relations things bear to him just are their reality. It is what it is for them to be made and also what it is for them to be redeemed. In him this creative and reconciliatory work is already accomplished, when viewed under the aspect of eternity. It is also still to come for us, pilgrims in the order of time.

This work has proceeded under these twin aspects—viewing all things considered as *conditio* and as *administratio*. This division is the powerful tool afforded us by Augustine's imaginative and difficult account of the days of creation. Insisting on an *ad litteram* reading of the hexaëmeron in Genesis 1 means interpreting the text as metaphorical speech about God's eternal act of creation. That act creates all things and all times from nothing. This offers us a way to read the first creation account in Scripture in a way that can bear the burdens of a modern cosmology. By allowing us to see what the angels see, the vast ordered beauty of the past, present, and future of the cosmos oriented toward its final rest in him on the seventh day, God points out the

2. *ST* I.49.2 *resp*: "Sed quod dicitur Sap. I, quod *Deus mortem non fecit*, intelligitur quasi per se intentam."

mysteriousness of us to ourselves. To be creatures is to be what we always will have been in God's eternal knowing and willing of us in our particularity.

With this division between time and eternity in place, we can look with fresh eyes at God's administration of all things in the order of time. We can see the source of natural evils in the voluntary evil of rational creatures—the sin of the angels. We can also see how the existence of natural evil is no threat to God's providential care of his creatures. He works in and through time and the countdown toward death to make *this* cosmos. He uses death to shape creation according to his purposes. God does not make death, but he will not let the possibilities sin opens up go to waste. God wields death as a tool—an *instrumentum*—just as he does on the cross. In doing so, he brings about the existence of the many and various kinds of life we encounter in the natural world. This is also how God shapes humans *de limo terrae*. God molds us out of the evolutionary processes common to all living creatures on earth, and so humans are both like and unlike all other living things.

The Augustinian reading of Genesis is uniquely able to answer the kinds of questions contemporary Christians are interested in throwing at the doctrine of creation. It allows us to take seriously the darkness that permeates this fallen world. We are not forced into dismissing the concerns of those like Tennyson, who tremble in the face of the horror of death. We are able to see the damaged cosmos for what it is, and also see it for what it might be. Knowing that "in everything God works for good" (Rom 8:28), we are also able to hope the real evils confronting us are not finally determinative.

BIBLIOGRAPHY

Alcuin of York. *Commentariorum in Apocalypsin.* In *Patrologiae cursus completus, series latina.* Edited by J.-P. Migne. Vol. 100. Paris: Ateliers catholiques, 1863.

Anselm of Canterbury. *Cur Deus Homo.* In *Patrologiae cursus completus, series latina.* Edited by J.-P. Migne. Vol. 158. Paris: Ateliers catholiques, 1853.

Augustine of Hippo. *Confessions.* Translated by Maria Boulding. Hyde Park, NY: New City Press, 1997.

———. *Confessions.* Translated by Henry Chadwick. Oxford: Oxford University Press, 1991.

———. *Confessionum.* In *Corpus scriptorum ecclesiasticorum latinorum.* Edited by Pius Knöll. Vol. 33. Vienna: Academiae Litterarum Caesareae, 1896.

———. *De civitate Dei.* In *Corpus scriptorum ecclesiasticorum latinorum.* Edited by Emanual Hoffman. Vol. 40.1. Vienna: Academiae Litterarum Caesareae, 1899.

———. *De civitate Dei.* In *Corpus scriptorum ecclesiasticorum latinorum.* Edited by Emanual Hoffman. Vol. 40.2. Vienna: Academiae Litterarum Caesareae, 1900.

———. *De diversis quaestionibus octoginta tribus.* In *Corpus christianorum, series latina.* Edited by A. Mutzenbecher. Vol. 44A. Turnholti: Typographi Brepols, 1975.

———. *De doctrina christiana.* In *Patrologiae cursus completus, series latina.* Edited by J.-P. Migne. Vol. 34. Paris: Ateliers catholiques, 1845.

———. *De Genesi ad litteram.* In *Patrologia cursus completus, series latina.* Edited by J.-P. Migne. Vol. 34. Paris: Ateliers catholiques, 1845.

———. *De Genesi ad litteram.* In *Corpus scriptorum ecclesiasticorum latinorum.* Edited by Joseph Zycha. Vol. 33. Vienna: Academiae Litterarum Caesareae, 1894.

———. *De Genesi ad litteram imperfectus.* In *Patrologia cursus completus, series latina.* Edited by J.-P. Migne. Vol. 34. Paris: Ateliers catholiques, 1845.

———. *De Genesi contra Manichaeos.* In *Patrologia cursus completus, series latina.* Edited by J.-P. Migne. Vol. 34. Paris: Ateliers catholiques, 1845.

———. *De libero arbitrio.* In *Patrologia cursus completus, series latina.* Edited by J.-P. Migne. Vol. 32. Paris: Ateliers catholiques, 1845.

———. *De ordine.* In *Patrologia cursus completus, series latina.* Edited by J.-P. Migne. Vol. 32. Paris: Ateliers catholiques, 1845.

———. *De peccatorum meritis et remissione et de baptismo parvulorum.* In *Corpus scriptorum ecclesiasticorum latinorum.* Edited by Carolo Urba and Joseph Zycha. Vol. 60. Vienna: Academiae Litterarum Caesareae, 1913.

———. *De trinitate*. In *Corpus christianorum, series latina*. Edited by W. Mountain and F. Glorie. Vol. 50. Turnholti: Typographi Brepols, 1968.

———. *De utilitate credendi*. In *Corpus scriptorum ecclesiasticorum latinorum*. Edited by Joseph Zycha. Vol. 25. Vienna: Academiae Litterarum Caesareae, 1891.

———. *In Evangelium Ioannis tractatus*. In *Patrologia cursus completus, series latina*. Edited by J.-P. Migne. Vol. 35. Paris: 1845.

———. "The Literal Meaning of Genesis." Translated by Edmund Hill. In *On Genesis: The Works of Saint Augustine: A Translation for the 21st Century*, edited by John E. Rotelle, 168–506. Hyde Park, NY: New City Press, 2002.

Bataille, Georges. *L'histoire de l'érotisme*. In *Œuvres complètes*. Vol. 10. Paris: Gallimard, 1976.

Bonaventure. *Breviloquium*. In *Opera Omnia*, vol. V, 199–292. Quarrachi: Typographia Collegii S. Bonaventurae, 1891.

Bonino, Serge-Thomas. *Les anges et les démons: quatorze leçons de théologie*. Bibliothèque de la Revue Thomiste. Paris: Éditions Parole et Silence, 2007.

Cavanaugh, William, and James K. A. Smith. *Evolution and the Fall*. Grand Rapids, MI: William B. Eerdmans, 2017.

Cavell, Stanley. "The Avoidance of Love: A Reading of *King Lear*." In *Must We Mean What We Say?*, 1–40. Cambridge: Cambridge University Press, 2012.

———. *The Claim of Reason: Wittgenstein, Skepticism, Morality, and Tragedy*. New York: Oxford University Press, 1979.

Cohen, Leonard. "Anthem." From *The Future* (studio album). Columbia Records. Released November 24, 1992.

Council of Florence. "Cantate Domino." In Heinrich Denzinger, *Compendium of Creeds, Definitions, and Declarations on Matters of Faith and Morals*. 43rd ed. San Francisco: Ignatius Press, 2012.

Council of Trent. "Decree on Original Sin." In Heinrich Denzinger, *Compendium of Creeds, Definitions, and Declarations on Matters of Faith and Morals*. 43rd ed. San Francisco: Ignatius Press, 2012.

Cyprian. *De Dominica* oratione. In *Corpus scriptorum ecclesiasticorum latinorum*. Edited by William Hartel. Vol. 3.1. Vienna: Academiae Litterarum Caesareae, 1868.

———. *De zelo et livore*. In *Corpus scriptorum ecclesiasticorum latinorum*. Edited by William Hartel. Vol. 3.1. Vienna: Academiae Litterarum Caesareae, 1868.

Darwin, Charles. *On the Origin of Species by Means of Natural Selection, or the Preservation of Favoured Races in the Struggle for Life*. London: John Murray, 1859.

———. *The Variations of Animals and Plants under Domestication*. Vol. 2. London: John Murray, 1868.

Davidson, Donald. "What Metaphors Mean." In *Inquiries into Truth and Interpretation*, 245–64. Oxford: Oxford University Press, 2001.

Dawkins, Richard. *The Greatest Show on Earth: The Evidence for Evolution*. New York: Free Press, 2009.

Deane-Drummond, Celia. "In Adam All Die? Questions at the Boundary of Niche Construction, Community Evolution, and Original Sin." In *Evolution and the Fall*, edited by William Cavanaugh and James K. A. Smith, 23–47. Grand Rapids, MI: William B. Eerdmans, 2017.

———. *Christ and Evolution: Wonder and Wisdom*. Minneapolis: Fortress Press, 2009.

Denzinger, Heinrich. *Compendium of Creeds, Definitions, and Declarations on Matters of Faith and Morals*. 43rd ed. San Francisco: Ignatius Press, 2012.

Diamond, Cora. "Ethics, Imagination and the Method of Wittgenstein's *Tractatus*." In *The New Wittgenstein*, edited by Alice Crary and Rupert Read, 95–114. London: Routledge, 2000.

———. "What Nonsense Might Be." In *The Realistic Spirit*, 149–73. Cambridge, MA: The MIT Press, 1991.

Dickinson, Emily. "Tell All Truth but Tell It Slant — (1263)." Poetry Foundation. https://www.poetryfoundation.org/poems/56824/tell-all-the-truth-but-tell-it-slant-1263.

Eagleton, Terry. *Sweet Violence: The Idea of the Tragic*. Malden: Blackwell Publishers, 2003.

Edwards, Jonathan. *The "Miscellanies": 833–1152*. Works of Jonathan Edwards Online. New Haven, CT: Yale University, Jonathan Edwards Center, 2008. Available at http://edwards.yale.edu.

———. *The "Miscellanies": (Entry Nos. 1153–1360)*. Works of Jonathan Edwards Online. New Haven, CT: Yale University, Jonathan Edwards Center, 2008. http://edwards.yale.edu.

———. *The "Miscellanies": (Entry Nos. A–Z, Aa–Zz, 1–500)*. Works of Jonathan Edwards Online. New Haven, CT: Yale University, Jonathan Edwards Center, 2008. http://edwards.yale.edu.

———. *The Works of Jonathan Edwards*, vol. 26: *Catalogues of Books*. New Haven, CT: Yale University Press, 2008.

Elam, Michael. "The *Ainulindalë* and J. R. R. Tolkien's Beautiful Sorrow in Christian Tradition." *VII: An Anglo-American Literary Review* 28, no. 1 (2011): 61–78.

Fourth Lateran Council. In Heinrich Denzinger, *Compendium of Creeds, Definitions, and Declarations on Matters of Faith and Morals*. 43rd ed. San Francisco: Ignatius Press, 2012.

Gennadius of Marseille, *Statuta Ecclesiae Antiqua*. In Heinrich Denzinger, *Compendium of Creeds, Definitions, and Declarations on Matters of Faith and Morals*. 43rd ed. San Francisco: Ignatius Press, 2012.

Greene, Graham. *The Power and the Glory*. New York: Penguin Books, 1983.

Gregory of Nyssa. *The Catechetical Oration of St. Gregory of Nyssa*. Translated by J. H. Srawley. Early Church Classics. London: Society for Promoting Christian Knowledge, 1917.

———. *De hominis opificio*. In *Patrologiae cursus completus, series graeca*. Edited by J.-P. Migne. Vol. 44. Paris: Ateliers catholiques, 1863.

———. *Discours catéchétique*. Translated by Raymond Winling. Vol. 453. Sources Chrétiennes. Paris: Les Éditions du Cerf, 2000.

Gregory the Great. *Moralia in Job*. In *Corpus christianorum, series latina*. Edited by M. Adriaen. Vol. 143. Turnholti: Typographi Brepols, 1979.

———. *Regulae pastoralis*. In *Patrologia cursus completus, series latina*. Edited by J.-P. Migne. Vol. 77. Paris: Ateliers catholiques, 1862.

Griffiths, Paul J. *Decreation: The Last Things of All Creatures*. Waco: Baylor University Press, 2014.

———. *Intellectual Appetite: A Theological Grammar*. Washington, DC: The Catholic University of America Press, 2009.

Guardini, Romano. *Der Herr: Betrachtungen über die Person und das Leben Jesu Christi*. Würzburg: Werkbund-Verlag, 1949.

———. *The Last Things: Death, Purification, Resurrection, Judgment, & Eternity*. Translated by Charlotte Forsyth and Grace Branham. Richmond, VA: Preservation Books, 2019.

Hart, David Bentley. *The New Testament: A Translation*. New Haven, CT: Yale University Press, 2017.

———. *You Are Gods: On Nature and Supernature*. Notre Dame: Notre Dame University Press, 2022.

Hauerwas, Stanley. *The Peaceable Kingdom: A Primer in Christian Ethics*. Notre Dame: University of Notre Dame Press, 1983.

Hill, Edmund. "Introduction" to "The Literal Meaning of Genesis." In *On Genesis*, edited by John E. Rotelle, 155–66. Hyde Park, NY: New City Press, 2002.

International Commission on English in the Liturgy. "Rite of Christian Initiation of Adults." In *The Rites of the Catholic Church*, 15–358. Collegeville, MN: The Liturgical Press, 1990.

———. "Rite of Marriage." In *The Rites of the Catholic Church*, 717–58. Collegeville, MN: The Liturgical Press, 1990.

Jerome. *Commentariorum in Esaiam*. In *Corpus christianorum, series latina*. Edited by M. Adriaen. Vol. 73. Turnholti: Typographi Brepols, 1963.

John Cassian. *Collationes*. In *Corpus scriptorum ecclesiasticorum latinorum*. Edited by Michael Petschenig. Vol. 13. Vienna: Academiae Litterarum Caesareae, 1886.

Kelsey, David H. *Eccentric Existence: A Theological Anthropology*. Vol. 1. Louisville, KY: Westminster John Knox Press, 2009.

Kerrigan, John. *Shakespeare's Binding Language*. Oxford: Oxford University Press, 2016.

Lash, Nicholas. "On Re-Reading Vatican II." In *Theology for Pilgrims*, 249–52. Notre Dame: University of Notre Dame Press, 2008.

Lawrence, D. H. "Self-Pity." In *The Complete Poems of D. H. Lawrence*, 382. Ware, UK: Wordsworth Editions, 1994.

Leo I. *Quam Laudibiliter*. In Heinrich Denzinger, *Compendium of Creeds, Definitions, and Declarations on Matters of Faith and Morals*. 43rd ed. San Francisco: Ignatius Press, 2012.

Leo XIII. *Libertas praestantissimum*. In Heinrich Denzinger, *Compendium of Creeds, Definitions, and Declarations on Matters of Faith and Morals*. 43rd ed. San Francisco: Ignatius Press, 2012.

MacKinnon, Donald M. "Atonement and Tragedy." In *Borderlands of Theology and Other Essays*, edited by George W. Roberts and Donovan E. Smucker, 52–58. Philadelphia: J. B. Lippincott, 1968.

Marlowe, Christopher. *Doctor Faustus*. London: Routledge, 1965.

Marshall, Bruce. *Trinity and Truth*. Cambridge: Cambridge University Press, 2000.

McCabe, Herbert. "Creation." In *God Matters*, 2–9. London: Geoffrey Chapman, 1987. Reprint, London: Continuum International, 2012.

———. "Evil." In *God Matters*, 25–38. London: Geoffrey Chapman, 1987. Reprint, London: Continuum International, 2012.

———. *The New Creation*. London: Continuum International, 2010.

McKeough, Michael J. *The Meaning of the Rationes Seminales in St. Augustine*. Washington, DC: Catholic University of America, 1926.

Milton, John. "Paradise Lost." In *The Poems of John Milton*, edited by Helen Darbishire, 1–281. London: Oxford University Press, 1958.

Missale Romanum Cum Lectionibus. Vol. 2. Vatican City: Libreria Editrice Vaticana, 1977.

Mivart, St. George. *The Genesis of Species*. London: Macmillan & Co., 1871.

Moi, Toril. *Revolution of the Ordinary: Literary Studies after Wittgenstein, Austin, and Cavell*. Chicago: University of Chicago Press, 2017.

Niceno-Constantinopolitan Creed. In Heinrich Denzinger, *Compendium of Creeds, Definitions, and Declarations on Matters of Faith and Morals*. 43rd ed. San Francisco: Ignatius Press, 2012.

Nightingale, Andrea. "Augustine on Extending Oneself to God through Intention." *Augustinian Studies* 46, no. 2 (2015): 185–209.

O'Connor, Flannery. *The Habit of Being: The Letters of Flannery O'Connor*. New York: Farrar, Straus & Giroux, 1979.

O'Daly, Gerard J. P. "Time as *Distentio* and St. Augustine's Exegesis of *Philippians* 3,12–14." *Revue d'Etudes Augustiniennes et Patristiques* 23, no. 3–4 (1977): 265–71.

Phillips, D. Z. *The Problem of Evil & the Problem of God*. Minneapolis: Fortress Press, 2005.

Pius XII. *Munificentissimus Deus*. http://w2.vatican.va/content/pius-xii/la/apost_constitutions/documents/hf_p-xii_apc_19501101_munificentissimus-deus.html.

Robbins, Frank Egleston. *The Hexaemeral Literature: A Study of the Greek and Latin Commentaries on Genesis*. Chicago: The University of Chicago Press, 1912.

The Roman Missal. Collegeville, MN: Liturgical Press, 2011.

Scheeben, Matthias. *Handbuch der katolischen Dogmatik*. Buch 3, Band 2. Freiburg im Breisgau: Herder Verlagshaudlung, 1878.

———. *Die Mysterien des Christenthums: Wesen, Bedeutung und Zusammenhang Derselben nach der in ihrem übernatülichen Charakter gegebenen Perspective.* Freiburg im Breisgau: Herder, 1865.

———. *The Mysteries of Christianity.* Translated by Cyril Vollert. New York: Herder & Herder, 1946.

Schmitz, Kenneth. *The Gift: Creation.* Milwaukee: Marquette University Press, 1982.

Second Synod of Orange. *Canons.* In Heinrich Denzinger, *Compendium of Creeds, Definitions, and Declarations on Matters of Faith and Morals.* 43rd ed. San Francisco: Ignatius Press, 2012.

Second Vatican Council. *Gaudium et Spes.* In Heinrich Denzinger, *Compendium of Creeds, Definitions, and Declarations on Matters of Faith and Morals.* 43rd ed. San Francisco: Ignatius Press, 2012.

Shakespeare, William. *Hamlet.* In *The Riverside Shakespeare.* 2nd ed. Boston: Houghton Mifflin, 1997.

———. *Troilus and Cressida.* In *The Riverside Shakespeare.* 2nd ed. Boston: Houghton Mifflin, 1997.

Simpson, Richard. "Darwin on the Origin of Species." *The Rambler* 2, no. 6 (1860): 361–76.

Suárez, Francisco. "Tractatus De Angelis." In *Commentarii Et Disputationes in Primam Partem D. Thomae.* Opera Omnia. Paris: Vivès, 1856.

Synod of Carthage. *Canons.* In Heinrich Denzinger, *Compendium of Creeds, Definitions, and Declarations on Matters of Faith and Morals.* 43rd ed. San Francisco: Ignatius Press, 2012.

Tanner, Tony. *Prefaces to Shakespeare.* Cambridge, MA: The Belknap Press of Harvard University Press, 2010.

Taylor, Charles. *A Secular Age.* Cambridge, MA: The Belknap Press of Harvard University Press, 2007.

Tennyson, Alfred. "In Memoriam A. H. H. Obit MDCCCXXXIII." In *Tennyson: Poems and Plays*, 230–66. London: Oxford University Press, 1965.

Thomas Aquinas. *Expositio super Iob ad litteram.* Lander, WY: The Aquinas Institute for the Study of Sacred Doctrine, 2016.

———. *Quaestiones disputate de potentia.* https://www.corpusthomisticum.org/qdp4.html.

———. *Summa Contra Gentiles.* https://aquinas.cc/la/en/~SCG2.

———. *Summa Theologiae.* Lander, WY: The Aquinas Institute for the Study of Sacred Doctrine, 2012.

Tolkien, J. R. R. *The Letters of J. R. R. Tolkien.* Boston: Houghton Mifflin, 1981.

———. *The Silmarillion.* 2nd ed. Boston: Houghton Mifflin, 1999.

Wippel, John F. *The Metaphysical Thought of Thomas Aquinas: From Finite Being to Uncreated Being.* Monographs of the Society for Medieval and Renaissance Philosophy. Washington, DC: The Catholic University of America Press, 2000.

Wittgenstein, Ludwig. *Philosophical Investigations*. Translated by G. E. M. Anscombe, P. M. S. Hacker, and Joachim Schulte. Oxford: Wiley Blackwell, 2009.

Woods, Henry. *Augustine and Evolution: A Study in the Saint's "De Genesi ad Litteram" and "De Trinitate."* New York: Universal Knowledge Foundation, 1924. Reprint, Eugene, OR: Wipf & Stock, 2009.

BIBLICAL INDEX

INDEX OF ANCIENT AND MEDIEVAL SOURCES

GENERAL INDEX